TOP STOCKS 2004

10th YEAR of PUBLICATION

TOP STOCKS 2004

10th YEAR of PUBLICATION

Martin Roth

Wrightbooks

The author and publisher would like to thank Aspect Huntley for permission to include the five-year shareholder return figures, and Alan Hull (author of *Active Investing*) for supplying the five-year share price graphs (www.alanhull.com).

This tenth edition first published 2003 by Wrightbooks
an imprint of John Wiley & Sons Australia, Ltd
33 Park Road, Milton, Qld 4064

Offices also in Sydney and Melbourne

First edition published as *Top Stocks* by Wrightbooks in 1995.
New edition published annually.
This edition reprinted November 2003.

Typeset in 10.9/12.3 pt Berkeley LT

ISBN: 0 7314 0022 4

Cover design by Rob Cowpe

Printed in Australia by McPherson's Printing Group

10 9 8 7 6 5 4 3 2

Disclaimer

The material in this publication is of the nature of general comment only, and neither purports nor intends to be advice. Readers should not act on the basis of any matter in this publication without considering (and if appropriate taking) professional advice with due regard to their own particular circumstances. The authors and publisher expressly disclaim all and any liability to any person, whether a purchaser of this publication or not, in respect of anything and of the consequences of anything done or omitted to be done by any such person in reliance, whether in whole or part, upon the whole or any part of the contents of this publication.

CONTENTS

(Cont'd...)

CONTENTS *(Cont'd...)*

Preface

Ten Years of Top Stocks

Welcome to the tenth edition of *Top Stocks*.

The first edition appeared in mid 1995, based on company results for June 1994. In those days I would send letters to more than 100 companies requesting a copy of the annual report. Some years later, with the financial results becoming available on the internet, we moved publication of the book forward to year-end.

Now the book gets written as the results are appearing. For companies whose financial year ends in June, the last possible date to report is mid September, and the manuscript goes to the printers the following week. The book you are holding was on sale early in October.

That initial edition comprised 80 companies. The first two? Advance Bank Australia and Allgas Energy. There were many more, too, that no longer exist.

But 13 'superstocks' have been in every edition – a noteworthy achievement, as the qualifying criteria are strict. Here they are:

- ANZ
- Commonwealth Bank of Australia
- CSR
- Harvey Norman
- Hills Industries
- Incitec (now Incitec Pivot)
- National Australia Bank
- QBE Insurance
- Santos

- Suncorp-Metway
- Wesfarmers
- Westpac
- Woolworths.

Not all those companies' shares have done well (and, in any case, share price performance has never been one of the criteria for inclusion in the book). But certainly a portfolio of the above 13 companies would have rewarded you richly.

Top Stocks was originally launched to help investors locate stocks offering security, through the presentation of an independent and objective evaluation of leading companies. Whatever may be happening in the market, the fact remains that there are plenty of good, solid companies with excellent long-term records of regular dividends and capital growth. They may not double or triple in price within the space of months, but so long as a company's business continues to flourish its shares should come to represent excellent value.

There are some minor changes to this edition. Over the past couple of years I have become aware that *Top Stocks* is increasingly being bought by market traders, who use it as a screening tool for choosing companies with good fundamentals for their trading activities. (I am particularly indebted to author and trader Alan Hull, who commended *Top Stocks* most highly to readers of his book *Active Investing*. I am privileged that Alan has contributed to this and last year's editions of *Top Stocks*, and I wish to thank him.)

To help traders, I have added some extra figures to the tables in this book. There's now the cashflow per share for most companies, along with the current ratio and the market capitalisation. See the Introduction to this book for more information on how these figures are calculated.

Also, for those companies whose latest financial results are interim (half-year) results, I have used those more recent figures to calculate the debt-to-equity and current ratios, rather than the older full-year results.

How were the 91 companies in this book selected? The criteria were as follows:

- All must be included in the All Ordinaries Index, which comprises Australia's 500 largest stocks (out of approximately 1,500). The reason for excluding smaller companies is that there is often little investor information available on many of them and some are so thinly traded as to be almost illiquid. In fact, the 500 All Ordinaries companies comprise, by market capitalisation, around 98% of the entire market.
- It was necessary that all companies be publicly listed since at least the end of 1998, and have a five-year record of profits and dividend payouts. An exception, introduced for this edition of the book, is companies demerged from another company in the All Ordinaries Index. These require just a two-year record of profits and dividend payouts. Two such companies are in this edition – PaperlinX (formerly part of Amcor) and Origin Energy (formerly part of Boral).
- All companies were required to post a return-on-equity ratio of at least 9% in their latest financial year.
- No company should have a debt-to-equity ratio of more than 75%.
- All companies must have an interest cover ratio of at least three.

As noted already, share price performance is not one of the criteria for inclusion in this book. The purpose is to select companies with good profits and a strong balance sheet. These may not offer the spectacular share price returns of a biotech start-up, but they should present far less risk. To use an Olympics analogy, the stocks in this book are more like marathon runners than sprinters. They should last the distance, providing solid – if unflashy – performance over the long term.

There are several notable exclusions. Investment trusts like Australian Foundation Investment Company are out, as these mainly buy other shares or investments. Also omitted are property trusts.

A further exclusion are the foreign stocks listed on the Australian Stock Exchange. There is sometimes a lack of information available about such companies. In addition, their stock prices tend to move on events and trends in their home countries, making it difficult at times for local investors to follow them.

Fully 20 companies from *Top Stocks 2003* have been dropped from the present edition, with 22 new entries.

Six of the exclusions were because the companies have been taken over. They are:

- AurionGold
- Bank of Western Australia
- Bristile
- BRL Hardy
- Goodman Fielder
- Sabre Group.

A further eight companies from the previous edition were excluded because their return on equity fell below the required 9%, they made a loss or they did not pay any dividends for the year. They are:

- Brazin
- Computershare
- CSL
- Equity Trustees
- Oil Company of Australia
- Sons of Gwalia
- Southern Cross Broadcasting
- Trust Company of Australia.

And a further six companies have been eliminated because their debt-to-equity ratio was above 75%. They are:

- Centennial Coal
- Jupiters
- Oroton International

- Plaspak
- Ramsay Health Care
- Tempo Services.

There are 22 new companies in *Top Stocks 2004* (although 10 have appeared in earlier editions, but were not in *Top Stocks 2003*). They are:

- Alesco
- Amcor
- Australian Gas Light
- Australian Stock Exchange
- BHP Billiton
- Casinos Austria
- Coal & Allied Industries
- Coates Hire
- Coles Myer
- Downer EDI
- K&S
- McGuigan Simeon Wines
- McPherson's
- Miller's Retail
- Origin Energy
- PaperlinX
- SDI
- Spotless Group
- Telstra
- Toll Holdings
- Wadepack
- Washington H. Soul Pattinson.

I hope this book will serve you well.

Martin Roth
Melbourne
September 2003

Introduction

The 91 companies in this book have been placed as much as possible into a common format, for ease of comparison. Please study the following explanations in order to get as much as possible from the large amount of data.

Each page begins with a brief introduction to the company and its activities. Then follow the highlights of its latest business results. For the majority of the companies these are their June 2003 results, which were issued between July and September 2003. Finally there is a section on the outlook for the company, sometimes including comment on the performance of the shares.

Tables

The tables have been made as concise as possible, though they repay careful study, as they contain large amounts of information. Note that the tables for the banks have been arranged a little differently from the others; details of these are later in this Introduction.

At the top of each page is a small table with the following data.

Share Price

This is the closing price on 20 August 2003. Also included are the 12-month high and low prices, as of the same date.

Market Capitalisation

This is the size of the company, as determined by the stock market. It is the share price (again, as of 20 August 2003) multiplied by the number of shares on issue. All companies in this book must be in the All Ordinaries Index, which comprises Australia's 500 largest stocks as measured by market capitalisation.

Price to Net-Tangible-Assets-per-Share Ratio

The NTA-per-share figure expresses the worth of a company's net tangible assets – that is, its assets minus its liabilities and intangible assets – for each share of the company. The price-to-NTA-per-share ratio relates this figure to the share price.

A ratio of one means that the company is valued exactly according to the value of its assets. A ratio below one suggests that the shares are a bargain, though usually there is a good reason for this. Profits are more important than assets.

Two companies in this book, Spotless Group and Tabcorp Holdings, have a negative NTA-per-share figure – as a result of having intangible assets valued at more than their remaining net assets – and a price-to-NTA-per-share ratio cannot be calculated.

See Table O, in the second part of this book, for a little more detail on this ratio.

Five-Year Share Price Return

This is the total return you could have received from the stock in the five years to 19 September 2003. It includes reinvested dividends, bonus stock, rights issues and capital gain from the stock's appreciation. It is expressed as a compounded annual rate of return. These figures have been supplied by Aspect Huntley.

Price-Earnings Ratio

The price-earnings ratio (PER) is one of the most popular measures of whether a share is cheap or expensive. It is calculated by dividing the share price – in this case the closing price for 20 August 2003 – by the earnings per share figure. Obviously the share price is continually changing, so the PER figures in this book are for guidance only. Many newspapers publish each morning the latest PER for every stock.

Dividend Yield

This is the latest full-year dividend expressed as a percentage of the share price. Like the PER, it changes as the share price moves. It is a useful figure, especially for investors who are buying shares for income, as it allows you to compare this income with alternative investments, such as a bank term deposit or a bond fund.

Sector Comparisons

It is often useful to compare a company's PER and its dividend yield with those of its sector. Often the stocks in a sector move together. Thus, if a particular stock is lagging the averages, this may – depending on the reasons – be a buying opportunity. Figures used in this book are those of the S&P/ASX sectors, again as of 20 August 2003.

Share Price Chart

Also at the top of each page is a five-year share price chart, provided by Alan Hull, author of *Active Investing* (www.alanhull.com).

Website

Most public companies now have websites, and the website addresses of companies in this book are placed under the share price chart. Some sites are little more than corporate brochures for the company, with glossy photos and beat-up prose. But increasingly, public companies are using the internet as a means of providing timely data to shareholders. Thus, you will often now find all the latest ASX company announcements – often placed on the site simultaneously to their ASX release – along with media releases and even, sometimes, speeches and presentations to stock market analysts.

If you are following a particular company it is certainly highly recommended that you become very familiar with that company's website.

Main Tables

Here is what you can find in the main tables.

Revenues

These are the company's revenues from its business activities, generally the sale of products or services. It does not usually include additional income from such sources as investments, bank interest or the sale of assets. If the information is available, the revenues figure has been broken down into the major product areas.

Earnings Before Interest and Taxation

Earnings before interest and taxation (EBIT) is the firm's profit from its operations before the payment of interest and tax. This figure is often used by analysts examining a company. The reason is that some companies have borrowed extensively to finance their activities, while others have opted for alternative means. By expressing profits before interest payments it is possible to compare more precisely the performance of these companies. The net interest figure – interest payments minus interest receipts – has been used for this calculation.

EBIT Margin

The EBIT margin is the company's EBIT expressed as a percentage of its revenues. It is a gauge of a company's efficiency. A high EBIT margin suggests that a company is achieving success in keeping its costs low.

Gross Margin

The gross margin is the company's gross profit as a percentage of its sales. The gross profit is the amount left over after deducting from a company's sales figure its cost of sales: that is, its manufacturing costs or, for a retailer, the cost of purchasing the goods it sells. The cost of goods sold figure does not usually include marketing or administration costs.

As there are different ways of calculating the cost of goods sold figure, this ratio is best used for year-to-year comparisons of a single company's efficiency, rather than in comparing one company with another. Not all companies present a cost of goods sold figure, so a gross margin ratio is not given for every stock in this book. The revenues for some companies include a mix of sales and services. Where a breakdown is possible, the gross profit figure will reflect sales only.

Operating Profit Before Tax

The operating profit before tax is simply the EBIT figure minus net interest payments. As much as possible, I have adjusted this to exclude non-recurring profits and losses, which are called significant items. Unfortunately, not all companies provide enough data to allow me to do this.

Profit After Tax

The profit after tax is the company's profit after the payment of tax, and also after the deduction of minority interests. Again, as far as possible, it does not include non-recurring profits or losses. Minority interests are that part of a company's profit that is claimed by outside interests, usually the other shareholders in a subsidiary which is not fully owned by the company. Many companies do not have any minority interests, and for those that do it is generally a tiny figure.

Earnings Per Share

Earnings per share (EPS) is the after-tax profit divided by the number of shares. Because the profit figure is for a 12-month period the number of shares used is a weighted average of those on issue during the year. This number is provided by the company in its annual report and results announcements.

Cashflow Per Share

Newly introduced to this edition of the book, the cashflow per share ratio tells – in theory – how much actual cash the company has generated from its operations.

In fact, the ratio in this book is not exactly a true measure of cashflow. It is simply the company's depreciation and amortisation figures for the year added to the after-tax profit, and then divided by a weighted average of the number of shares. (Depreciation and amortisation are expenses that do not actually utilise cash, so can be added back to after-tax profit to give a kind of indication of the company's cashflow.)

By contrast, a true cashflow – including such items as newly raised capital and money received from the sale of assets – would require quite complex calculations based on the company's statement of cashflows. However, many analysts use the ratio as I present it, because it is easy to calculate, and it is certainly a useful guide to how much funding the company has available from its operations. (Note that a depreciation figure was not available for some companies, and no cashflow per share ratio could be calculated for these.)

Dividend

The dividend figure is the total for the year, interim and final. However, it does not include special dividends. The level of franking is also provided.

Net Tangible Assets Per Share

The NTA per share figure tells the theoretical value of the company – per share – if all assets were sold and then all liabilities paid. It is very much a theoretical figure, as there is no guarantee that corporate assets are really worth the price put on them in the balance sheet. Intangible assets such as goodwill, newspaper mastheads and patent rights are excluded because of the difficulty in putting a sales price on them, and also because they may in fact not have much value if separated from the company.

As already noted, two companies in this book – Spotless Group and Tabcorp Holdings – have a negative NTA, due to the fact that their intangible assets are so great, and no figure can be listed for them.

Where a company's most recent financial results are the half-year figures, these are used to calculate this ratio.

Interest Cover

The interest cover ratio indicates how many times a company could make its interest payments from its pre-tax profit. A rough rule of thumb says a ratio of at least three times is desirable. Below that and fast-rising interest rates could imperil profits. The ratio is derived by dividing the EBIT figure by net interest payments. Some fortunate companies have interest receipts that are higher than their interest payments, which turns the interest cover into a negative figure, and so it is not listed.

Return on Equity

Return on equity (ROE) is the after-tax profit expressed as a percentage of the shareholders' equity. In theory, it is the amount that the company's managers have made for you – the shareholder – on your money. The shareholders' equity figure used is an average for the year.

Debt-to-Equity Ratio

The debt-to-equity ratio is one of the best-known measures of a company's debt levels. It is total borrowings minus the company's cash holdings, expressed as a percentage of the shareholders' equity. Some companies have no debt at all, or their cash position is greater than their level of debt, which results in a negative ratio, so no figure is listed for them. Where a company's most recent financial results are the half-year figures, these are used to calculate this ratio.

Current Ratio

Also new to this edition of the book, the current ratio is simply the company's current assets divided by its current liabilities. Current assets are cash or assets that can, in theory, be converted quickly into cash. Current liabilities are normally those payable within a year. Thus, the current ratio measures the ability of a company to repay in a hurry its short-term debt, should the need arise. The surplus of current assets over current liabilities is referred to as the company's working capital.

Where a company's most recent financial results are the half-year figures, these are used to calculate this ratio.

Banks

The tables for the banks are somewhat different from those for most other companies. EBIT and debt-to-equity ratios have little relevance for them, as they have such high interest payments (to their customers). Other differences are examined below.

Operating Income

Operating income is used instead of sales revenues. Operating income is the bank's net interest income – that is, its total interest income minus its interest expense – plus other income, such as bank fees, fund management fees and income from businesses such as corporate finance and insurance.

Net Interest Income

Banks borrow money – that is, they accept deposits from savers – and they lend it to businesses, home buyers and other borrowers. They charge the borrowers more than they pay those who deposit money with them, and the difference is known as net interest income.

Operating Expenses

These are all the costs of running the bank. Banks have high operating expenses, and one of the keys to profit growth is cutting these expenses. Add the provision for doubtful debts to operating expenses, then deduct the total from operating income, and you get the pre-tax profit.

Non-Interest Income to Total Income

Banks have traditionally made most of their income from savers and from lending out money. But increasingly this is becoming a commodity business, with a growing number of entrants offering higher interest rates to savers and lower rates to borrowers. In response, the big banks are working to diversify into new fields, and the non-interest income to total income ratio is an indication of their success.

Cost-to-Income Ratio

As noted, the banks have high costs – numerous branches, expensive computer systems, many staff, and so on – and they are all striving to reduce these. The cost-to-income ratio expresses their expenses as a percentage of their operating income, and is one of the ratios most often used as a gauge of efficiency. The lower the ratio drops the better.

Return on Assets

Banks have enormous assets, in sharp contrast to, say, a dot-com start-up whose main physical assets may be little more than a set of computers. So the return on assets – the after-tax profit expressed as a percentage of the year's average total assets – is another measure of efficiency.

THE COMPANIES

PART I

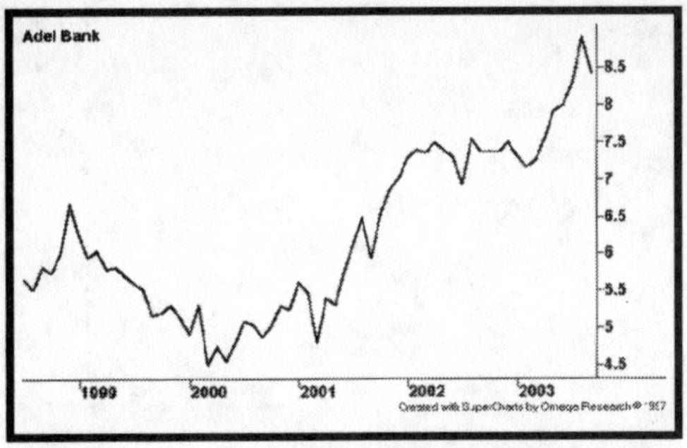

www.adelaidebank.com.au

ADELAIDE BANK LIMITED

Share price ($)	8.53
12-month high ($)	8.75
12-month low ($)	6.75
Market capitalisation ($mn)	752.5
Price-to-NTA-per-share ratio	1.8
5-year share price return (% p.a.)	13.6

Sector: Financials	Company	Sector
Price-earnings ratio (times)	14.6	16.2
Dividend yield (%)	4.3	4.5

Adelaide Bank dates back to its establishment as the Cooperative Building Society of South Australia in 1900. It achieved bank status in 1994. It occupies a strong position within South Australia, and is advancing into other states. Its Leveraged Equities subsidiary specialises in margin lending.

LATEST BUSINESS RESULTS (JUNE 2003, FULL YEAR)

Record home lending, lower cost ratios and improved margins combined to deliver a record profit to Adelaide Bank. Assets under management rose 14% to $12.25 billion, with loans under management up 17% to $11.1 billion, notably higher than the Australian average of 13%. The housing boom drove this growth, with the home loan portfolio up 21% to $8.5 billion. Total loan approvals jumped 22% to $5.3 billion. There was also strong growth in retail deposits, which rose 25% to $6.4 billion. The Leveraged Equities margin lending business generated $7.65 million in pre-tax profit, up 4% from the previous year. This would have been higher, but for $115,000 in writeoffs due to operational errors during the year, and the cost of integrating the Hartleys Limited margin lending book. Despite global uncertainty in stock markets, the margin lending portfolio grew 4% to $1.23 billion.

OUTLOOK

Adelaide Bank's particular strength is its nationwide home loan business, much of it through alliances with key mortgage brokers, and it continues to develop new partnerships. It claims 2.3% of the national mortgage market, and believes it can build this in the medium term to 5.0%. Though its business will certainly be hurt by a downturn in the housing sector, it says that it is confident about providing further double-digit profit gains in 2003–04. It expects modest growth in fee (non-interest) income, though its percentage of non-interest income to total income remains among the lowest of all the banks, and it sees little likelihood of this changing soon. It has invested heavily in new technology for its Leveraged Equities business to establish a platform that can facilitate significant future growth once markets recover. It continues to work at boosting productivity, and believes it can lower its cost-to-income ratio to 56% by June 2004.

ADB Year to 30 June	2002	2003
Operating income ($mn)	173.2	201.1
Net interest income ($mn)	128.8	167.5
Operating expenses ($mn)	107.2	120.1
Operating profit before tax ($mn)	61.3	74.3
Profit after tax ($mn)	41.2	51.2
Earnings per share (¢)	47.1	58.3
Dividend (¢)	32	37
Percentage franked	100	100
Non-interest income to total income (%)	25.6	16.7
Net tangible assets per share ($)	3.15	4.63
Cost-to-income ratio (%)	61.9	59.7
Return on equity (%)	14.3	14.2
Return on assets (%)	0.6	0.7

Alesco Corporation Ltd

Share price ($)	5.56	
12-month high ($)	5.56	
12-month low ($)	3.60	
Market capitalisation ($mn)	253.5	
Price-to-NTA-per-share ratio	5.6	
5-year share price return (% p.a.)	14.1	
Sector: Industrials	**Company**	**Sector**
Price-earnings ratio (times)	17.2	12.1
Dividend yield (%)	4.7	3.9

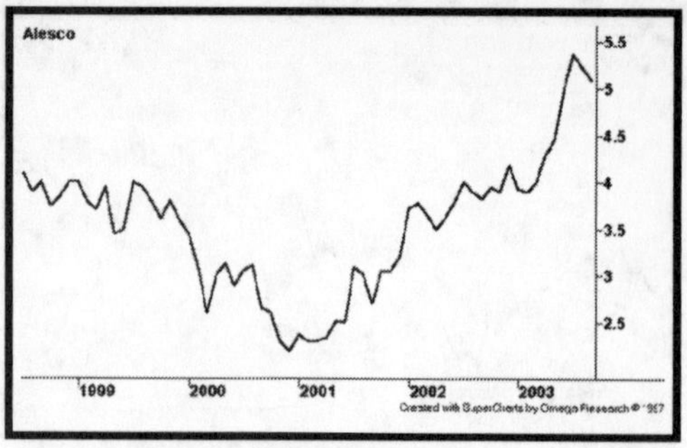

www.alesco.com.au

Alesco, formerly called Atkins Carlyle, was initially established as a general merchants business in Perth more than 100 years ago. Today, based in Sydney, it specialises in four broad areas. The largest of these, construction and mining, incorporates Marathon Tyres, which distributes heavy-duty tyres, and Parchem, which supplies chemical products to the construction industry. The building and renovations business is centred on Parbury, which distributes branded building products, and also includes the new Robinhood kitchen rangehood business. The automotive division markets auto-electrical components and branded motor cycle accessories. The new scientific and testing division was formed from the acquisition of Biolab, the largest distributor of scientific and testing equipment in Australia and New Zealand.

Latest Business Results (May 2003, Full Year)

The sale of some operations led to a decline in sales, but the company's increasing emphasis on high-margin businesses boosted profits. All divisions recorded higher earnings. The best result came from the buildings and renovations business, with profit (before interest and tax) up 25%, thanks to the continuing housing boom, the launch of a new range of products and cost-cutting initiatives. Construction and mining profits grew 6% and automotive was up 7%. There was an initial contribution from the new scientific and testing division.

Outlook

Alesco's strategy is to invest in and develop industrial businesses holding premium brands with high market shares within niche markets, as well as to dispose of underperforming operations. It is also working to diversify its operations – as with the recent acquisition of Biolab – in order to reduce dependence on any one business segment or industry. The Marathon Tyre business has signed a new distribution agreement with Michelin for industrial and earthmoving tyres that continues until at least July 2006. Alesco will restructure Biolab, with increasing emphasis on high-growth areas like biosciences and environmental technologies. At the time of acquisition, the Robinhood business had a limited distribution network. Following its integration into the Parbury operation, the products now have wider access to new markets and more extensive distribution services.

ALS Year to 31 May	2002	2003
Revenues ($mn)	400.4	392.1
Construction & mining (%)	48	39
Building & renovations (%)	27	30
Automotive (%)	25	26
Scientific & testing (%)	0	5
EBIT ($mn)	20.4	23.0
EBIT margin (%)	5.1	5.9
Gross margin (%)	31.1	34.7
Operating profit before tax ($mn)	15.2	18.7
Profit after tax ($mn)	9.2	12.7
Earnings per share (¢)	27.5	32.4
Cashflow per share (¢)	65.3	64.0
Dividend (¢)	24	26
Percentage franked	100	100
Net tangible assets per share ($)	1.37	1.00
Interest cover (times)	3.9	5.4
Return on equity (%)	8.7	10.0
Debt-to-equity ratio (%)	66.0	53.4
Current ratio	1.4	1.3

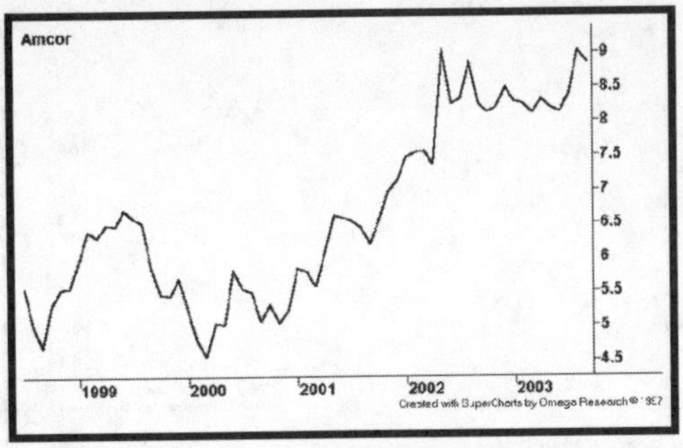

www.amcor.com.au

AMCOR LIMITED

Share price ($)	8.61
12-month high ($)	8.93
12-month low ($)	7.68
Market capitalisation ($mn)	7,437.7
Price-to-NTA-per-share ratio	2.9
5-year share price return (% p.a.)	19.1

Sector: Materials	Company	Sector
Price-earnings ratio (times)	16.7	16.0
Dividend yield (%)	3.5	2.9

Melbourne-based Amcor, started in the 1860s as a paper maker, is today one of the world's three largest manufacturers of packaging. It has operations in 36 countries, and around 75% of its revenues come from abroad. It is the world's biggest producer of PET (polyethylene terephthalate) plastic bottles and jars, and a global force in three other areas: closures (lids for glass bottles and jars), flexible plastic packaging and specialty printed cartons.

LATEST BUSINESS RESULTS (JUNE 2003, FULL YEAR)

Profits were up strongly, thanks to the company's strategy of focusing on specific high value-added products, predominantly targeting food and beverage customers. The PET packaging operations had a very strong year. First-year synergy benefits from the $2.9 billion Schmalbach-Lubeca PET plastic bottles acquisition meant this has already become earnings per share positive. Australian business was also strong, after three years of rationalisation and restructuring. There was a successful first year of operations from the new wine bottle plant in Gawler, South Australia. The European tobacco carton business – for which Amcor is the market leader – performed well, especially in Russia. However, the closures business in Europe was hurt by the introduction of deposit legislation in Germany. Amcor Asia had a difficult year, with the impact of SARS severely reducing earnings in the second half.

OUTLOOK

Amcor continues to grow by acquisition, and the challenge for the company now is the successful integration of all its new businesses. In August 2003, it announced the purchase from British packaging giant Rexam of its medical and health products flexible packaging business, for $330 million. This makes Amcor the world leader in that niche. Strong volume growth is anticipated in the current year for the global PET business, with $290 million approved for new capital expenditure, which will also help underpin the continued expansion in custom products, and will support cost-reduction initiatives to counter market pricing pressures. With the Asian region recovering from the SARS epidemic, it is anticipated that results will gradually improve during the year.

AMC Year to 30 June	2002	2003
Revenues ($mn)	7,472.4	10,709.9
EBIT ($mn)	567.9	730.5
EBIT margin (%)	7.6	6.8
Operating profit before tax ($mn)	446.4	575.3
Profit after tax ($mn)	316.9	431.4
Earnings per share (¢)	47.5	51.7
Cashflow per share (¢)	98.7	124.4
Dividend (¢)	28	30
Percentage franked	50	45
Net tangible assets per share ($)	4.47	2.93
Interest cover (times)	4.7	4.7
Return on equity (%)	9.4	9.8
Debt-to-equity ratio (%)	–	40.4
Current ratio	2.2	1.0

Angus & Coote (Holdings) Limited

Share price ($)	6.12	
12-month high ($)	6.41	
12-month low ($)	5.33	
Market capitalisation ($mn)	73.3	
Price-to-NTA-per-share ratio	1.4	
5-year share price return (% p.a.)	25.1	
Sector: Consumer Discretion.	**Company**	**Sector**
Price-earnings ratio (times)	12.9	20.2
Dividend yield (%)	5.9	3.7

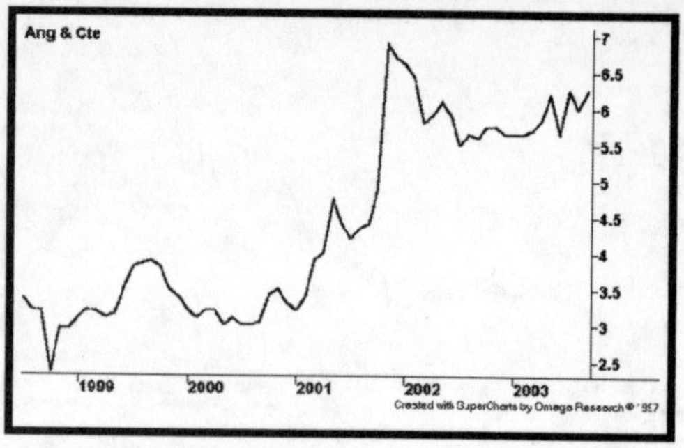

www.anguscoote.com.au

Sydney-based Angus & Coote, founded in 1895, is Australia's dominant specialist jewellery retailer, with a 15% market share. It operates through two main divisions: the A&C division markets jewellery, watches, clocks, silverware, crystal and related products through 139 jewellery stores throughout Australia, under the names Angus & Coote, Dunklings the Jewellers, Amies the Family Jewellers, Edments and Angus & Coote Tax Free. The Goldmark division operates 114 jewellery stores throughout Australia, and is the country's largest national jewellery brand. Angus & Coote has launched a joint venture retail operation in the US, with four pilot stores.

Latest Business Results (July 2003, Full Year)

Revenues and the after-tax profit only just edged up, masking a significant improvement in the company's finances. By Angus & Coote's own estimates, profit before tax from core businesses increased 50.3%, and underlying profit after tax from core businesses increased 57.9%. However, writedowns from its US venture put a dent in profits, and the company was also hurt by a substantially increased taxation rate, due to an income tax credit of $1.2 million in the July 2002 year. The A&C division had a particularly strong year, largely as a result of improved sales of higher margin products. There was also a favourable impact from the strength of the dollar. But sales to international travellers remained weak.

Outlook

Angus & Coote's business is quite dependent on trends in consumer discretionary spending. This has remained strong, although the company could be hurt by any economic slowdown, and especially by a rise in interest rates. It is working to position some of its Goldmark stores to attract those in the fashion-conscious 15- to 29-years age group, with new ranges of contemporary fashion accessory products, and new, smaller concept stores in major shopping centres. It is also seeking to export this model to the US, with four new stores having opened there in late 2002, in a joint venture with Too Inc, a leading specialty retailer of branded apparel and lifestyle products for girls. However, in mid 2003, Too Inc decided to withdraw from the joint venture. Angus & Coote has said it will announce in November the venture's future.

ANC Year to 27 July*	2002	2003
Revenues ($mn)	215.6	217.9
EBIT ($mn)	7.9	10.4
EBIT margin (%)	3.6	4.8
Gross margin (%)	57.1	59.6
Operating profit before tax ($mn)	6.5	8.7
Profit after tax ($mn)	5.6	5.7
Earnings per share (¢)	46.6	47.5
Cash flow per share (¢)	101.6	110.7
Dividend (¢)	32	36
Percentage franked	100	100
Net tangible assets per share ($)	4.11	4.41
Interest cover (times)	5.9	5.9
Return on equity (%)	11.4	11.0
Debt-to-equity ratio (%)	37.2	45.9
Current ratio	1.5	1.6

** 28 July, 2002.*

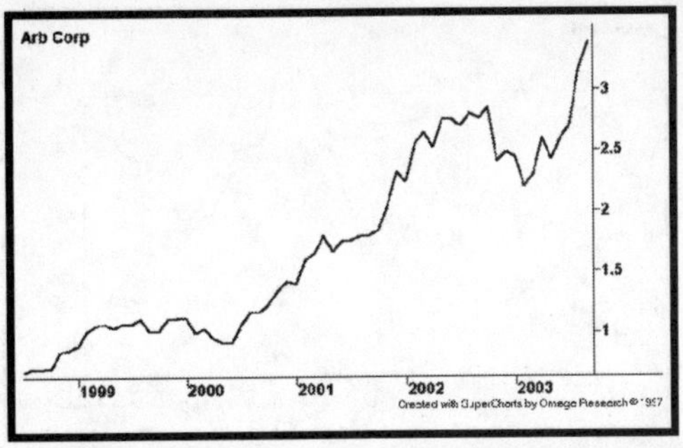

www.arb.com.au

ARB Corporation Limited

Share price ($)	3.14
12-month high ($)	3.20
12-month low ($)	2.01
Market capitalisation ($mn)	200.5
Price-to-NTA-per-share ratio	5.6
5-year share price return (% p.a.)	40.2

Sector: Consumer Discretion.	Company	Sector
Price-earnings ratio (times)	19.2	20.2
Dividend yield (%)	2.5	3.7

Melbourne-based ARB is a small manufacturer of specialty automotive accessories, and an international leader in the design and production of equipment for four-wheel-drive vehicles. Its products are divided into five broad groupings: mechanical products, notably the prize-winning 'air locker' air-operated locking differential system; fabricated metal products, such as bull bars, roof racks and tow bars; the Old Man Emu range of suspension products, such as springs and shock absorbers; ARB canopies; and trade products, which include a large range of imported and locally produced accessories, for which ARB acts as local distributor.

Latest Business Results (June 2003, Full Year)

ARB posted its 12th straight profit rise, despite a negative impact on business from the drought in Australia, the war in the Middle East and the rapid appreciation of the Australian dollar. Domestically, all areas recorded some growth, with particularly strong contributions from Queensland and the ACT. Export sales for the year (not including the USA) were up 24%. American sales grew by about 10%, but growth was flat when converted to Australian dollars.

Outlook

ARB has become a major beneficiary of the growing popularity of four-wheel-drive vehicles in Australia, America and many other countries, and the result has been continuing strong increases in sales and profits, and a soaring share price. Boasting a large range of products, it has roughly a third of the local market for four-wheel-drive accessories. It is seeing strong overseas demand for its profitable air locker unit, with about 80% of production exported to some 50 countries. Though making up around 20% of company sales, this product represents more than a quarter of profit. ARB has started manufacturing its own windows and doors for canopies, and with demand for canopies growing it is boosting capacity. Numerous new suspensions, locking differentials, bull bars and other products are expected to support growth in 2004 and beyond. A new Brisbane office and warehouse was opened in mid 2003, and new warehousing and production capacity is planned for Victoria. A share split has boosted liquidity of the company's shares.

ARP Year to 30 June	2002	2003
Revenues ($mn)	78.8	88.0
EBIT ($mn)	12.0	14.7
EBIT margin (%)	15.2	16.7
Operating profit before tax ($mn)	11.7	14.5
Profit after tax ($mn)	8.3	10.3
Earnings per share (¢)	13.1	16.3
Cashflow per share (¢)	17.3	21.1
Dividend (¢)	6.5	8.0
Percentage franked	100	100
Net tangible assets per share ($)	0.47	0.56
Interest cover (times)	40.9	62.1
Return on equity (%)	27.9	29.5
Debt-to-equity ratio (%)	6.2	10.5
Current ratio	1.5	1.6

Australand Holdings Limited

Share price ($)	1.82	
12-month high ($)	1.85	
12-month low ($)	1.30	
Market capitalisation ($mn)	960.6	
Price-to-NTA-per-share ratio	1.4	
5-year share price return (% p.a.)	20.2	
Sector: Financials	**Company**	**Sector**
Price-earnings ratio (times)	10.4	16.2
Dividend yield (%)	6.6	4.5

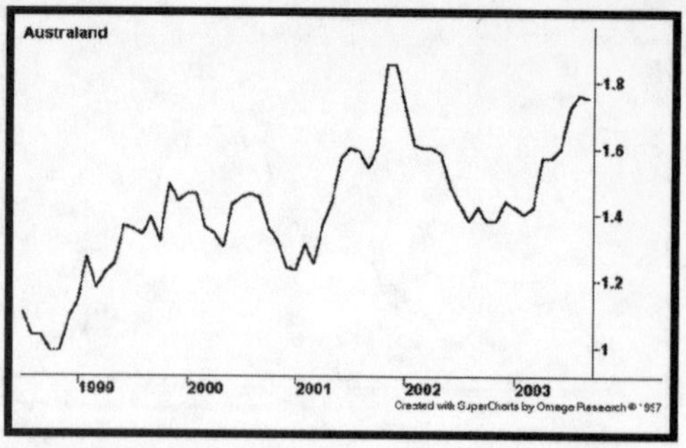

www.australand.com.au

Sydney-based Australand is one of Australia's largest property development companies with operations covering: large-scale land development projects; medium density and detached housing projects in Sydney, Melbourne, Brisbane and Perth; apartment buildings; commercial office buildings; and purpose-built industrial facilities. It also manages property trusts. Australand is listed on the Singapore Stock Exchange.

Latest Business Results (June 2003, Half Year)

Profits rose sharply, with all businesses strong. The land and housing division saw profits (before interest and tax) up 10% to $49 million, principally due to an increase in the number of housing sales brought to account. The apartments division recorded a $13.5 million profit, compared to a loss of more than $8.0 million in the 2002 first half, thanks to a sharp increase in sales, from $85 million to nearly $220 million. The commercial and industrial division saw profit soar from $0.7 million to more than $8.0 million, on the back of increased sales, from $73 million to $159 million. The company has announced that it expects 2003 full-year revenues and profit to be up by around 10% on the 2002 result.

ALZ Year to 31 December	2001	2002
Revenues ($mn)	1,233.5	1,138.5
EBIT ($mn)	129.6	132.1
EBIT margin (%)	10.5	11.6
Gross margin (%)	17.9	17.9
Operating profit before tax ($mn)	114.9	131.2
Profit after tax ($mn)	81.4	90.4
Earnings per share (¢)	16.8	17.4
Cashflow per share (¢)	18.9	19.4
Dividend (¢)	12	12
Percentage franked	91	88
Interest cover (times)	8.8	138.9
Return on equity (%)	12.1	12.4
Half Year to 30 June	**2002**	**2003**
Revenues ($mn)	347.4	615.1
Operating profit before tax ($mn)	37.3	66.3
Profit after tax ($mn)	24.7	41.2
Earnings per share (¢)	4.4	7.4
Dividend (¢)	6	6
Percentage franked	75	100
Net tangible assets per share ($)	1.29	1.31
Debt-to-equity ratio (%)	59.2	55.0
Current ratio	2.0	2.8

Outlook

As a housing developer, Australand will be hurt by any downturn in this cyclical business. It is working to diversify its earnings base, to cushion the impact. It usually has more than 90 residential projects and 30 commercial and industrial projects in the planning or development phase at any time, and it maintains a spread throughout the major regions of Australia. It has also created four wholesale property trusts holding 30 properties with a total value of $800 million. Australand retains a minority stake in each trust as part of its strategy to progressively increase recurrent income and reduce its dependence on profits from development activities.

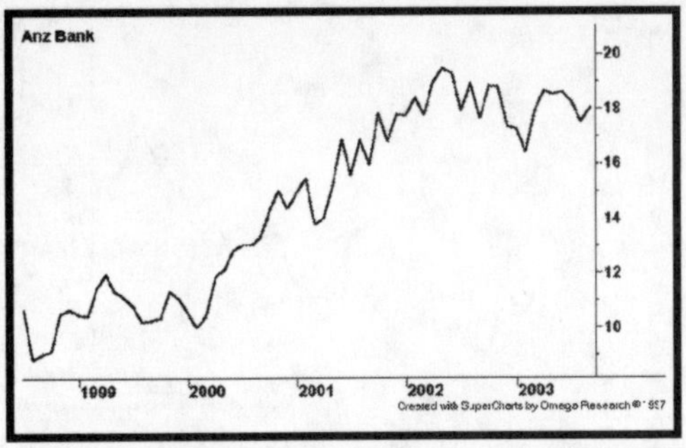

www.anz.com.au

Australia & New Zealand Banking Group Limited

Share price ($)	17.87	
12-month high ($)	19.63	
12-month low ($)	15.69	
Market capitalisation ($mn)	27,612.9	
Price-to-NTA-per-share ratio	2.2	
5-year share price return (% p.a.)	20.4	
Sector: Financials	**Company**	**Sector**
Price-earnings ratio (times)	11.5	16.2
Dividend yield (%)	4.8	4.5

ANZ is one of Australia's four banking giants, with significant interests in numerous areas of finance. It has a stake in online stockbroker E*Trade Australia, and has launched a major funds management joint venture with Dutch giant ING.

Latest Business Results (March 2003, Half Year)

Profits rose again, in a good result. The housing boom helped fuel the growth. Net interest income rose 9% – even though the net interest margin worsened a little – with housing loans up 19% to $57 billion. Non-housing loans rose 12% to $37 billion. Non-interest income actually declined 4%, to $1.35 billion, as a result of reduced fee revenues and a one-off charge of $27 million to credit card reward partners, relating to the under-accrual of loyalty points in past years. Particularly strong results came from the bank's institutional, corporate, mortgages, asset finance and Asia Pacific division. The new ING joint venture was subdued in a difficult equity market. The consumer finance and treasury businesses recorded profit decreases. The cost-to-income ratio declined further to 45.6%, confirming ANZ as Australia's most efficient bank. It claims its productivity is among the top 5% of banks worldwide.

Outlook

ANZ's immediate challenge is to sustain growth in the event of a housing downturn. The company has announced several strategies for future growth. In particular, it is working to revitalise its personal banking business, where it lags its three large rivals. It has invested heavily in this business, and is reducing some fees, as part of its Restoring Customer Faith program, which it believes will deliver long-term enhanced market share. It has announced that it will try to boost its New Zealand presence by bidding for the National Bank of New Zealand, and its chances of success have been greatly helped by Westpac's decision to withdraw from the bidding. It is also working to expand in Asia.

ANZ Year to 30 September	2001	2002
Operating income ($mn)	6,406.0	6,988.0
Net interest income ($mn)	3,833.0	4,018.0
Operating expenses ($mn)	3,092.0	2,905.0
Operating profit before tax ($mn)	2,783.0	3,223.0
Profit after tax ($mn)	1,870.0	2,322.0
Earnings per share (¢)	125.3	155.1
Dividend (¢)	73	85
Percentage franked	100	100
Non-interest income to total income (%)	40.2	42.5
Cost-to-income ratio (%)	48.3	41.6
Return on equity (%)	18.4	21.1
Return on assets (%)	1.0	1.3
Half Year to 31 March	**2002**	**2003**
Operating income ($mn)	3,374.0	3,492.0
Operating profit before tax ($mn)	1,493.0	1,587.0
Profit after tax ($mn)	1,050.0	1,141.0
Earnings per share (¢)	66.3	72.0
Dividend (¢)	39	44
Percentage franked	100	100
Net tangible assets per share ($)	7.05	8.13

The Australian Gas Light Company

Share price ($)	11.02	
12-month high ($)	11.64	
12-month low ($)	9.56	
Market capitalisation ($mn)	4,821.1	
Price-to-NTA-per-share ratio	4.0	
5-year share price return (% p.a.)	3.3	
Sector: Utilities	**Company**	**Sector**
Price-earnings ratio (times)	15.1	15.2
Dividend yield (%)	5.0	4.6

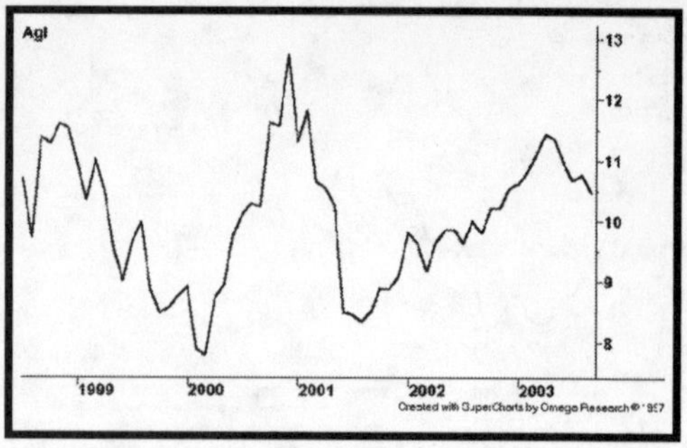

www.agl.com.au

AGL, established in 1837 to light the streets of Sydney, is one of the nation's oldest business enterprises. It now operates a major supply network for gas and electricity, with more than three million customers in Australia and New Zealand. It owns 30% of the listed Australian Pipeline Trust, and 50% of Elgas, Australia's largest liquefied petroleum gas distributor. It also operates energy assets in Chile.

Latest Business Results (June 2003, Full Year)

AGL enjoyed a strong result, thanks mainly to its $880 million acquisition in 2002 of Victorian energy retailer Pulse Energy, which made a better-than-expected contribution. Without Pulse, AGL would have reported profits roughly in line with the previous year. Cost-cutting and streamlining initiatives in New Zealand led to a 2% increase in profits, offsetting the reduction in revenue resulting from the sale of retail gas and generation assets. There was a good result from the small Agility subsidiary, which provides advisory and support services for energy infrastructure schemes. The company took a $17 million writedown on its TransACT telecommunications investment, and reported a $52.5 million equity-accounted loss on its COMindico telecommunications venture.

Outlook

For some years, AGL has been taking advantage of government moves to deregulate the energy and telecommunications industries. However, the company's forays into telecommunications have generally proven unsuccessful, and it is now working to rationalise its energy assets. In many cases, it is hampered by government regulations, which allow for fairly predictable revenue streams but provide only minimal scope for growth. As a result, it is seeking to diversify its operations. It is looking to take a 35% stake in Victoria's $3.5 billion Loy Yang A power station, but is facing objections from the Australian Competition and Consumer Commission. It has sold some $800 million worth of non-core assets, and is looking to sell more, including its telecommunications businesses and its Western Australian electricity generation facilities. The company has already announced that it expects further growth in profits in the 2003–04 year.

AGL Year to 30 June	2002	2003
Revenues ($mn)	2,906.2	3,872.4
EBIT ($mn)	537.8	679.9
EBIT margin (%)	18.5	17.6
Gross margin (%)	32.2	32.1
Operating profit before tax ($mn)	379.9	514.0
Profit after tax ($mn)	247.1	320.8
Earnings per share (¢)	66.4	73.2
Cashflow per share (¢)	125.4	130.1
Dividend (¢)	52	55
Percentage franked	67	62
Net tangible assets per share ($)	3.17	2.77
Interest cover (times)	3.4	4.1
Return on equity (%)	12.3	12.8
Debt-to-equity ratio (%)	107.2	63.1
Current ratio	0.7	1.1

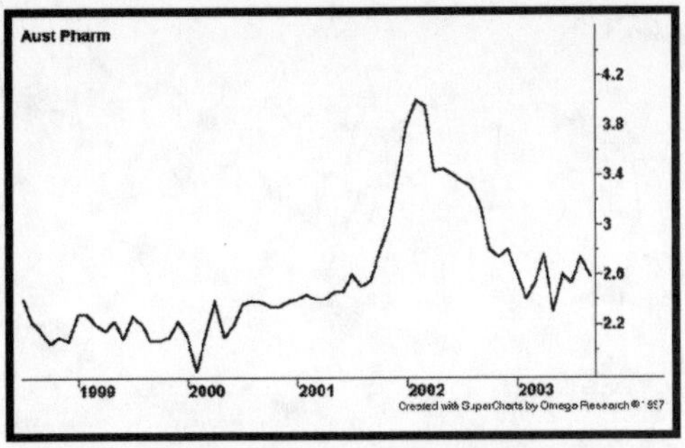

www.api.net.au

Australian Pharmaceutical Industries Limited

Share price ($)	2.68	
12-month high ($)	3.49	
12-month low ($)	2.16	
Market capitalisation ($mn)	612.3	
Price-to-NTA-per-share ratio	2.7	
5-year share price return (% p.a.)	9.9	
Sector: Health Care	**Company**	**Sector**
Price-earnings ratio (times)	16.9	40.6
Dividend yield (%)	4.9	2.9

Sydney-based Australian Pharmaceutical is one of Australia's largest wholesalers and distributors of pharmaceutical products. It was listed on the stock exchange in 1997, after 87 years as a co-operative owned and controlled by chemists. In 2000 it acquired the pharmaceutical wholesaling and manufacturing operations of Washington H. Soul Pattinson, which now owns 22% of the company's equity. In 2001 it bought Hospital Services Australia, another national wholesaler and distributor, in 2002 it acquired the Australian and New Zealand pharmaceutical operations of Interpacific and in mid 2003 it bought the Pharmacy Health brand of 87 over-the-counter health products.

Latest Business Results (April 2003, Full Year)

Revenues grew solidly, thanks to the company's string of acquisitions. But integration costs, lower than forecast earnings from the Hospital Services Australia acquisition and costs associated with moving to a new head office and distribution centre all combined to bring profits down. The company was also hit by a $2 million charge relating to the Therapeutic Goods Administration recall of products manufactured by Pan Pharmaceuticals. There was a good contribution from the new Interpacific acquisitions. The company reported that on a normalised basis profits rose approximately 5%.

Outlook

Following the Australian Competition and Consumer Commission's refusal to allow the planned merger between Australian Pharmaceutical and one of its main rivals, Sigma, the company is now looking to fresh ways to boost business and cut costs. Its move to a new 30,000–square-metre home at Camellia in Sydney is expected to lead eventually to productivity gains, though it has caused a higher-than-expected hit to costs. The company has also restructured itself into six new operating divisions – API Pharmacy, Hospital and Medical Supplies, Halas Dental, Zuellig Pharma, Healthcare Logistics and Healthcare Manufacturing – designed to streamline its business. It has sold its API Finance loan book, in order to concentrate on its core areas of expertise. However, continuing government moves to reduce the cost of the Pharmaceutical Benefits Scheme – which applies to about 75% of drug sales in Australia – will have a negative impact on business.

API Year to 30 April	2002	2003
Revenues ($mn)	1,906.3	2,471.5
EBIT ($mn)	43.9	43.4
EBIT margin (%)	2.3	1.8
Gross margin (%)	7.0	7.4
Operating profit before tax ($mn)	50.0	46.5
Profit after tax ($mn)	34.7	34.0
Earnings per share (¢)	17.6	15.9
Cashflow per share (¢)	21.1	20.6
Dividend (¢)	13	13
Percentage franked	100	100
Net tangible assets per share ($)	1.00	0.98
Interest cover (times)	–	–
Return on equity (%)	13.2	11.1
Debt-to-equity ratio (%)	34.8	–
Current ratio	1.2	1.4

Australian Stock Exchange Limited

Share price ($)	13.31	
12-month high ($)	13.78	
12-month low ($)	10.22	
Market capitalisation ($mn)	1,364.0	
Price-to-NTA-per-share ratio	6.5	
5-year share price return (% p.a.)	–	
Sector: Financials	**Company**	**Sector**
Price-earnings ratio (times)	22.2	16.2
Dividend yield (%)	3.0	4.5

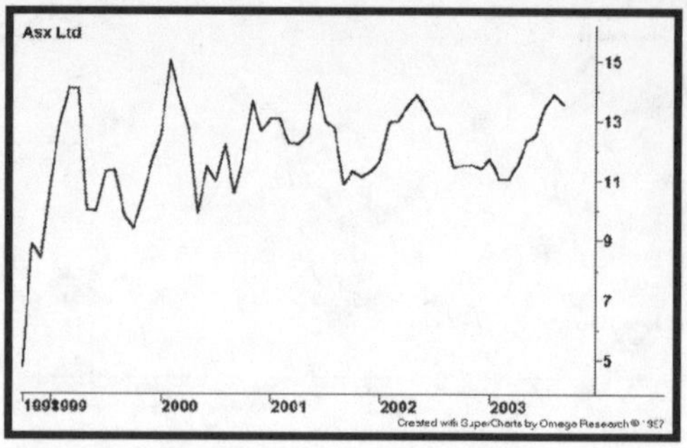

www.asx.com.au

The Australian Stock Exchange was formed in 1987 through the amalgamation of six independent stock exchanges that formerly operated in the state capital cities. Each of those exchanges had a history of share trading dating back to the 19th century. Originally a mutual organisation of stockbrokers, in 1998 the ASX became a listed company, with its shares traded on its own market. As well as operating Australia's primary national stock exchange for equities, derivatives and fixed-interest securities, it also provides a comprehensive market data service.

Latest Business Results (June 2003, Full Year)

In a dismal year for the stock market, the ASX saw its revenues essentially flat, though it managed a small rise in profits. Its core equities trading business recorded a 1% decline in revenues, to $90 million. There was a daily average during the year of 54,633 equities trades, compared with 56,144 in the previous year. Derivatives trading revenues were flat, with a 13% increase in options trading offset by reduced warrants business. Though there were only 81 new listings on the ASX, compared to 91 in the previous year, new listings revenues actually rose 5%. However, market data revenues fell 4%. The company treated as a significant item a $5 million writeoff of its discontinued funds management transaction project ASX FundConnect.

Outlook

Renewed stock market strength from July 2003 – with volumes some 25% higher than in the same period of the previous year – suggests the ASX could experience strong organic growth in the June 2004 year. The company is also working to introduce a range of new products, such as its new property trust index futures contract and its agricultural futures contracts. It sees great potential from its ASX Perpetual joint venture share registry operation, despite a decline in profit in the June 2003 year. Demand for its investor education courses is growing as investors become more sophisticated. The company is already able to give Australian investors access to Singapore and US markets, and has initiated talks on links with Japanese and Canadian markets.

ASX Year to 30 June	2002	2003
Revenues ($mn)	195.6	195.1
Equities trading (%)	47	46
Listings (%)	19	20
Derivatives trading (%)	20	20
Market data (%)	14	14
EBIT ($mn)	78.4	79.2
EBIT margin (%)	40.1	40.6
Operating profit before tax ($mn)	82.7	85.6
Profit after tax ($mn)	59.1	61.3
Earnings per share (¢)	58.3	60.1
Cashflow per share (¢)	76.7	77.0
Dividend (¢)	40.6	39.6
Percentage franked	100	100
Net tangible assets per share ($)	1.93	2.06
Interest cover (times)	–	–
Return on equity (%)	33.2	29.9
Debt-to-equity ratio (%)	–	–
Current ratio	1.9	2.6

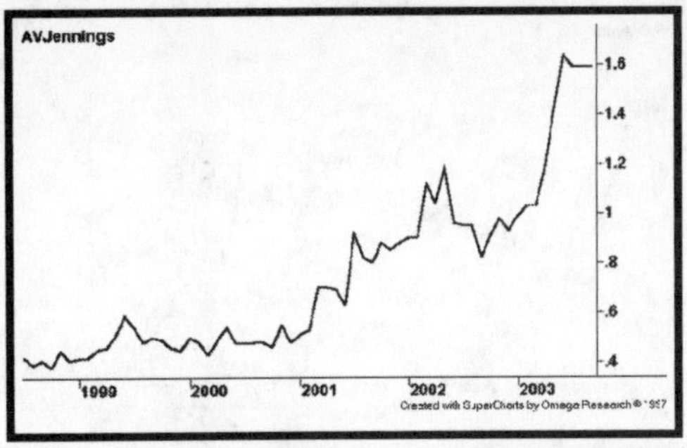

www.avjennings.com.au

AV Jennings Homes Limited

Share price ($)	1.59
12-month high ($)	1.71
12-month low ($)	0.81
Market capitalisation ($mn)	342.2
Price-to-NTA-per-share ratio	1.6
5-year share price return (% p.a.)	45.2

Sector: Financials	Company	Sector
Price-earnings ratio (times)	6.0	16.2
Dividend yield (%)	6.3	4.5

Melbourne-based AV Jennings, one of Australia's best-known names in housing developments, was founded in Victoria in 1932. It is today one of Australia's largest home builders and creators of residential communities, offering around 3,000 new homes each year. It operates in four states: New South Wales, Victoria, Queensland and South Australia.

Latest Business Results (March 2003, Full Year)

The continuing housing boom handed another solid gain in profits to AV Jennings. Revenues were up, thanks to an increase in project housing and land sales. However, the main boost to profits came from the company's moves into urban redevelopment activity. Gross margins on turnover for project housing increased slightly when compared to the previous period. However, for redevelopment products (including land and housing), the gross margin increased significantly. The company also benefited from just a negligible change in administrative overheads and from a mandatory change in Australian accounting standards relating to residential property development projects. This change, which requires the use of the percentage of completion method of accounting in certain circumstances, resulted in an increase in revenue of $33 million, pre-tax profit of $9.3 million and profit after tax of $6.5 million.

Outlook

AV Jennings has spent several years transforming itself into a developer of 'urban infill' projects, generally for existing home owners who want to move into a bigger and/or newer dwelling in their own suburb. This involves finding suitable suburban land sites, and then developing them. Previously, the company concentrated on building cheap homes for customers – usually first home buyers – who had already bought a plot of land. The latter work involved low margins and a great degree of volatility, in line with the housing cycle. Now, however, the company is enjoying stability of earnings and far higher margins. One of its main problems is locating suitable development sites, and during the March 2003 year it increased its land holdings from 5,900 lots to 6,650 lots, resulting in a higher debt-to-equity ratio but providing ample scope for future growth.

AVJ Year to 31 March	2002	2003
Revenues ($mn)	466.0	529.5
Developments (%)	79	72
Projects (%)	21	28
EBIT ($mn)	43.6	80.8
EBIT margin (%)	9.4	15.3
Gross margin (%)	47.1	55.9
Operating profit before tax ($mn)	43.5	80.7
Profit after tax ($mn)	29.3	56.8
Earnings per share (¢)	13.6	26.4
Cashflow per share (¢)	14.9	27.6
Dividend (¢)	9.5	10
Percentage franked	100	100
Net tangible assets per share ($)	0.77	1.00
Interest cover (times)	807.1	598.6
Return on equity (%)	17.5	28.8
Debt-to-equity ratio (%)	27.1	43.3
Current ratio	1.6	2.6

AXA Asia Pacific Holdings Limited

Share price ($)	2.54	
12-month high ($)	2.68	
12-month low ($)	1.87	
Market capitalisation ($mn)	6,230.9	
Price-to-NTA-per-share ratio	1.2	
5-year share price return (% p.a.)	-1.2	
Sector: Financials	**Company**	**Sector**
Price-earnings ratio (times)	13.5	16.2
Dividend yield (%)	3.8	4.5

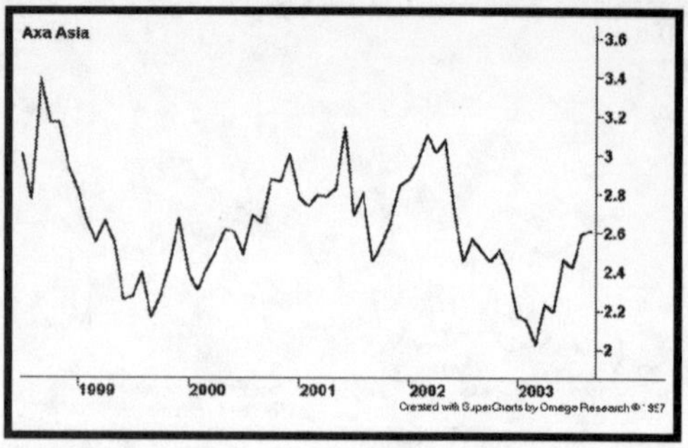

www.axa.com.au

AXA Asia Pacific is one of Australia's insurance giants. Established in 1869 as the National Mutual Life Association of Australasia, it is now a 51%-owned subsidiary of the French insurance and financial services giant AXA. It is a leading supplier of life insurance and superannuation products in Australia and New Zealand, with a big funds management operation and a growing financial planning business. It has a major insurance business in China, and is also active in Indonesia, the Philippines, Singapore and Thailand.

Latest Business Results (June 2003, Half Year)

Profits surged, thanks mainly to powerful gains in investment earnings from Asia. Altogether, investment profits (after tax) expanded from $27 million to $188 million, thanks in large measure to favourable movements in the bond markets. But operating earnings actually fell 10%, though this reflected the sale in February 2003 of the company's health insurance business. Excluding this, operating earnings were flat on the June 2002 half, with business up both locally and abroad, but the strong dollar had a negative impact on overseas earnings. Australian and New Zealand funds under management edged up to $42 billion. The company treated as a significant item an after-tax $368 million profit on the sale of its health insurance business.

Outlook

AXA Asia Pacific is working to transform itself, with the sale of its health insurance operations and the acquisition of the financial advisory firm ipac Securities. It views wealth management as offering great potential, not only in Australia but also throughout Asia, and is moving to acquire other similar businesses. It is working to launch ipac-style operations in Asia. The company is achieving success in boosting acceptance of its funds among advisers, and believes it has laid a foundation for strong growth as markets recover. In the Hong Kong/China market it is boosting business through salaried marketing staff, rather than relying on commissioned agents, which led to problems several years before when rival firms poached many AXA agents.

AXA Year to 31 December*	2001	2002
Revenues ($mn)	5,253.0	2,992.0
Operating profit before tax ($mn)	321.0	253.0
Profit after tax ($mn)	395.0	330.0
Earnings per share (¢)	17.9**	18.8
Dividend (¢)	12.25	9.75
Percentage franked	61	60
Return on equity (%)	10.4**	10.8

** 15 months to 31 December 2001.*
*** Annualised figure.*

Half Year to 30 June	2002	2003
Revenues ($mn)	1,125.0	2,486.0
Operating profit before tax ($mn)	107.0	293.0
Profit after tax ($mn)	134.0	287.0
Earnings per share (¢)	7.6	16.5
Dividend (¢)	4.75	4.75
Percentage franked	60	60
Net tangible assets per share ($)	1.71	2.05
Debt-to-equity ratio (%)	–	–

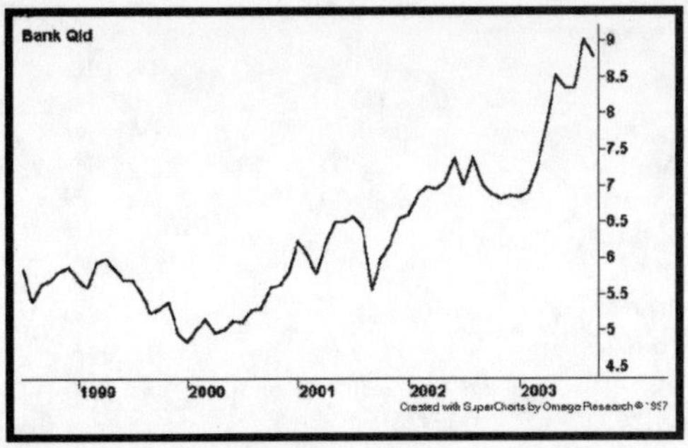

www.boq.com.au

Bank of Queensland Limited

Share price ($)	9.02
12-month high ($)	9.05
12-month low ($)	6.50
Market capitalisation ($mn)	676.6
Price-to-NTA-per-share ratio	2.5
5-year share price return (% p.a.)	14.6

Sector: Financials	Company	Sector
Price-earnings ratio (times)	19.7	16.2
Dividend yield (%)	3.2	4.5

The Bank of Queensland was established in 1874 as a building society, later gaining a banking licence. It has an estimated 6% share of the banking market in Queensland, with some 110 branches.

Latest Business Results (February 2003, Half Year)

Bank of Queensland rode the state's housing boom to a strong surge in revenues and profits. The result was aided by higher productivity, increased branch numbers, new products and business banking investment, combined with the success of the bank's Performance Enhancement Program in controlling expenses. Revenues grew at 20% compared to an increase in costs of only 7% for the same period. Lending approvals rose 51% to $2.3 billion, making the company one of Australia's fastest growing banks over the period. Total assets under management grew by 10% to $7.3 billion. Deposit growth was also strong, up 22%. The bank's cost-to-income ratio improved from 73% in the first half of 2002 to 65%.

Outlook

The bank is enjoying superb growth, thanks especially to its mortgage business. It is now responsible for some 14% of all new housing loans in the booming southeast Queensland housing market. It continues its new branch roll-out, with 12 planned for the 2003 second half, and a further 10 by August 2004. It has also put in place a series of strong cost-control initiatives, and is expecting $24 million in annual benefits from these moves. It is striving to boost its business banking loan book, which grew by 31% in the 12 months to March 2003. In August 2003, the bank announced the $13 million acquisition of UFJ Finance Australia, which leases equipment to small and medium-sized businesses. The acquisition is expected to expand the bank's business lending by about one-third. Bank of Queensland shares have been supported by speculation that it may become a takeover target, perhaps by the Commonwealth Bank, which already owns 13% of the equity.

BOQ Year to 31 August	2001	2002
Operating income ($mn)	163.2	173.9
Net interest income ($mn)	106.6	109.1
Operating expenses ($mn)	124.1	124.0
Operating profit before tax ($mn)	36.5	40.6
Profit after tax ($mn)	27.5	28.7
Earnings per share (¢)	43.2	45.8
Dividend (¢)	28	29
Percentage franked	100	100
Non-interest income to total income (%)	34.7	37.2
Cost-to-income ratio (%)	76.0	71.3
Return on equity (%)	14.1	12.3
Return on assets (%)	0.7	0.6
Half Year to 28 February	**2002**	**2003**
Operating income ($mn)	84.1	101.1
Operating profit before tax ($mn)	18.9	30.7
Profit after tax ($mn)	13.3	21.3
Earnings per share (¢)	18.7	28.1
Dividend (¢)	14	17
Percentage franked	100	100
Net tangible assets per share ($)	2.90	3.58

Bendigo Bank Limited

Share price ($)	8.95	
12-month high ($)	9.05	
12-month low ($)	7.00	
Market capitalisation ($mn)	1,092.8	
Price-to-NTA-per-share ratio	2.4	
5-year share price return (% p.a.)	21.4	
Sector: Financials	**Company**	**Sector**
Price-earnings ratio (times)	19.1	16.2
Dividend yield (%)	3.7	4.5

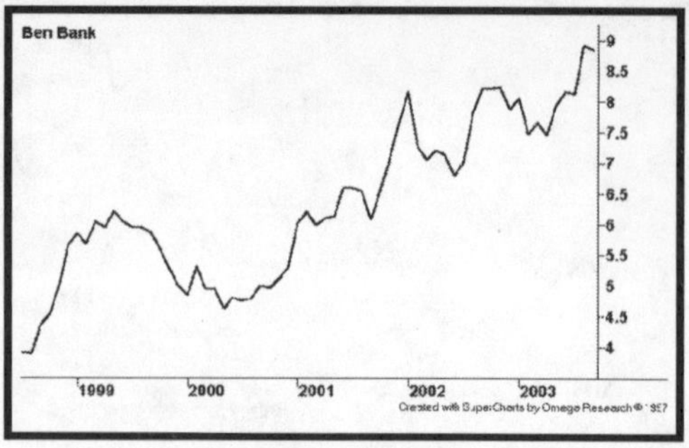

www.benbank.com.au

Established as a building society in 1858, Victoria's Bendigo Bank is today Australia's only remaining regionally based bank, and is also one of the smallest of all the listed banks. It has a network of more than 250 branches, concentrated in Victoria, southern NSW and Queensland. It has moved into various niche businesses, including the establishment of Elders Rural Bank in a joint venture with Futuris Corporation, to provide banking services to rural Australia. Its Sandhurst Trustees subsidiary, founded in 1888, provides a wide range of financial products and services to individuals, trusts and corporate bodies. It has developed a community bank model, launching new bank branches together with local communities.

Latest Business Results (June 2003, Full Year)

Its high gearing to housing handed Bendigo an excellent increase in revenues and profits. Total bank lending approvals were $4.8 billion, a 33% increase over the previous year, with lending approvals secured by mortgage over residential property representing 70% of the total. Total deposits rose 18% to $8.2 billion. All of this increase was in retail deposits, and the ratio of retail deposits to total deposits rose to 92.5%. New customer numbers were up 13%. Superannuation and managed funds controlled by Sandhurst Trustees grew $450 million to $1.7 billion. Altogether, bank assets grew 16% to $9.3 billion.

Outlook

Bendigo Bank continues its impressive expansion, though the focus now is organic growth, rather than increasing in size through acquisition. It opened 30 new community bank branches in the June 2003 year – bringing the total to 100 – with at least 30 more planned by June 2004. However, the bank's costs remain stubbornly high, and among the highest of all the banks. In addition, its strong gearing to housing makes Bendigo very vulnerable to any downturn in that sector. It is working to boost its business banking and wealth management operations. It is also striving to reduce its dependence on Victoria, which still represents more than 60% of business. Bendigo Bank could realise windfall profits from the likely public float of the venerable financial institution IOOF, of which it owns 9% of the equity.

BEN Year to 30 June	2002	2003
Operating income ($mn)	291.6	346.6
Net interest income ($mn)	192.6	222.3
Operating expenses ($mn)	205.2	241.9
Operating profit before tax ($mn)	64.4	89.3
Profit after tax ($mn)	48.8	59.0
Earnings per share (¢)	41.1	46.8
Dividend (¢)	29	33.5
Percentage franked	100	100
Non-interest income to total income (%)	34.0	35.9
Net tangible assets per share ($)	3.52	3.80
Cost-to-income ratio (%)	70.4	69.8
Return on equity (%)	10.6	11.3
Return on assets (%)	0.7	0.7

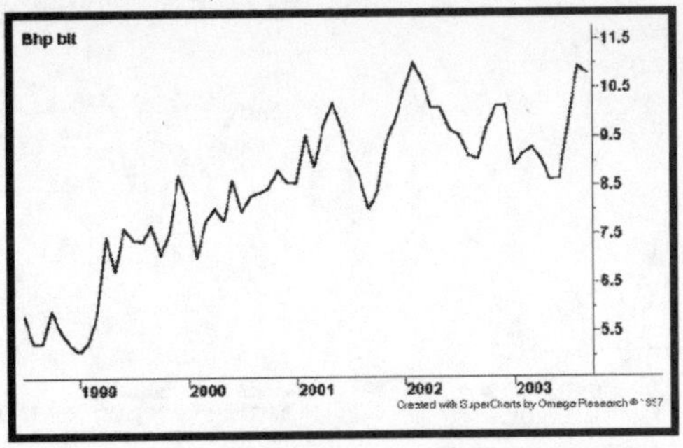

www.bhpbilliton.com

BHP BILLITON LIMITED

Share price ($)	10.55
12-month high ($)	10.84
12-month low ($)	8.22
Market capitalisation ($mn)	66,465.0
Price-to-NTA-per-share ratio	3.7
5-year share price return (% p.a.)	17.5

Sector: Materials	Company	Sector
Price-earnings ratio (times)	23.5	16.0
Dividend yield (%)	2.1	2.9

BHP Billiton, formed from the merger in 2001 of Australian resources giant BHP and British-based mining major Billiton, is now the world's largest diversified resources company. It has more than 100 operations in approximately 20 countries, and occupies industry leader or near industry leader positions in major commodity businesses, including aluminium, energy coal and metallurgical coal, copper, ferro-alloys, iron ore and titanium minerals, along with substantial interests in oil, gas, liquefied natural gas, nickel, diamonds and silver.

LATEST BUSINESS RESULTS (JUNE 2003, FULL YEAR)

BHP Billiton reports its financial results in US dollars. For the purposes of this book, these have been converted into Australian dollars at the rates of A$1 = US$0.565 for the June 2002 results and A$1 = US$0.667 for the June 2003 results. Thus, figures in this book should be used for general guidance only. Profits in June 2003 were up (though were down when translated into Australian dollars for this book). The company achieved higher sales volumes of iron ore, energy coal, copper, aluminium, diamonds and manganese and higher prices for petroleum products, nickel, ferrochrome, copper, hot briquetted iron and manganese alloy. Partly offsetting these were lower sales volumes of petroleum products and lower prices for export energy coal and iron ore.

OUTLOOK

BHP Billiton has become a big beneficiary of booming demand from China for alumina, iron ore, manganese and nickel, with sales more than doubling in 2002–03. The company believes this growth is sustainable. It maintains considerable strength in petroleum products – which provided a third of the company's earnings in 2002-03 – and is planning a major new oil drilling program in Australia's Bass Strait and North West Shelf. It currently has 14 massive projects under developments in seven countries that it believes will power company growth in coming years. With the merger of BHP and Billiton, the company announced a major cost-savings program with a target of US$500 million of annual savings by June 2005. The company says it has already realised US$375 million in annual savings.

BHP Year to 30 June*	2002	2003
Revenues ($mn)	28,134.5	23,400.3
Carbon steel materials (%)	21	21
Aluminium (%)	18	19
Petroleum (%)	18	18
Energy coal (%)	12	12
Base metals (%)	12	11
Diamonds & specialty products (%)	9	8
Stainless steel materials (%)	5	6
EBIT ($mn)	4,982.3	4,841.1
EBIT margin (%)	31.3	31.0
Operating profit before tax ($mn)	4,614.2	4,172.4
Profit after tax ($mn)	2,916.8	2,788.6
Earnings per share (¢)	48.4	44.9
Cashflow per share (¢)	100.3	85.7
Dividend (¢)	23.01	21.74
Percentage franked	100	100
Net tangible assets per share ($)	3.58	2.86
Interest cover (times)	24.0	10.9
Return on equity (%)	13.6	15.3
Debt-to-equity ratio (%)	49.8	46.6
Current ratio	1.1	1.6

** BHP Billiton reports its financial results in US dollars. For this book they have been converted to Australian dollars.*

Blackmores Limited

Share price ($)	6.77	
12-month high ($)	7.20	
12-month low ($)	5.48	
Market capitalisation ($mn)	104.1	
Price-to-NTA-per-share ratio	4.5	
5-year share price return (% p.a.)	13.2	
Sector: Health Care	**Company**	**Sector**
Price-earnings ratio (times)	16.5	40.6
Dividend yield (%)	5.2	2.9

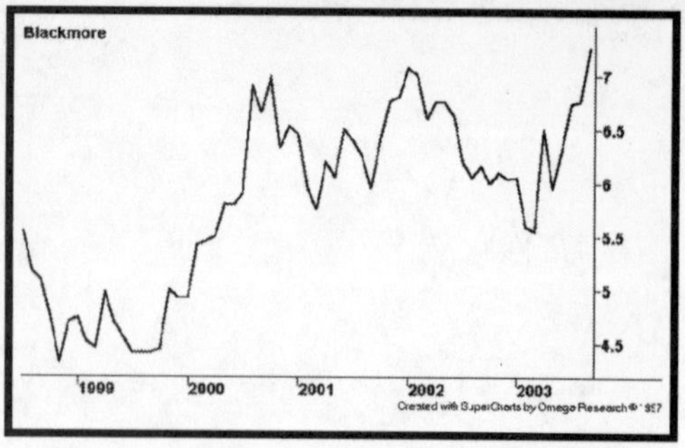

www.blackmores.com.au

Founded in the 1930s, Blackmores is a leading manufacturer and distributor of a wide range of natural healthcare products, nutritional supplements and cosmetics. Its brands include Vitaglow and BioACE. It exports to New Zealand (5% of total company revenues) and South East Asia (14%).

Latest Business Results (June 2003, Full Year)

Turmoil in the health products market, following the mass recall of Pan Pharmaceuticals products, helped boost business for its rival Blackmores. For some weeks after the recall, Blackmores was the only major brand unaffected, with some of its products in short supply, and domestic sales jumping 18% for the year. However, a $1.5 million communications campaign during the recall period meant domestic profits rose only modestly. There was a strong gain from New Zealand, and a big turnaround in South East Asia, with sales there up 19% and this business moving into the black.

Outlook

Blackmores has come through the Pan recall episode with its reputation considerably enhanced. It makes many of its products in it own facilities, and exercises strict controls over outside suppliers. With low debt levels, the company is now seen as being ready to take advantage of the disruption of the natural products industry with a takeover bid for any faltering rival, at a time when total industry sales remain down. The company has started to realise a huge increase in visitor numbers to its website, where it dispenses medical advice. In 2002–03 it gained as many new subscribers to its online newsletter as it had in the previous six years combined. Despite difficult trading conditions in parts of South East Asia, following the SARS outbreak, Blackmores achieved excellent growth, thanks to new products and strong retail partnerships, and it sees the region as offering further strong potential. New Zealand too offers new promise as a result of a strategic partnership from January with PSM Healthcare, New Zealand's leading pharmaceuticals and toiletries manufacturer, allowing it to sell the full range of Blackmores products. Blackmores provides a shareholders card that gives a 25% discount on its products.

BKL Year to 30 June	2002	2003
Revenues ($mn)	81.4	94.7
EBIT ($mn)	8.6	10.1
EBIT margin (%)	10.5	10.7
Gross margin (%)	60.4	63.0
Operating profit before tax ($mn)	7.5	8.9
Profit after tax ($mn)	5.1	6.2
Earnings per share (¢)	34.0	41.1
Cashflow per share (¢)	44.3	53.5
Dividend (¢)	33	35
Percentage franked	100	100
Net tangible assets per share ($)	1.24	1.50
Interest cover (times)	7.7	8.4
Return on equity (%)	27.3	29.9
Debt-to-equity ratio (%)	56.1	36.2
Current ratio	1.1	1.2

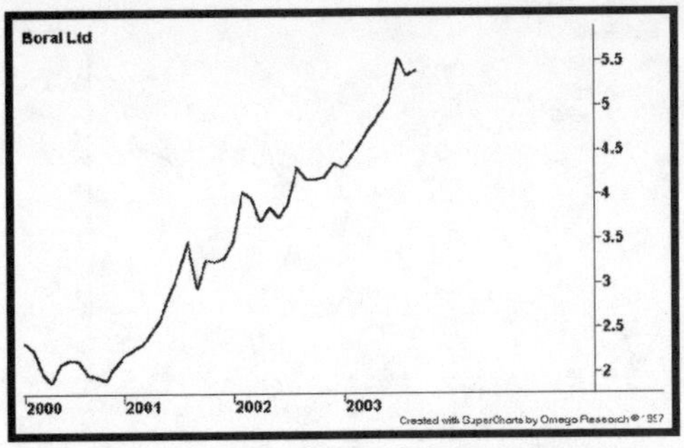

www.boral.com.au

Boral Limited

Share price ($)	5.53
12-month high ($)	5.75
12-month low ($)	3.85
Market capitalisation ($mn)	3,179.5
Price-to-NTA-per-share ratio	1.7
5-year share price return (% p.a.)	18.7

Sector: Materials	Company	Sector
Price-earnings ratio (times)	11.3	16.0
Dividend yield (%)	4.2	2.9

Sydney-based Boral is one of Australia's largest producers of building and construction materials, and it also has operations in several countries. It is one of this country's biggest brick, clay paver and concrete masonry producers, and is also one of the largest in America. It owns half of a large plasterboard joint venture in Asia. The Australian housing market accounts for approximately one-third of total revenues, the Australian non-dwelling building market for 15% to 20%, and the Australian roads, highways, subdivisions and bridges construction market for 15% to 20%. About a third of total sales revenues come from abroad.

Latest Business Results (June 2003, Full Year)

The domestic housing and construction boom lay behind a big jump in profits, along with price increases, productivity gains and some strategic acquisitions. The company also benefited from a resilient housing market in the US and strengthening conditions in Asia. Australian profits (before interest and tax) were up 56%. US profits were up 14%, supported by the new Franklin Brick acquisition, though when translated into Australian dollars there was no growth. The relatively small Asian operation (about 5% of earnings) saw a 39% jump in profits.

Outlook

Boral has already forecast that a weakening of the domestic housing market will limit growth, and it sees 2003–04 profits rising by a single-digit amount only. In Australia, it continues to work to raise prices. In the US, it is trying to diversify from its reliance on the low-margin brick business into other products, such as clay terracotta tiles. US brick-making operations are being hit by substantially higher natural gas prices, and the company believes this might offset profit gains made from higher sales. Much will also depend on currency movements. Boral's earnings from its Asian plasterboard joint venture are expected to benefit from continued growth in plasterboard demand, and the Indonesian construction materials businesses should benefit from increased volumes. The company expects annual spending on growth initiatives, including acquisitions and productivity enhancements, of around $200 million annually for some years.

BLD Year to 30 June	2002	2003
Revenues ($mn)	3,488.8	3,831.0
EBIT ($mn)	343.2	477.7
EBIT margin (%)	9.8	12.5
Gross margin (%)	35.1	36.9
Operating profit before tax ($mn)	280.0	409.9
Profit after tax ($mn)	192.4	283.2
Earnings per share (¢)	33.7	49.1
Cashflow per share (¢)	66.6	82.8
Dividend (¢)	19	23
Percentage franked	56	88
Net tangible assets per share ($)	3.02	3.27
Interest cover (times)	5.4	7.0
Return on equity (%)	10.1	13.9
Debt-to-equity ratio (%)	45.2	35.7
Current ratio	1.4	1.4

Brickworks Limited

Share price ($)	8.25	
12-month high ($)	8.35	
12-month low ($)	5.69	
Market capitalisation ($mn)	1,097.3	
Price-to-NTA-per-share ratio	1.8	
5-year share price return (% p.a.)	32.3	
Sector: Materials	**Company**	**Sector**
Price-earnings ratio (times)	15.0	16.0
Dividend yield (%)	2.4	2.9

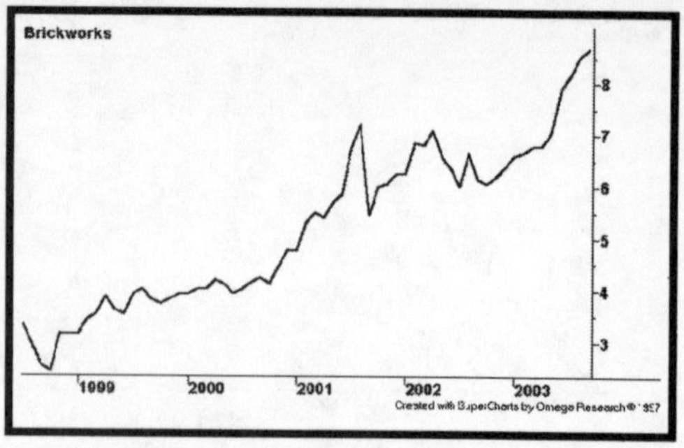

www.brickworks.com.au

Sydney-based Brickworks, founded in 1934, has become Australia's largest brick producer, following its acquisition of rival Bristile. It was already the country's largest producer of floor tiles, and is one of the largest roof tile manufacturers. It also manages an extensive land and equity portfolio. In a cross-shareholding arrangement designed to prevent takeovers, it owns 41% of the equity of Washington H. Soul Pattinson, while Soul Pattinson owns nearly 50% of the equity in Brickworks.

Latest Business Results (June 2003, Full Year)

The housing boom handed Brickworks a big jump in sales and profits. The company's clay products operations enjoyed their best year ever, with sales up 21%, and were unable to meet all domestic demand. Exports were up 78%. Clay products pre-tax profit jumped 29% to $34 million. Investment income (dividends and realised gains) surged 45% to $35 million. At the end of June 2003, the company's investment portfolio was valued at $872 million, slightly down from $880 million a year before. The portfolio returned 3.8% over the year, including unrealised gains, compared to a decline of 1.6% in the benchmark S&P/ASX 300 Accumulation Index.

Outlook

Brickworks now has the task of integrating the Bristile business into its own operations. With Brickworks strong on the east coast, and Bristile based in Western Australia, the prospects are for a powerful nationwide business. But the company has said that with its plants already operating at full capacity, there is little scope for organic growth in the June 2004 year, other than through price rises and increased efficiencies. Overseas sales are growing rapidly, with particularly good demand in Hong Kong for the Silk Road paver range. The company has undertaken a major restructuring of its outdoor tile distribution network, and says strategies are in place to minimise the impact of competition from a large new tile factory being built in NSW by a South African–owned rival. Brickworks is also developing its extensive land holdings, which are concentrated in Sydney's western suburbs. To help pay for the Bristile acquisition, it plans to float $150 million worth of equity holdings as a new investment company.

BKW Year to 30 June	2002	2003
Revenues ($mn)	147.3	179.6
EBIT ($mn)	63.6	78.7
EBIT margin (%)	43.2	43.8
Gross margin (%)	39.7	40.2
Operating profit before tax ($mn)	60.7	75.3
Profit after tax ($mn)	51.9	72.7
Earnings per share (¢)	39.4	55.2
Cashflow per share (¢)	46.9	63.8
Dividend (¢)	15.5	20
Percentage franked	100	100
Net tangible assets per share ($)	4.13	4.61
Interest cover (times)	21.3	23.0
Return on equity (%)	9.9	12.6
Debt-to-equity ratio (%)	12.6	5.0
Current ratio	0.6	1.0

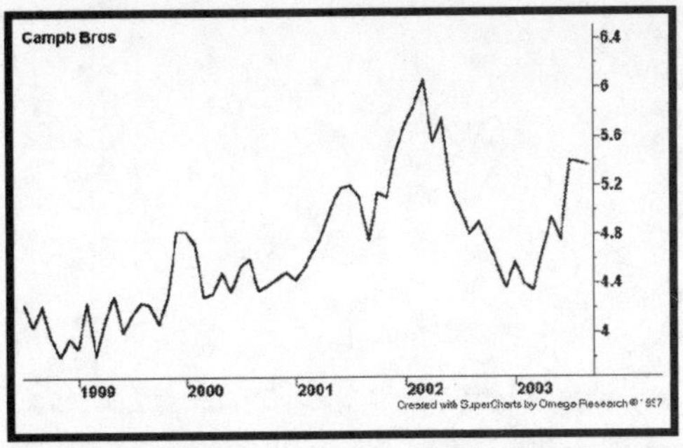

www.campbell.com.au

Campbell Brothers Limited

Share price ($)	5.45	
12-month high ($)	5.48	
12-month low ($)	4.20	
Market capitalisation ($mn)	212.9	
Price-to-NTA-per-share ratio	3.6	
5-year share price return (% p.a.)	12.3	
Sector: Materials	**Company**	**Sector**
Price-earnings ratio (times)	17.9	16.0
Dividend yield (%)	5.5	2.9

Established in 1863, Brisbane-based Campbell Brothers makes cleaning products and provides laboratory services. It is the largest Australian-owned manufacturer and distributor of household laundry and cleansing products, offers sales and marketing systems to grocery manufacturers and retailers and distributes consumer and industrial goods throughout the South Pacific. It is also one of Australia's leaders in the importation, manufacture and distribution of chemical and associated products and the provision of engineering system services and water treatment technologies and it has become the world's largest provider of laboratory analysis services to the minerals industry.

Latest Business Results (March 2003, Full Year)

Continuing strong growth in its laboratory operations – particularly in the second half – handed Campbell Brothers a pleasing boost to its sales and profits. Despite initial disruption and commissioning delays in the integration of the new Bondar Clegg Laboratories acquisition, the laboratory services division recorded excellent profit growth of 42%, with revenues up 18%. The industrial division also performed well, thanks to changes made to the organisational structure during the year, along with the centralisation of manufacturing and distribution operations at Darra, Queensland. Division profits were up 28% and revenues rose 13%. However, the consumer products division struggled in a highly competitive market. Despite improvements in the second half, division profits crashed 42%, with sales slipping 5%.

Outlook

Facing intense competitive pressures in its core cleaning products businesses, Campbell Brothers has for some years been engaged in a strategy of growth through acquisition. It has made 26 acquisitions over 10 years, and is actively seeking more. It is also working to move further away from manufacture and into the provision of services. The company now operates 42 laboratories in 17 countries, and the laboratory services division, though just a third of revenues, accounts for 54% of company profit. It believes it has halted the decline in consumer products profitability, although its new pest control and carpet cleaning initiatives have yet to make the expected contribution and are the subject of continuing review.

CPB Year to 31 March	2002	2003
Revenues ($mn)	336.2	359.3
Consumer (%)	43	37
Laboratory services (%)	28	32
Industrial (%)	29	31
EBIT ($mn)	23.5	25.0
EBIT margin (%)	7.0	7.0
Gross margin (%)	22.2	26.0
Operating profit before tax ($mn)	18.6	19.9
Profit after tax ($mn)	11.2	11.9
Earnings per share (¢)	29.8	30.5
Cashflow per share (¢)	66.8	70.1
Dividend (¢)	30	30
Percentage franked	100	100
Net tangible assets per share ($)	1.59	1.53
Interest cover (times)	4.8	4.9
Return on equity (%)	9.9	9.4
Debt-to-equity ratio (%)	65.1	67.8
Current ratio	2.2	2.0

Casinos Austria International Limited

Share price ($)	0.61	
12-month high ($)	0.63	
12-month low ($)	0.49	
Market capitalisation ($mn)	110.7	
Price-to-NTA-per-share ratio	2.7	
5-year share price return (% p.a.)	18.7	
Sector: Consumer Discretion.	**Company**	**Sector**
Price-earnings ratio (times)	13.7	20.2
Dividend yield (%)	4.9	3.7

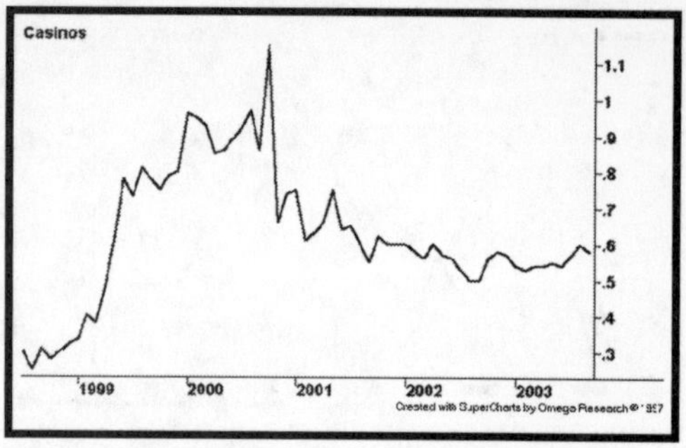

www.casinosaustria.com

Casinos Austria International is a 70%-owned Australian subsidiary of Casinos Austria, a giant global force in the gaming industry. The local company holds investments in gambling operations around the world, sometimes in partnership with its parent, and sometimes in partnership with other companies. Its three flagship operations are the Reef Hotel Casino in Cairns, the Great Blue Heron Casino near Toronto, and four casinos in South Africa. However, it holds many other investments, including in cruise ship gambling, in Casino Canberra in Australia and in several middle-eastern casino businesses.

Latest Business Results (June 2003, Half Year)

The company overcame a series of negative events, including the Iraq war and the SARS outbreak, to post higher profits. The Great Blue Heron Casino recorded solid results following the launch of 24-hour operations. Domestic visitors to the Reef Hotel Casino in Cairns more than offset a drop in foreign tourists, helping that business realise a big jump in profits. Higher revenues were recorded in South Africa, and Casino Canberra posted improved results too. The two Egyptian casinos recorded lower revenues, due to the Iraq War. The Oasis Casino in Palestine's Jericho remained closed due to the ongoing conflict.

CAI Year to 31 December	2001	2002
Revenues ($mn)	92.9	41.2
EBIT ($mn)	18.6	14.4
EBIT margin (%)	20.0	35.0
Operating profit before tax ($mn)	18.2	14.2
Profit after tax ($mn)	13.3	7.9
Earnings per share (¢)	7.5	4.5
Cashflow per share (¢)	8.7	5.4
Dividend (¢)	3	3
Percentage franked	56	17
Interest cover (times)	47.3	58.0
Return on equity (%)	20.3	11.1
Half Year to 30 June	**2002**	**2003**
Revenues ($mn)	19.2	19.8
Operating profit before tax ($mn)	5.7	6.9
Profit after tax ($mn)	3.0	4.3
Earnings per share (¢)	1.7	2.4
Dividend (¢)	0	0
Percentage franked	–	–
Net tangible assets per share ($)	0.20	0.22
Debt-to-equity ratio (%)	8.5	5.1
Current ratio	1.4	1.1

Outlook

The Reef Hotel Casino, one of the main contributors to Casino Austria's business, looks set for good growth, with a strong revival of Asian tourist numbers to Cairns and a new attraction, the rainforest dome, due to open by the end of the year. The South African businesses, too, remain strong, with the opening of the fourth casino proving a solid boost to business. The company is investigating the launch of a fifth operation. A new game at Casino Canberra, Rapid Roulette, is proving popular, and the company is trying to get permission to add gaming machines to this operation.

Central Equity Limited

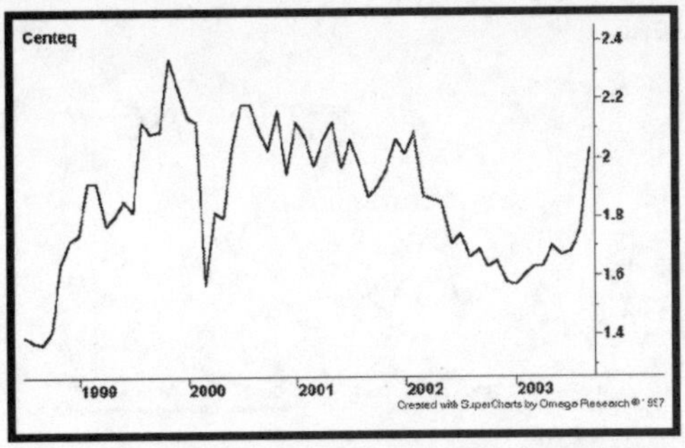

www.centralequity.com.au

Share price ($)	1.72
12-month high ($)	1.80
12-month low ($)	1.54
Market capitalisation ($mn)	151.7
Price-to-NTA-per-share ratio	0.8
5-year share price return (% p.a.)	15.2

Sector: Financials	Company	Sector
Price-earnings ratio (times)	4.5	16.2
Dividend yield (%)	7.6	4.5

Melbourne-based property developer Central Equity was founded in 1987, and has been responsible for some $2 billion worth of residential property developments in the city. It has achieved renown for its pioneering innercity apartment projects, including the conversion of older buildings into residential properties. Its real estate subsidiary Melbourne Inner City Management has an extensive business managing many of the properties the company has sold. Some 30% of company sales come from previous purchasers or referrals.

Latest Business Results (June 2003, Full Year)

The continuing housing boom handed Central Equity a record profit. At June 2003 it had an additional $433 million of contracted sales not yet reflected in the financial statements.

Outlook

Central Equity shares have been volatile. In some years they have been among the top-performing shares among larger companies on the ASX, at other times among the worst. It will suffer in any housing downturn, although it believes its policy of selling off-the-plan gives it a substantial time lag. It also believes that selling off-the-plan has led to the abandonment of many rival projects, which could not garner enough sales to proceed, thus introducing an element of regulation to the housing market. However, concerns have been growing about a glut of innercity apartments in Melbourne, with claims that values of apartments in some recent developments have fallen below their sales prices. In mid 2003 the company completed its Southpoint development in the Melbourne Southbank precinct. Funds totalling approximately $65 million from settlements were used to retire construction finance. The company has four other developments in Southbank, worth $550 million, with 95% of the apartments already sold. Completion of the first two will be in late 2003 and of the remaining two in late 2004. It has also sold over half of the apartments in its latest development, Market Square Condos in Dudley Street, West Melbourne, with construction to begin in early 2004. Central Equity is also continuing to expand its land subdivision development work with land for subdivision comprising approximately $140 million in end sale value.

CEQ Year to 30 June	2002	2003
Revenues ($mn)	209.3	220.5
EBIT ($mn)	33.0	42.5
EBIT margin (%)	15.8	19.3
Gross margin (%)	23.5	25.8
Operating profit before tax ($mn)	34.9	46.9
Profit after tax ($mn)	24.1	32.8
Earnings per share (¢)	28.9	38.0
Cashflow per share (¢)	29.8	39.4
Dividend (¢)	12	13
Percentage franked	100	100
Net tangible assets per share ($)	1.84	2.13
Interest cover (times)	–	–
Return on equity (%)	16.3	19.1
Debt-to-equity ratio (%)	57.3	46.6
Current ratio	1.8	1.7

CMI Limited

Share price ($)	1.70	
12-month high ($)	1.75	
12-month low ($)	1.19	
Market capitalisation ($mn)	47.3	
Price-to-NTA-per-share ratio	0.8	
5-year share price return (% p.a.)	27.5	
Sector: Industrials	**Company**	**Sector**
Price-earnings ratio (times)	6.4	12.1
Dividend yield (%)	5.9	3.9

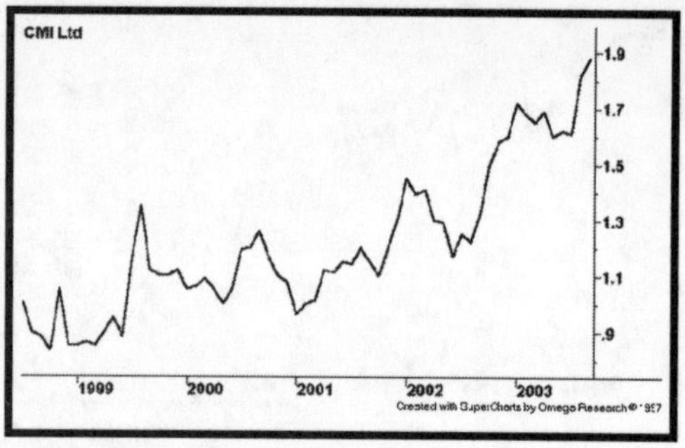

www.cmilimited.com.au

Brisbane-based CMI, established in 1991, is a manufacturer and distributor of a range of specialist industrial components, with 80% of sales to Australian and international automotive companies. It also supplies the white goods, mining, construction and IT industries. Its operations are conducted through four divisions: engineered components, electrical components, four-wheel-drive components and US operations. It has manufacturing and/or distribution centres in Australia, New Zealand and the US, and sells its products to around 20 countries.

Latest Business Results (June 2003, Full Year)

Record Australian car sales, recent acquisitions and an improved performance from its four-wheel-drive business all combined to hand CMI a big increase in sales and profits. There was continued strong sales growth from the company's electrical components division, particularly to the mining sector, as well as a strong performance by its New Zealand–based spring manufacturing business. American sales were up 25%.

Outlook

CMI is a beneficiary of the continuing strength in the Australian economy, which is flowing through to strong demand for new cars. The company is also realising growing success in its efforts to penetrate the US market for auto components. It sees another bright year ahead, with increased sales both domestically and in the US. Two acquisitions made during 2002–03 – Toowoomba Metal Technologies (TMT) and CMI Forge – have been fully integrated into the company's operations, and are expected to boost sales revenues by at least $60 million annually. In May 2003 the company raised approximately $11 million through an entitlement offer of new convertible preference shares, to reduce bank borrowings associated with the two acquisitions and fund future growth. However, TMT's sales of heavy transport wheels to North America have been hurt by the strong dollar. Since acquisition, CMI has been working to reduce TMT's cost structure, and expects benefits from these measures to accrue during 2003–04. The relocation during the year of CMI's Campbellfield automotive components plant to larger, state-of-the-art premises adjoining Ford Australia's Broadmeadows factory has further strengthened the company's supply arrangements with Ford and other key customers. The opening of CMI's second US distribution centre in South Carolina will boost US business.

CMI Year to 30 June	2002	2003
Revenues ($mn)	124.0	191.2
EBIT ($mn)	9.5	13.8
EBIT margin (%)	7.6	7.2
Gross margin (%)	20.0	18.7
Operating profit before tax ($mn)	7.8	10.8
Profit after tax ($mn)	5.2	7.2
Earnings per share (¢)	17.9	26.8
Cashflow per share (¢)	32.6	47.8
Dividend (¢)	10	10
Percentage franked	100	100
Net tangible assets per share ($)	1.59	2.10
Interest cover (times)	5.7	4.5
Return on equity (%)	11.1	12.4
Debt-to-equity ratio (%)	55.8	63.3
Current ratio	2.0	1.9

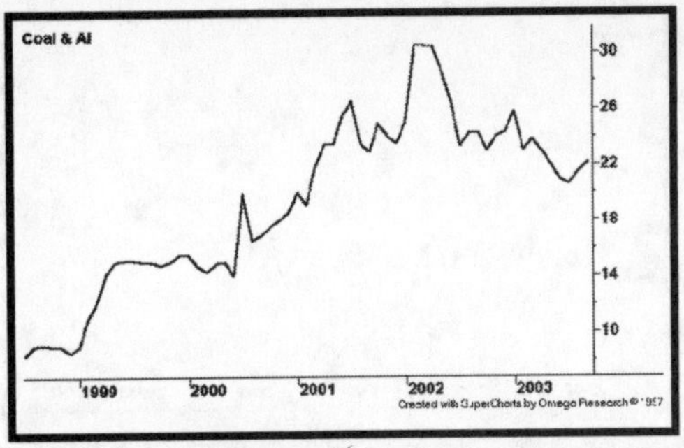

www.coalandallied.com.au

Coal & Allied Industries Limited

Share price ($)	21.00
12-month high ($)	25.80
12-month low ($)	20.00
Market capitalisation ($mn)	1,857.2
Price-to-NTA-per-share ratio	2.3
5-year share price return (% p.a.)	26.7

Sector: Materials	Company	Sector
Price-earnings ratio (times)	11.4	16.0
Dividend yield (%)	3.8	2.9

Coal & Allied is a 76%-owned subsidiary of minerals giant Rio Tinto, and is one of Australia's leading coal mining companies. Its activities are mainly in NSW, and are centred on the Hunter Valley. It also operates a joint venture mine at Mount Thorley with Pohang Iron and Steel of South Korea, and it has other interests at Bengalla and Warkworth.

Latest Business Results (June 2003, Half Year)

Revenues were down and profits fell sharply, in a dismal result that reflected the intense competition that has arisen in the coal business. The company was hit by a lethal combination of a stronger dollar, generally lower contract prices for export thermal coal, higher shipping costs and the increasing shift to lower priced spot sales of Australian coal. Actual coal production fell by 900,000 tonnes to 13.8 million tonnes.

Outlook

Demand for coal remains firm, but strong competition from Chinese and Indonesian exports is pushing prices down, at a time when the Australian dollar has strengthened. This has forced the company to reduce stockpiles and adjust production levels, and it was expecting to produce approximately 28 million tonnes of coal in 2003, compared to its installed capacity of just over 32 million tonnes. It is also being forced to make changes in work patterns, including a decrease in the use of contract labour. The trend to spot or indexed sales, rather than contract tonnes, continued to gather pace in Asia, led by the Japanese power utilities. The result is that only 35% of sales now are by contract, compared to 85% just five years ago. The company is addressing the problem of port congestion, caused by fluctuations in the arrival of vessels. Each one-cent increase in the value of the Australian dollar against the US dollar reduces the company's profit by $9 million.

CNA Year to 31 December	2001	2002
Revenues ($mn)	1,443.2	1,181.4
EBIT ($mn)	390.2	330.3
EBIT margin (%)	27.0	28.0
Gross margin (%)	77.7	79.9
Operating profit before tax ($mn)	328.0	306.4
Profit after tax ($mn)	212.5	159.7
Earnings per share (¢)	245.4	184.5
Cashflow per share (¢)	413.9	332.4
Dividend (¢)	75	80
Percentage franked	100	100
Interest cover (times)	6.3	13.8
Return on equity (%)	33.3	21.1
Half Year to 30 June	**2002**	**2003**
Sales revenues ($mn)	674.6	463.0
Operating profit before tax ($mn)	221.7	20.8
Profit after tax ($mn)	104.7	7.2
Earnings per share (¢)	121.0	8.3
Dividend (¢)	40	0
Percentage franked	100	–
Net tangible assets per share ($)	9.03	9.33
Debt-to-equity ratio (%)	69.0	62.3
Current ratio	0.8	0.5

Coates Hire Limited

Share price ($)	2.48	
12-month high ($)	2.66	
12-month low ($)	1.68	
Market capitalisation ($mn)	496.2	
Price-to-NTA-per-share ratio	1.7	
5-year share price return (% p.a.)	6.3	
Sector: Industrials	**Company**	**Sector**
Price-earnings ratio (times)	14.8	12.1
Dividend yield (%)	4.0	3.9

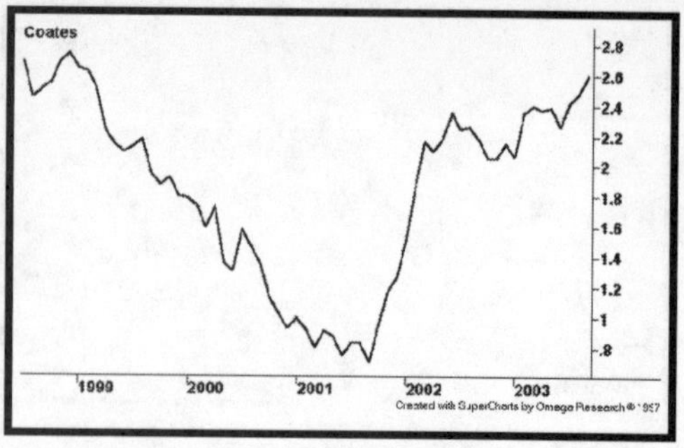

www.coates.com.au

Sydney-based Coates Hire Limited is Australia's largest hire equipment company with more than 130 branches. Following the acquisition of its largest rival Wreckair, it now has around a third of the market. Domestically, it divides its operations into four businesses: Coates Hire provides a large range of general equipment; Coates Shorco Sykes supplies specialist pumps and excavation support equipment; Coates Prestige provides portable buildings and toilets; and Coates Conrent is a leading supplier of construction hoists. The company also has operations in Britain (9% of turnover) and Indonesia (2%).

Latest Business Results (June 2003, Full Year)

Australia's buoyant construction environment gave Coates a booming year, with revenues and profits up strongly. The Coates Hire business recorded sales up 36%, with profits soaring 115%. The result was aided by the first full year of contributions from the Wreckair business. A large number of new infrastructure projects in the eastern states provided a particularly potent boost to business. Coates Shorco Sykes had an excellent year, with sales up by 27% and profit rising 45%. The events market helped improve Coates Prestige revenues by 47% and profit by 123%, while the growth in the high-rise construction market – boosting the demand for hoists – gave Coates Conrent one of its best years ever, with sales up 32% and profit up 141%. However, a weak economy and problems with a major customer hurt the British business, which recorded a large loss.

Outlook

Several years of acquisitions and productivity improvements are now handing Coates superior growth. The company itself says that its market data points towards at least three more years of continuing strong growth in the domestic construction sector, and it views itself as ideally placed to reap further rewards. It is working to raise its prices and is also actively seeking further bolt-on acquisitions. Though it sees excellent prospects for all its domestic units, it rates as 'dynamic' the growth forecast for its portable buildings business. It is making major changes to its British subsidiaries, with the aim of achieving a turnaround in profitability. It believes the Indonesian market will offer solid long-term potential.

COA Year to 30 June	2002	2003
Revenues ($mn)	291.6	378.4
EBIT ($mn)	36.2	43.1
EBIT margin (%)	12.4	11.4
Operating profit before tax ($mn)	25.0	32.5
Profit after tax ($mn)	16.4	33.2
Earnings per share (¢)	10.7	16.7
Cashflow per share (¢)	40.6	51.5
Dividend (¢)	9	10
Percentage franked	51	78
Net tangible assets per share ($)	1.29	1.49
Interest cover (times)	3.2	4.1
Return on equity (%)	7.0	11.3
Debt-to-equity ratio (%)	47.2	35.8
Current ratio	1.0	1.0

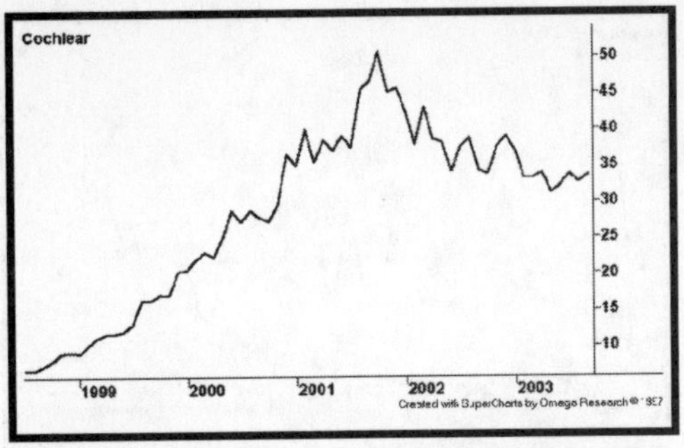

www.cochlear.com.au

Cochlear Limited

Share price ($)	34.01
12-month high ($)	39.80
12-month low ($)	29.60
Market capitalisation ($mn)	1,806.9
Price-to-NTA-per-share ratio	15.1
5-year share price return (% p.a.)	37.9

Sector: Health Care	Company	Sector
Price-earnings ratio (times)	30.9	40.6
Dividend yield (%)	2.3	2.9

Cochlear, founded in 1981 and formerly a subsidiary of Pacific Dunlop (now Ansell), has two-thirds of the world market for cochlear bionic-ear implants, which are intended to assist the communication ability of people suffering from severe hearing impediments. It has sold around 50,000 of its Nucleus 22 and Nucleus 24 implant systems in around 80 countries. Overseas business accounts for over 80% of sales and profits.

Latest Business Results (June 2003, Full Year)

Once again, profits rose strongly. System sales grew by 19% to 9,328 units, though the strengthening Australian dollar limited sales revenues growth to 13%. The Americas region was the standout result for the year, with revenues up 19% (33% in US dollars), reflecting the ongoing industry growth in the region and market share gains made over the year. European sales were up 13% (16% in local currency), while Asian sales revenues were flat. The company reported that the Asian SARS outbreak had an impact on business in the final quarter of the financial year. As an elective surgical procedure, cochlear implantation was delayed by potential recipients (especially children), who stayed away from hospitals during the epidemic, and approximately 250 unit sales were lost as a result.

Outlook

Cochlear is one of Australia's most successful high-tech companies, with continuing long-term sales growth of around 20% annually. However, the share price has received several hits recently from US research linking ear implants with an increased incidence of meningitis. Fortunately, Cochlear has been able to distance itself from these findings, and has actually gained some market share, which it says has risen to 65% to 70% of the global market. It sees enormous potential in the US, and is boosting its marketing budget there. With some 50,000 units of its implant systems now in use, it expects the supply of accessories and upgrades to recipients to become an important revenue stream. It is also striving to make its products as simple to operate as possible, through the continual development of new software for implant recipients.

COH Year to 30 June	2002	2003
Revenues ($mn)	255.0	288.6
EBIT ($mn)	51.5	80.1
EBIT margin (%)	20.2	27.8
Gross margin (%)	71.1	77.2
Operating profit before tax ($mn)	51.0	80.0
Profit after tax ($mn)	43.7	58.2
Earnings per share (¢)	83.4	110.0
Cashflow per share (¢)	92.5	124.6
Dividend (¢)	51	77
Percentage franked	100	100
Net tangible assets per share ($)	1.44	2.26
Interest cover (times)	111.9	576.6
Return on equity (%)	66.5	59.7
Debt-to-equity ratio (%)	18.2	–
Current ratio	1.5	1.8

Coles Myer Limited

Share price ($)	7.32	
12-month high ($)	7.55	
12-month low ($)	5.27	
Market capitalisation ($mn)	8,935.6	
Price-to-NTA-per-share ratio	2.7	
5-year share price return (% p.a.)	4.7	
Sector: Consumer Staples	**Company**	**Sector**
Price-earnings ratio (times)	20.5	17.9
Dividend yield (%)	3.6	3.6

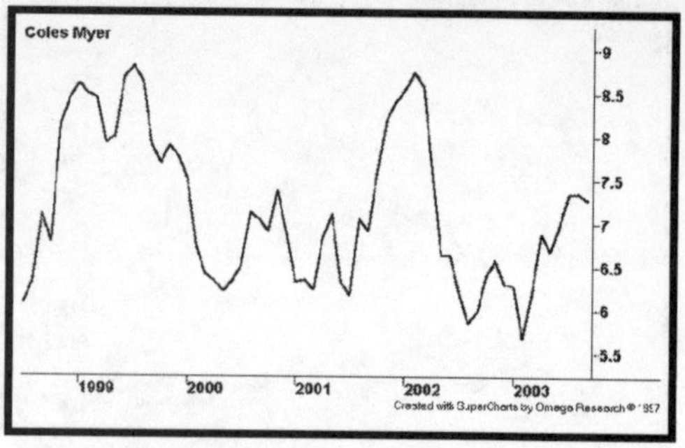

www.colesmyer.com

Melbourne-based Coles Myer is Australia's largest retailer and one of the biggest in the world. It operates more than 1,900 stores, including Coles, Myer, Grace Bros, Kmart, Target, Bi-Lo, Liquorland, Vintage Cellars, Theo's Liquor, Harris Technology and Officeworks.

Latest Business Results (July 2003, Full Year)

Coles Myer's business powered ahead, with all divisions performing well. The core food and liquor business saw little change in total revenues, but with profits (before interest and tax) up nearly 4%, thanks to strong growth in higher margin home-brand products, the phasing out of the shareholder discount card and enhanced efficiencies. A most impressive result came from the Kmart & Officeworks division, with sales up 9% and profits soaring 66%, thanks especially to initiatives to improve the product mix at Kmart stores. The Myer Grace Bros & Megamart division saw revenues actually edge down, but a buoyant fourth quarter helped this business move from the red into profit. Target stores achieved 8% sales growth with profits rocketing ahead 74%, with a significant improvement in sales margins, as the company continued to close underperforming stores. The small emerging businesses division, representing less than 1% of total sales, remained in the red.

Outlook

A major restructuring of all its businesses is leading to some impressive gains in sales and profits. Going forward, the company is placing renewed emphasis on its core food and liquor business. A major alliance with Shell means the introduction of discounted petrol, which it is hoped will boost supermarket turnover. However, fears have been expressed that this could lead to a petrol price war, and no extra profit. The company is planning to introduce its own Coles Myer MasterCard, which will be linked to an upgraded Fly Buys program. It is following Woolworths in placing increased pressure on suppliers to cut costs, in response to new, low-cost rivals like the German chain Aldi, and is raising the percentage of home-brand goods on its shelves. Despite the popularity of the company's shareholder discount card, it is being phased out, and this is expected to bring annual savings of $150 million to $200 million.

CML Year to 27 July*	2002	2003
Revenues ($mn)	25,688.7	27,016.6
Food & liquor (%)	62	60
Kmart & Officeworks (%)	15	16
Myer Grace Bros & Megamart (%)	13	12
Target (%)	9	10
EBIT ($mn)	566.5	680.4
EBIT margin (%)	2.2	2.5
Gross margin (%)	24.4	27.4
Operating profit before tax ($mn)	491.0	617.2
Profit after tax ($mn)	353.8	429.5
Earnings per share (¢)	30.0	35.8
Cash flow per share (¢)	71.0	77.8
Dividend (¢)	25.5	26
Percentage franked	100	100
Net tangible assets per share ($)	2.59	2.71
Interest cover (times)	7.5	10.8
Return on equity (%)	11.6	12.1
Debt-to-equity ratio (%)	51.5	6.6
Current ratio	1.4	1.4

** 28 July 2002.*

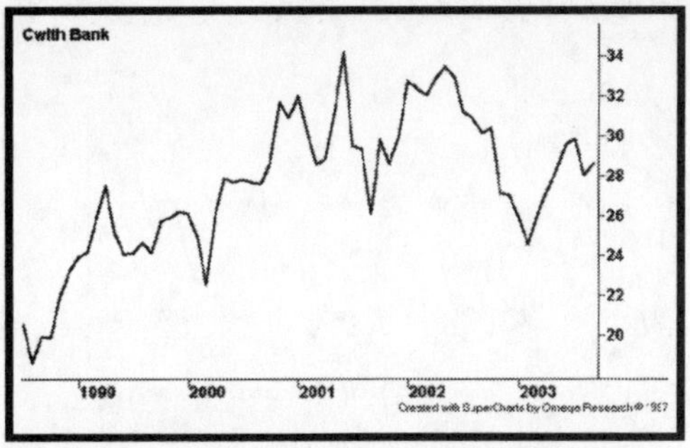

www.commbank.com.au

COMMONWEALTH BANK OF AUSTRALIA

Share price ($)	29.80	
12-month high ($)	32.46	
12-month low ($)	23.05	
Market capitalisation ($mn)	37,156.2	
Price-to-NTA-per-share ratio	2.5	
5-year share price return (% p.a.)	13.1	
Sector: Financials	**Company**	**Sector**
Price-earnings ratio (times)	18.6	16.2
Dividend yield (%)	5.2	4.5

Australia's second-largest bank, with over seven million retail customers, the CBA is the country's top provider of home loans, personal loans and credit cards, and the largest holder of deposits. It is also Australia's largest fund manager, through Commonwealth Financial Services and Colonial First State, and the third-largest life insurer. Commonwealth Securities has become Australia's largest online stockbroker. It has significant interests in New Zealand through ASB Bank.

LATEST BUSINESS RESULTS (JUNE 2003, FULL YEAR)

The bank announced a fall in profits, due mainly to a $245 million writedown of the value of its wealth management business. By contrast, there was a strong result for other businesses. Banking operations delivered a 16% increase in underlying net profit after tax, driven by solid home loan growth. Total lending assets increased 9% to $175 billion, with home lending up 16% to $100 billion, although the bank said its high market share had weakened slightly. It also said it had lost some market share in business banking. Life insurance showed excellent growth, and New Zealand banking was strong. But fund management profits slumped 37%.

OUTLOOK

Its strong position in domestic banking means the bank could suffer disproportionately in the event of a downturn in housing or in other businesses. It is also threatened by the growth in non-bank lending and third-party mortgage brokers and by tighter profit margins for many products. In response, the bank has said it is planning a major transformational change to deliver the outstanding service levels, with enhanced staff engagement and simple and efficient processes, that it believes are required to be more competitive. It says this new strategy will be designed to give customers more convenient and informed access to financial services, through wealth management advice, products to respond to the ageing of the population, and personalised banking services for payments, savings and investments. It is having particular success with its master trust offering FirstChoice, which was launched in mid-2002 and had achieved $3.2 billion in funds by June 2003. Around 40% of all inflows were sourced from the bank's branch network.

CBA Year to 30 June	2002	2003
Operating income ($mn)	9,068.0	9,399.0
Net interest income ($mn)	4,710.0	5,026.0
Operating expenses ($mn)	5,201.0	5,551.0
Operating profit before tax ($mn)	3,572.0	2,976.0
Profit after tax ($mn)	2,655.0	2,012.0
Earnings per share (¢)	212.4	160.6
Dividend (¢)	150	154
Percentage franked	100	100
Non-interest income to total income (%)	48.1	46.5
Net tangible assets per share ($)	10.89	11.96
Cost-to-income ratio (%)	57.4	59.1
Return on equity (%)	14.2	10.3
Return on assets (%)	1.1	0.8

Crane Group Limited

Share price ($)	11.01	
12-month high ($)	11.08	
12-month low ($)	7.52	
Market capitalisation ($mn)	581.9	
Price-to-NTA-per-share ratio	1.8	
5-year share price return (% p.a.)	15.2	
Sector: Industrials	**Company**	**Sector**
Price-earnings ratio (times)	12.2	12.1
Dividend yield (%)	5.4	3.9

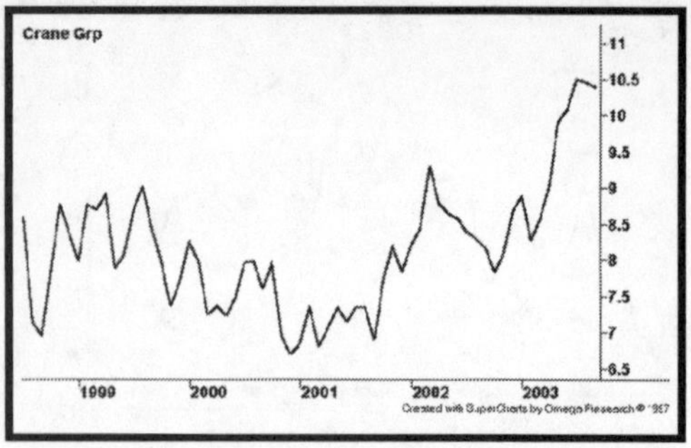

www.crane.com.au

Sydney-based Crane, founded in 1867, is a leading manufacturer and distributor of non-ferrous metal products and of plastic pipeline systems. Its Tradelink division is Australia's largest distributor of plumbing supplies, with 188 outlets. It has extensive operations in Australia, New Zealand and Singapore, and it exports non-ferrous metal products to more than 15 countries.

Latest Business Results (June 2003, Full Year)

The housing boom, along with recent acquisitions and cost-cutting moves, handed Crane a powerful boost to its profits. Both Australian and New Zealand operations were strong. Though second-half business was not as strong as in the first half, due to slower new housing activity, this was cushioned significantly by the continued strength of the renovations and additions market. The best performance came from the company's distribution businesses, with sales up 20% and profits soaring 47%. Tradelink was particularly strong, assisted by the opening of four new branches and the upgrading or relocation of 34 more. There was also the first full-year contribution from the New Zealand distributor MasterTrade, which was acquired in January 2002, along with a buoyant irrigation pipeline market. Profit growth was partially offset by an increase in systems-related expenses of $7 million, reflecting the progression of the company's new enterprise-wide computer system.

Outlook

Crane continues to expand through new store openings and acquisition. Tradelink expanded its branch network by eight stores with the acquisition of Warlay Plumbing Supplies in March 2003 and Boots Plumbing in June 2003. In addition, the metals group has acquired three businesses from MCK Pacific, and in August 2003 Iplex Pipelines Australia, which is 75% owned by Crane, acquired the listed pipeline manufacturer Milnes Holdings. At the same time, there has been considerable market speculation that Crane itself could be acquired by Wesfarmers. The company continues to spend heavily on its new computer system, and has said that this expense, along with additional bolt-on acquisitions, could mean no profit growth in the June 2004 year. A housing slowdown would also hurt business. The company believes its new computer network could add $15 million annually to pre-tax profit by 2006.

CRG Year to 30 June	2002	2003
Revenues ($mn)	1,645.3	1,911.7
EBIT ($mn)	76.5	96.2
EBIT margin (%)	4.7	5.0
Gross margin (%)	19.0	20.2
Operating profit before tax ($mn)	59.3	75.9
Profit after tax ($mn)	33.6	46.4
Earnings per share (¢)	67.3	90.1
Cashflow per share (¢)	146.8	162.8
Dividend (¢)	50	60
Percentage franked	100	100
Net tangible assets per share ($)	5.58	6.03
Interest cover (times)	4.4	4.7
Return on equity (%)	9.8	11.8
Debt-to-equity ratio (%)	49.2	57.5
Current ratio	1.7	1.5

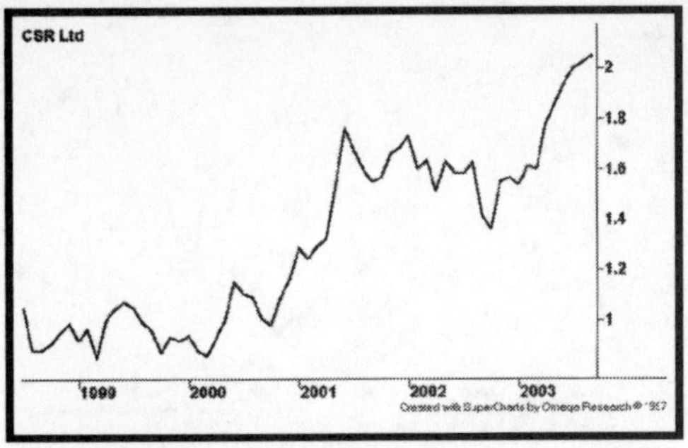

www.csr.com.au

CSR Limited

Share price ($)	2.06
12-month high ($)	2.12
12-month low ($)	1.21
Market capitalisation ($mn)	1,983.8
Price-to-NTA-per-share ratio	1.9
5-year share price return (% p.a.)	23.7

Sector: Materials	Company	Sector
Price-earnings ratio (times)	3.4	16.0
Dividend yield (%)	8.3	2.9

CSR, founded in 1855 as a sugar refiner, has returned to its roots with the 2003 demerger of its Rinker construction materials business into a separate company, also listed on the stock exchange. CSR now operates in three separate industries: it is one of the world's leading sugar producers; it makes building products, such as bricks, pavers, plasterboard and roofing tiles; and it owns 70% of Gove Aluminium Finance, which holds more than a third of the equity of NSW's Tomago Aluminium Smelter.

Latest Business Results (March 2003, Full Year)

The Rinker demerger took place at the end of March, so the results included this business. In the United States, Rinker Materials enjoyed good growth in revenues and profits, though a strong Australian dollar meant there was only a small extra contribution to the accounts. Domestically, the Readymix concrete business – now included in the new Rinker entity – achieved extremely strong profit growth, thanks to higher demand, price rises and operational efficiencies. CSR Building Products was a beneficiary of the booming housing market, with revenues and profits up. Aluminium sales and profits were also up, despite generally low world prices. However, falling world sugar prices meant a profit decline for this business.

Outlook

The new CSR will derive roughly 45% of its revenues from buildings products, 35% from sugar and 20% from aluminium. With a strong gearing towards residential construction, the building products business should continue to prosper as long as the housing market remains buoyant. The company is hoping to take advantage of strong market shares for most of its products to raise prices. However, the sugar business is at the mercy of weak international prices, the stronger Australian dollar and weather conditions, and the near-term outlook is not good. CSR is exploring a project to increase the co-generation of electricity at sugar mills, using waste sugar cane fibre. Aluminium demand remains firm. The company is deciding whether to participate in a major upgrade of the Tomago smelter.

CSR Year to 31 March	2002	2003
Revenues ($mn)	6,984.7	7,282.9
Rinker Materials (%)	59	58
Readymix (%)	13	14
Building products (%)	12	12
Sugar (%)	10	10
Aluminium (%)	6	6
EBIT ($mn)	925.8	975.8
EBIT margin (%)	13.3	13.4
Gross margin (%)	36.4	36.9
Operating profit before tax ($mn)	818.5	870.5
Profit after tax ($mn)	552.6	561.0
Earnings per share (¢)	58.5	59.8
Cashflow per share (¢)	105.0	108.8
Dividend (¢)	24	17
Percentage franked	56	70
Net tangible assets per share ($)	3.11	1.10
Interest cover (times)	8.6	9.3
Return on equity (%)	13.8	22.0
Debt-to-equity ratio (%)	42.3	19.7
Current ratio	1.4	1.2

Danks Holdings Limited

Share price ($)	13.99	
12-month high ($)	14.30	
12-month low ($)	9.50	
Market capitalisation ($mn)	91.0	
Price-to-NTA-per-share ratio	1.8	
5-year share price return (% p.a.)	17.9	
Sector: Consumer Discretion.	**Company**	**Sector**
Price-earnings ratio (times)	17.5	20.2
Dividend yield (%)	3.9	3.7

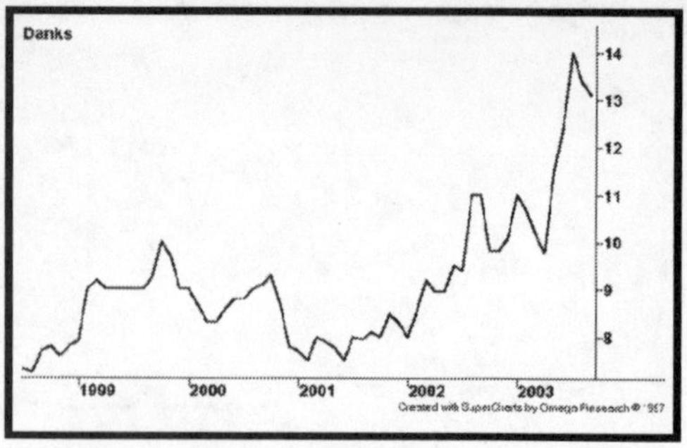

www.danks.com.au

Melbourne-based Danks Holdings has roots that date back to 1859, and is Australia's largest independent hardware wholesale distributor, with six warehouses in Victoria, NSW and Western Australia. It carries a range of some 25,000 products, which it distributes to more than 700 group stores, all independently owned. These include HOME Timber and Hardware stores, Thrifty-Link Hardware stores and Plants Plus Garden Centre nurseries. It also distributes its products to more than 1,000 other independent retailers.

Latest Business Results (June 2003, Full Year)

The continuing housing and home renovation boom delivered increased sales revenues to Danks. However, higher capital spending costs meant flat profit growth. The company's rural and gardening businesses were also affected by the drought. The company reported a 21% rise in timber and building product sales, a 30% increase in sales of its exclusive JDS-brand products and a 70% jump in its new Plumbworx range of plumbing products. The company said that its retailer customer numbers grew further during the year, thanks to new operators, independent retailers and stores from competitor groups converting to Danks under one of its three marketing banners.

Outlook

Still managed conservatively by the original Danks family, the company has over some years considerably restructured its business, in the process successfully defending its position against the warehouse-type operations of its big rival Bunnings. The moves towards warehouse stores by its other main rival, Mitre 10, could lead to a renewed customer appreciation of the attractions of the smaller, more personalised stores in the Danks group. A heavy investment in information technology has considerably streamlined the ordering and distribution processes. Thanks to buoyant business conditions, the company has leased new warehouses in Sydney and Perth, which has significantly boosted its distribution capacity. Additional specialist staff have also been recruited, with the particular aim of assisting group retailers with the design and layout of the next evolution of hardware stores. The introduction of its exclusive JDS-brand products is intended to strengthen the ability of its retailer customers to compete successfully with larger rivals. Danks shares are very thinly traded.

DKS Year to 30 June	2002	2003
Revenues ($mn)	389.5	433.3
EBIT ($mn)	8.4	8.6
EBIT margin (%)	2.2	2.0
Gross margin (%)	10.2	9.8
Operating profit before tax ($mn)	7.6	7.6
Profit after tax ($mn)	5.3	5.2
Earnings per share (¢)	80.7	80.1
Cashflow per share (¢)	115.4	112.4
Dividend (¢)	55	55
Percentage franked	100	100
Net tangible assets per share ($)	7.35	7.90
Interest cover (times)	10.6	8.2
Return on equity (%)	11.2	10.5
Debt-to-equity ratio (%)	27.5	18.8
Current ratio	1.8	1.9

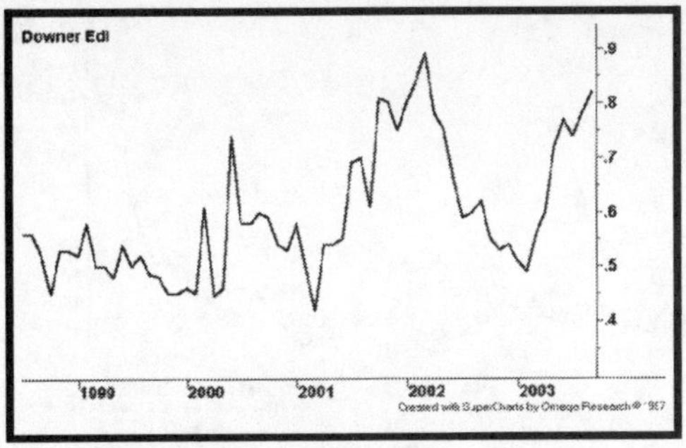

www.downergroup.com.au

Downer EDI Limited

Share price ($)	0.70	
12-month high ($)	0.78	
12-month low ($)	0.44	
Market capitalisation ($mn)	679.2	
Price-to-NTA-per-share ratio	1.6	
5-year share price return (% p.a.)	14.6	
Sector: Industrials	**Company**	**Sector**
Price-earnings ratio (times)	10.2	12.1
Dividend yield (%)	4.1	3.9

Sydney-based Downer EDI – Australia's second-largest listed engineering, infrastructure and resource services company – has grown through a long series of mergers in Australia and New Zealand, most recently between Downer Group and Evans Deakin Industries. It provides engineering and infrastructure management services to the public and private power, rail, road, telecommunications, mining and mineral processing sectors in Australia, New Zealand, Asia and the Pacific. It operates through five broad divisions: Works Infrastructure, Downer Engineering, Roche Mining, Century Resources and EDI Rail.

Latest Business Results (June 2003, Full Year)

Downer recorded its sixth consecutive year of higher profits, thanks to a healthy business environment and continuing restructuring of its operations. The good result was achieved despite the sale of some businesses. The company reported that core businesses delivered around $500 million of incremental revenue, of which approximately 70% was organic. The best performance came from infrastructure services, with revenues up 37%. Engineering delivered a 16% sales rise, and mining and resources 6%. Rail revenues fell 8%. At year-end, the company held an order book worth $5.5 billion, which was 22% higher than a year before, and it was preferred bidder for a further $500 million of orders.

Outlook

Thanks to its healthy order book, Downer expects revenues and profits to rise by at least 15% in the year to June 2004. It sees promise in a recovering resources sector and in power generation and transmission infrastructure, along with increasing road and rail work. It has high hopes for CPG Corporation – formerly part of Singapore's public works department – which it acquired in early 2003. This company is a leader in facilities management and engineering consultancy, and Downer plans to use it to expand its activities in Asia (currently about 6% of total turnover). In September 2003 CPG won an order to design, build and commission a $90 million whole milk powder plant in New Zealand. Downer shares have been hurt by problems with its fleet of Millennium trains supplied to NSW's StateRail, though the company believes this will not affect profits.

DOW Year to 30 June	2002	2003
Revenues ($mn)	2,350.9	2,573.5
Mining & resources (%)	37	35
Engineering (%)	29	31
Infrastructure services (%)	17	21
Rail (%)	13	11
EBIT ($mn)	114.9	124.8
EBIT margin (%)	4.9	4.8
Operating profit before tax ($mn)	79.3	94.7
Profit after tax ($mn)	56.4	66.6
Earnings per share (¢)	6.4	6.9
Cashflow per share (¢)	18.7	19.2
Dividend (¢)	2.4	2.9
Percentage franked	0	41
Net tangible assets per share ($)	0.45	0.44
Interest cover (times)	3.2	4.2
Return on equity (%)	8.7	9.1
Debt-to-equity ratio (%)	63.0	39.0
Current ratio	1.8	1.4

FKP Limited

Share price ($)	2.51	
12-month high ($)	3.00	
12-month low ($)	1.12	
Market capitalisation ($mn)	287.6	
Price-to-NTA-per-share ratio	1.6	
5-year share price return (% p.a.)	33.7	
Sector: Financials	**Company**	**Sector**
Price-earnings ratio (times)	10.7	16.2
Dividend yield (%)	4.8	4.5

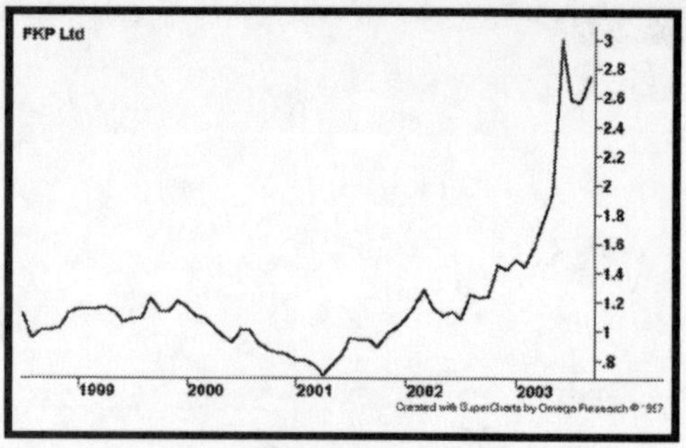

www.fkp.com.au

FKP, formerly called Forrester Kurts Properties, is a leading Queensland-based property developer, with activities that encompass construction, low-, medium- and high-density residential developments, commercial and retail projects, master planned residential communities and the ownership and management of retirement villages. It is active in all eastern states. Its subsidiary Australian Retirement Homes has become a leader in the aged care industry, with 23 retirement community properties, making FKP Australia's largest owner/operator of retirement villages. The company has launched its first property trust.

Latest Business Results (June 2003, Full Year)

The continuing housing boom handed FKP a sharp increase in sales and profits, though all other business areas were also strong. Residential property sales of $124 million were up 20% from the previous year. Commercial property sales were up 59% to $63 million, thanks mainly to the sale of 120 Edward Street, Brisbane, while the sale of the Mt Sheridan Shopping Centre in Cairns was the main contributor to a six-fold jump in retail property sales to $21.6 million. External construction contract turnover rose 47% to $44 million. Revenues from the rendering of services were up 37% to $25.4 million, including a 35% rise in deferred management fees from the resale of retirement village units and an initial $0.4 million in management fees from the establishment of its funds management business during the year.

Outlook

FKP is achieving success in its moves to diversify away from its traditional property development business, in order to provide stability to its earnings. In particular, it has become a leader in the development and management of aged care facilities, and has attracted stock market attention for its exposure to this high-growth and potentially high-margin business. Despite its booming construction businesses, aged care services remain one of the company's most profitable businesses. It has achieved a successful launch of its first property trust, and has a second due. The company has reported that in June 2003 it had sales of $130 million not yet brought to account, and it expected profits to rise by at least a further 15% in the 2003–04 year.

FKP Year to 30 June	2002	2003
Revenues ($mn)	195.5	278.6
Property development (%)	68	67
Construction (%)	15	15
Aged care services (%)	16	12
EBIT ($mn)	24.3	39.9
EBIT margin (%)	12.4	14.3
Gross margin (%)	19.3	18.7
Operating profit before tax ($mn)	24.1	38.7
Profit after tax ($mn)	17.1	26.7
Earnings per share (¢)	15.1	23.5
Cashflow per share (¢)	16.0	24.7
Dividend (¢)	10	12
Percentage franked	100	100
Net tangible assets per share ($)	1.35	1.53
Interest cover (times)	111.5	32.6
Return on equity (%)	11.3	16.2
Debt-to-equity ratio (%)	26.5	12.1
Current ratio	2.1	2.2

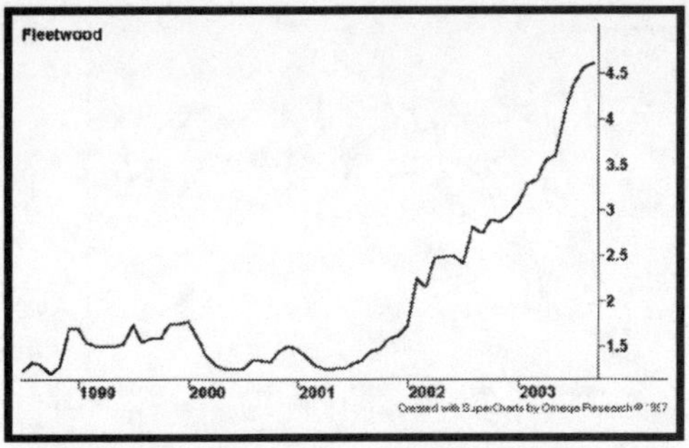

www.fleetwood.com.au

Fleetwood Corporation Limited

Share price ($)	4.71	
12-month high ($)	4.86	
12-month low ($)	2.60	
Market capitalisation ($mn)	206.6	
Price-to-NTA-per-share ratio	3.9	
5-year share price return (% p.a.)	39.9	
Sector: Consumer Discretion.	**Company**	**Sector**
Price-earnings ratio (times)	16.2	20.2
Dividend yield (%)	3.0	3.7

Western Australian company Fleetwood, established in 1964, is a leader in the caravan, recreational vehicle and portable accommodation businesses. Its Coromal Caravans division is the second-largest caravan manufacturer in Australia and its Camec brand is a major supplier of parts and accessories to the recreational vehicle industry. It also holds the Hertz Campervan licence for Australia and New Zealand. Fleetwood Portables is a leader in the manufacture, sale and rental of transportable buildings, and Fleetwood Homes and Cabins is the largest manufacturer of park homes in Western Australia, with an 85% market share. The company is also the largest caravan park operator in Western Australia. It has an additional three parks in Karratha and one in Port Hedland providing accommodation for workers on resource projects. In mid 2003, it acquired Windsor Caravans, Australia's fourth-largest caravan maker.

Latest Business Results (June 2003, Full Year)

Profits continued their sharp upward trajectory, as the company rode the boom in caravan demand. Profits (before interest and tax) for recreational vehicles – mainly caravans – jumped 46%, with the company struggling to meet demand. Manufactured accommodation profits were up 22%, thanks to increased activity in the resources industry and strong demand by retirees for park homes. The company's small caravan parks division realised a 17% rise in profits.

Outlook

With its business geared to three areas with high growth potential – recreation, resource development and retirement – Fleetwood has been expanding rapidly, and the shares have performed very strongly. In July 2003 it had a nine-month backlog of caravan orders. It expects the $6 million acquisition of Melbourne-based Windsor Caravans to help meet growing demand. As 60% of Fleetwood's present output is shipped from Perth to the eastern states, the Windsor acquisition also hands it a key eastern production facility, with substantial cost benefits. Fleetwood has also acquired, for $7 million, Car-Van, its major rival in the supply of recreational vehicle components. A pick-up in the resources industry is delivering Fleetwood a stream of substantial new orders for on-site manufactured accommodation for workers on projects in Western Australia and the Northern Territory.

FWD Year to 30 June	2002	2003
Revenues ($mn)	158.4	188.5
Recreational vehicles (%)	61	62
Manufactured accommodation (%)	33	33
EBIT ($mn)	13.1	18.7
EBIT margin (%)	8.3	9.9
Gross margin (%)	30.9	23.0
Operating profit before tax ($mn)	11.2	16.6
Profit after tax ($mn)	7.6	11.2
Earnings per share (¢)	20.9	29.1
Cashflow per share (¢)	37.5	44.8
Dividend (¢)	13	14
Percentage franked	100	100
Net tangible assets per share ($)	0.69	1.20
Interest cover (times)	6.8	9.0
Return on equity (%)	16.4	17.4
Debt-to-equity ratio (%)	58.4	24.3
Current ratio	1.6	1.9

Flight Centre Limited

Share price ($)	22.90	
12-month high ($)	27.20	
12-month low ($)	17.30	
Market capitalisation ($mn)	2,122.1	
Price-to-NTA-per-share ratio	10.8	
5-year share price return (% p.a.)	50.4	
Sector: Consumer Discretion.	**Company**	**Sector**
Price-earnings ratio (times)	29.8	20.2
Dividend yield (%)	1.9	3.7

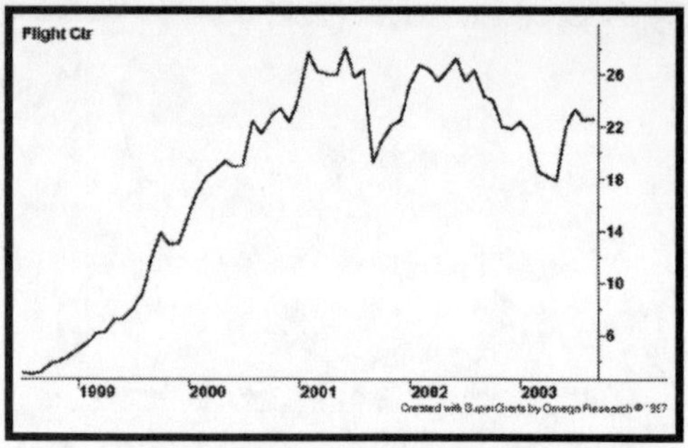

www.flightcentre.com.au

Brisbane-based Flight Centre is the largest independent retail travel agency in Australia and New Zealand, and has an estimated 20% market share. It operates under various brands, including Great Holiday Escape, Corporate Traveller, 24 Hour Flights/Flight Centre Direct, Student Flights, Travel Associates, SBT Business Travel Solutions and Stage and Screen Travel and Freight Services. It has expanded to South Africa – where its market share is estimated at 10% – and to Canada, the US and Britain.

Latest Business Results (June 2003, Full Year)

Turbulence in the global travel industry did not impede Flight Centre, which posted a further double-digit gain in revenues and profits. Following a strong first half, up 47% on the same period in the prior year, the second half was significantly affected by the war in Iraq, the SARS virus and concerns about terrorism. Yet despite this, the company in June 2003 recorded its highest-ever one-month profit. Business travel – which comprises about 30% of company profit – was hardest hit by world events. Profits from Australia (608 stores), New Zealand (121 stores) and South Africa (83 stores) rose 16%, 20% and 76% respectively. Revenue growth was in line with the growth in shop numbers. (Based on recent industry trends, the company has changed the way it presents its revenues, which appear differently in this edition of *Top Stocks* from previous editions.) The company reported that at the end of June 2003 it had 1,054 stores operating worldwide – up from 832 a year earlier – and 209 other businesses.

Outlook

With net cash reserves of more than $335 million, Flight Centre is in a position to maintain an ambitious expansion program, through both organic growth and acquisition. The British operation is expanding rapidly. The acquisition of corporate travel specialist Britannic Travel has delivered Flight Centre 42 stores, and it has opened a further 20. However, British business remains sluggish, and the company is working to effect a turn-around. US operations remain in the red. The company has acquired five stores in Hong Kong, and plans to use this as a launching pad for expansion into Asia.

FLT Year to 30 June	2002	2003
Revenues ($mn)	469.5	605.9
EBIT ($mn)	91.1	96.6
EBIT margin (%)	19.4	15.9
Operating profit before tax ($mn)	90.5	102.3
Profit after tax ($mn)	62.0	70.0
Earnings per share (¢)	71.9	77.0
Dividend (¢)	37.5	43.5
Percentage franked	100	100
Net tangible assets per share ($)	1.79	2.13
Interest cover (times)	159.5	–
Return on equity (%)	33.8	23.2
Debt-to-equity ratio (%)	–	–
Current ratio	1.4	1.5

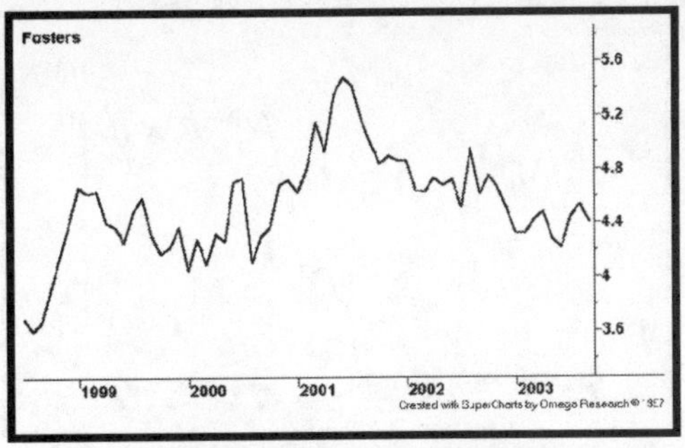

www.fosters.com.au

Foster's Group Limited

Share price ($)	4.51
12-month high ($)	4.97
12-month low ($)	4.12
Market capitalisation ($mn)	9,306.4
Price-to-NTA-per-share ratio	4.7
5-year share price return (% p.a.)	7.5

Sector: Consumer Staples	Company	Sector
Price-earnings ratio (times)	16.4	17.9
Dividend yield (%)	4.2	3.6

Melbourne-based Foster's, one of the world's leading winemakers and brewers, operates within four broad groupings: Beringer Blass Wine Estates is the company's international wine business; Carlton and United Breweries dominates the Australian beer market and has extensive hotel interests; Foster's Brewing International manages the Foster's Lager premium beer brand in more than 150 countries; and the Lensworth Group manages the company's extensive property assets. The group has brewing operations in Australia, Vietnam, India, China and the Pacific, and wine operations in Australia, Chile, the US, Britain, the Netherlands, France, Germany, Italy and New Zealand.

Latest Business Results (June 2003, Full Year)

A sluggish wine business held back profit growth for Foster's, despite a buoyant global beer market. The company was also hurt by the strong Australian dollar. The highly competitive California wine environment hurt Foster's, forcing it to cut prices there. This was only partially offset by double-digit expansion for wine in Asia-Pacific and Europe. Altogether, wine division profits fell 3%, though without the dollar's rise they would have been up 4%. Domestic beer volumes edged up 1%, but profits were up nearly 8%, thanks to higher prices and greater sales of high-margin premium beers. The global Foster's Lager business achieved an excellent 25.5% increase in profits, despite a slight dip in volume sales, thanks especially to increased license royalties and stringent cost controls. A $152 million significant loss reflected mainly restructuring of domestic brewing operations.

Outlook

Foster's looks set to transform itself. It expects to sell its $1.4 billion Australian Leisure and Hospitality division, which is Australia's largest hotel owner and gambling machine operator with 131 pub venues. There is speculation the company might use the proceeds to try to boost its wine assets, perhaps through a bid for rival Southcorp. It may eventually split its beer and wine businesses into separate companies. In the short term, the company faces continual turmoil in the US wine market, along with uncertain currency movements, which could again put pressure on company profits, despite a rosy outlook for beer sales.

FGL Year to 30 June	2002	2003
Revenues ($mn)	4,572.0	4,731.5
Wine (%)	41	39
Beer (%)	37	39
Leisure & hospitality (%)	18	18
EBIT ($mn)	990.9	972.0
EBIT margin (%)	21.7	20.5
Gross margin (%)	49.7	49.6
Operating profit before tax ($mn)	808.5	818.8
Profit after tax ($mn)	560.9	568.1
Earnings per share (¢)	27.6	27.5
Cashflow per share (¢)	38.6	37.9
Dividend (¢)	17	18.75
Percentage franked	100	100
Net tangible assets per share ($)	0.77	0.97
Interest cover (times)	5.4	6.3
Return on equity (%)	14.2	13.2
Debt-to-equity ratio (%)	73.8	58.9
Current ratio	1.6	1.3

Freedom Group Limited

Share price ($)	2.13
12-month high ($)	2.15
12-month low ($)	1.61
Market capitalisation ($mn)	227.5
Price-to-NTA-per-share ratio	3.9
5-year share price return (% p.a.)	17.2

Sector: Consumer Discretion.	Company	Sector
Price-earnings ratio (times)	12.3	20.2
Dividend yield (%)	4.7	3.7

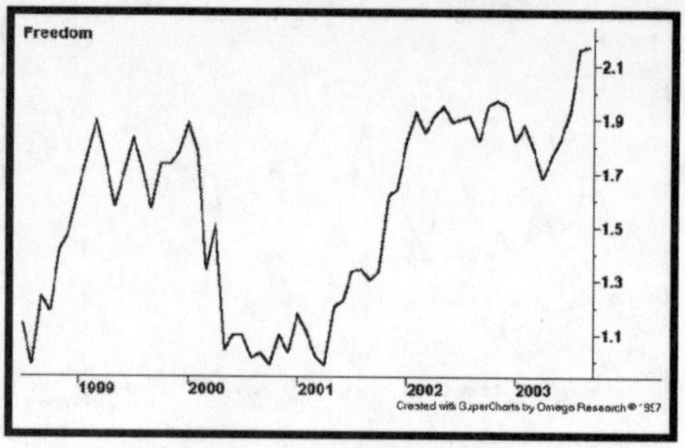

www.freedom.com.au

Sydney-based Freedom Group, founded in 1981, is one of Australia's leading furniture retailers. It operates 179 stores throughout Australia and New Zealand under the Freedom, Guests, Capt'n Snooze and Bayswiss names. It has a manufacturing alliance with the South African furniture giant Steinhoff Group, which has taken a 20% equity interest in Freedom. In August 2003, a group of Freedom managers offered to make a management buyout of the company.

Latest Business Results (June 2003, Full Year)

The housing boom and continuing restructuring delivered Freedom a firm increase in sales and profits. The 49 Freedom stores in Australia showed good growth, and the 15 in New Zealand produced an excellent result. However, the company's 19 Guests stores remained in the red. The new Bayswiss food and lifestyle store acquisition realised a lower-than-expected result, although the company pressed ahead with expansion plans and opened 10 new stores. The Capt'n Snooze business (76 stores) also had mixed results, after suffering high costs from its drive to establish a presence in Western Australia.

Outlook

The company has spent the past few years working to rationalise its operations and achieve increased efficiencies. It has enjoyed success with its Freedom outlets, but the Guests operation continues to struggle, and it plans to close several under-performing outlets. The acquisition in August 2002 of the Bayswiss chain of upmarket homeware and food stores has given Freedom exposure to a new business area with potentially high margins, and it intends to continue opening new stores, bringing the total to at least 26 by the end of 2003 with an eventual target of 50. It has bought some stores from the now-closed Foodchain operation of David Jones and converted these to Bayswiss outlets. Freedom management now wishes to expand further overseas. It sees opportunities in Asia, Europe, the Middle East and South Africa, but believes substantial financing would be required, and the added risk could put pressure on the shares. For this reason, a group of managers say they now wish to take the company private, in co-operation with the major shareholder, the Steinhoff Group.

FFL Year to 30 June	2002	2003
Revenues ($mn)	349.2	397.8
EBIT ($mn)	23.6	27.8
EBIT margin (%)	6.8	7.0
Gross margin (%)	47.3	50.1
Operating profit before tax ($mn)	22.5	26.1
Profit after tax ($mn)	15.6	18.0
Earnings per share (¢)	15.6	17.3
Cashflow per share (¢)	21.6	25.1
Dividend (¢)	10	10
Percentage franked	100	100
Net tangible assets per share ($)	0.41	0.54
Interest cover (times)	21.3	15.8
Return on equity (%)	23.8	20.8
Debt-to-equity ratio (%)	12.0	28.3
Current ratio	1.5	1.6

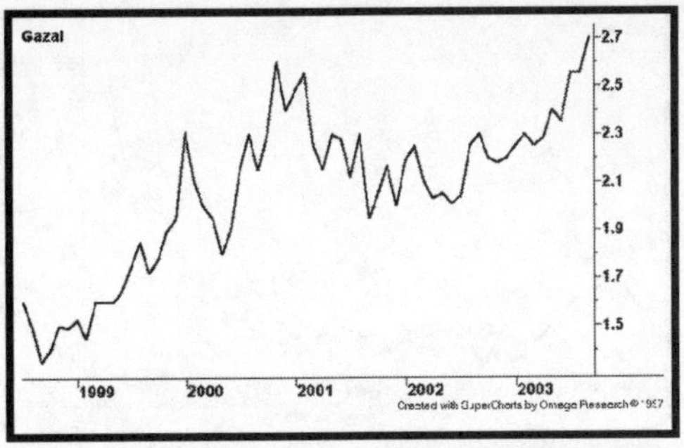

www.gazal.com.au

Gazal Corporation Limited

Share price ($)	2.65	
12-month high ($)	2.65	
12-month low ($)	2.10	
Market capitalisation ($mn)	144.1	
Price-to-NTA-per-share ratio	2.8	
5-year share price return (% p.a.)	22.0	
Sector: Consumer Discretion.	**Company**	**Sector**
Price-earnings ratio (times)	15.6	20.2
Dividend yield (%)	5.3	3.7

Sydney-based Gazal, founded in 1958, is one of Australia's largest publicly listed clothing companies, specialising mainly in business shirts, men's casual wear and surf wear, ladies' intimate apparel and school wear. It owns the Mambo label, and in Australia it is a licence holder for such well-known brands as Nautica, Van Heusen, Lovable, Crystelle, Maui and Sons, Bisley, Paramount, Midford, Oroton, Stamina, Tigerlily, Mariner and Kookai. It also makes house-brand merchandise for major retailers, and it has some sales in Asia and Europe. The controlling Gazal family hold more than 60% of the shares. It has sold its Asian joint venture manufacturing operation.

Latest Business Results (June 2003, Full Year)

Sales and profits rose modestly. Domestic sales (85% of the total) were up just 4%, though lower costs – partly a result of the stronger dollar – meant that domestic profits rose 13%. Sales of licensed products were generally strong, but the company's own Mambo brand suffered through intense competition in the youth and surf markets. Asian sales (6% of the total) were up 20%, but with a sharp decline in profits. In Europe, where the company is strongly promoting the Mambo brand, sales surged 48% to $17.6 million, though profitability was low.

Outlook

Gazal sees the purchase in 2000 of the Mambo label as marking a step in a new direction, from 'brand renter' to 'brand owner'. Its strategy now is to seek ownership of high-profile brands wherever the opportunity presents itself, with the aim of developing intellectual assets which can evolve into global brands with real long-term value. However, in the short term it has found Mambo falling well short of expectations. In particular, in its first year of company-owned operations in Europe, the start-up phase has proven more difficult than expected. In June 2003, Gazal sold its interest in its Asian manufacturing companies, following a decline in the proportion of product sourced from these factories. This move has freed up capital and also gives the company more flexibility in its product sourcing. Gazal is a significant beneficiary of the strength of the dollar.

GZL Year to 30 June	2002	2003
Revenues ($mn)	180.1	194.7
EBIT ($mn)	14.9	16.0
EBIT margin (%)	8.2	8.2
Gross margin (%)	38.9	43.8
Operating profit before tax ($mn)	13.5	14.2
Profit after tax ($mn)	9.1	9.7
Earnings per share (¢)	16.1	17.0
Cashflow per share (¢)	20.7	23.3
Dividend (¢)	13.75	14
Percentage franked	100	100
Net tangible assets per share ($)	0.76	0.93
Interest cover (times)	10.7	8.5
Return on equity (%)	12.0	11.8
Debt-to-equity ratio (%)	29.7	27.8
Current ratio	1.6	2.2

GUD Holdings Limited

Share price ($)	5.72	
12-month high ($)	5.80	
12-month low ($)	3.50	
Market capitalisation ($mn)	347.4	
Price-to-NTA-per-share ratio	4.5	
5-year share price return (% p.a.)	30.5	
Sector: Consumer Discretion.	**Company**	**Sector**
Price-earnings ratio (times)	12.7	20.2
Dividend yield (%)	4.5	3.7

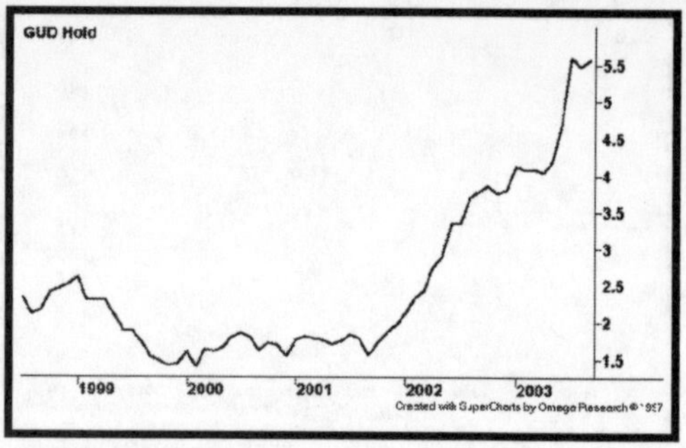

www.gud.com.au

GUD, based in Melbourne and founded in 1940, is a diversified manufacturer and distributor with five broad product lines: Sunbeam small electrical appliances; Victa lawnmowers; Ryco, Wesfil and Goss automotive filtration and associated products; Davey water pumps, pump sets and water pressure systems; and Lock Focus security products and associated hardware. It exports to more than 50 countries.

Latest Business Results (June 2003, Full Year)

GUD's continuing restructuring program and a stream of new products led to another large rise in profits, despite only modest sales growth. The core Sunbeam Victa division saw profits (before interest and tax) up 31%, thanks in particular to new manufacturing facilities for Sunbeam and strong consumer spending. This result was particularly impressive, as the drought led to a sharp decline in lawnmower demand. A healthy motoring environment gave the Ryco/Wesfil division a 20% jump in profit. Though representing only 23% of company revenues, Ryco/Wesfil actually generates more than a third of total profit. The Davey pump business was a beneficiary of the drought, along with stronger international sales, and profits were up 31%. Cost reductions and new products helped the Lock Focus division win back customers previously lost to cheap imports, leading to a 20% boost in profits.

Outlook

GUD has reaped enormous benefits from a major restructuring, with a massive turnaround in profits, and the question now is how much further this can continue. Nevertheless, while consumer spending remains firm the company looks set to do well. It is seeing good business from a range of novel home appliance products, and particularly its new Café Series line of coffee makers. The lifting of the drought is expected to boost lawnmower sales. The company believes it can achieve further operational improvements with its Ryco/Wesfil business. A new range of Davey products focusing on water efficiency is aimed at boosting demand both domestically and abroad. Having repaid much debt, GUD is now actively seeking acquisitions that will help fuel further growth.

GUD Year to 30 June	2002	2003
Revenues ($mn)	365.9	372.4
Sunbeam Victa (%)	56	54
Ryco/Wesfil (%)	23	23
Davey (%)	17	19
Lock Focus (%)	4	4
EBIT ($mn)	34.9	44.3
EBIT margin (%)	9.5	11.9
Gross margin (%)	30.9	35.9
Operating profit before tax ($mn)	29.6	40.6
Profit after tax ($mn)	20.8	27.4
Earnings per share (¢)	32.8	45.0
Cashflow per share (¢)	49.5	61.3
Dividend (¢)	16.5	26
Percentage franked	55	100
Net tangible assets per share ($)	1.14	1.26
Interest cover (times)	6.6	11.9
Return on equity (%)	16.5	22.1
Debt-to-equity ratio (%)	31.2	16.5
Current ratio	1.9	1.7

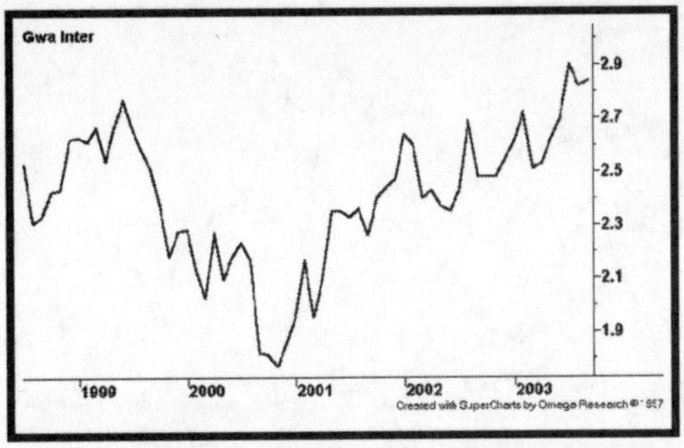

www.gwail.com.au

GWA International Limited

Share price ($)	2.91
12-month high ($)	2.99
12-month low ($)	2.36
Market capitalisation ($mn)	808.4
Price-to-NTA-per-share ratio	14.5
5-year share price return (% p.a.)	10.3

Sector: Industrials	Company	Sector
Price-earnings ratio (times)	14.7	12.1
Dividend yield (%)	5.3	3.9

Brisbane-based GWA is a manufacturer of a wide range of household products, including 90% of Australia's toilets. Its Caroma division is a leading supplier of bathroom fittings, and has operations in Asia, Europe and America. The Sebel contract furniture business provides seating for stadiums and auditoriums, and also operates in several countries. In addition, the company makes Rover lawnmowers, Dorf Clark tapware, Dux hot water systems and Gainsborough door fittings, and it owns the Wisa Beheer cistern producer in the Netherlands.

Latest Business Results (June 2003, Full Year)

GWA is a prime beneficiary of the housing boom, and sales and profits rose strongly. Caroma bathroom products achieved good profit growth, driven by domestic demand. However, a poor performance in Caroma's Stylus division hurt business, and the strong dollar erased much of the benefit of firm American demand. The Dorf Clark tapware business improved significantly on the previous year's lacklustre performance, thanks to successful new product introductions and operational savings. The Dux hot water system operation also grew. Sebel commercial furniture benefited from strong domestic demand, particularly in education and stadia, as well as commercial renovation work. However, the Rover lawnmower suffered from the drought, with profits down, despite growing overseas sales.

Outlook

The company itself believes the outlook is rosy, with few signs of a housing downturn. It notes that there is generally an approximate nine-month time lag between new home approvals and the time when GWA's products are bought. It also sees growing demand from renovation work, and notes that more kitchens and bathrooms are installed each year through renovations than through new housing construction. It is working to restructure the faltering Stylus operation, and expects a greatly improved result in the 2003–04 year. It also believes that just average domestic weather conditions are required to revive Rover lawnmower profits. GWA has expressed its desire to expand through acquisition, including a major purchase that would add a new business to its operations, as well as a series of bolt-on acquisitions. Overseas, it sees continuing growth, though with currency fluctuations remaining a complicating factor.

GWT Year to 30 June	2002	2003
Revenues ($mn)	609.5	659.6
Building fixtures & fittings (%)	82	83
Commercial furniture (%)	10	11
EBIT ($mn)	79.7	90.9
EBIT margin (%)	13.1	13.8
Gross margin (%)	44.5	44.2
Operating profit before tax ($mn)	66.6	78.6
Profit after tax ($mn)	46.7	55.0
Earnings per share (¢)	16.8	19.8
Cashflow per share (¢)	27.2	29.9
Dividend (¢)	14.5	15.5
Percentage franked	100	100
Net tangible assets per share ($)	0.10	0.20
Interest cover (times)	6.1	7.4
Return on equity (%)	12.1	13.7
Debt-to-equity ratio (%)	59.2	50.2
Current ratio	2.2	2.5

Harvey Norman Holdings Limited

Share price ($)	2.63	
12-month high ($)	3.30	
12-month low ($)	1.88	
Market capitalisation ($mn)	2,734.8	
Price-to-NTA-per-share ratio	2.9	
5-year share price return (% p.a.)	8.6	
Sector: Consumer Discretion.	**Company**	**Sector**
Price-earnings ratio (times)	18.4	20.2
Dividend yield (%)	1.9	3.7

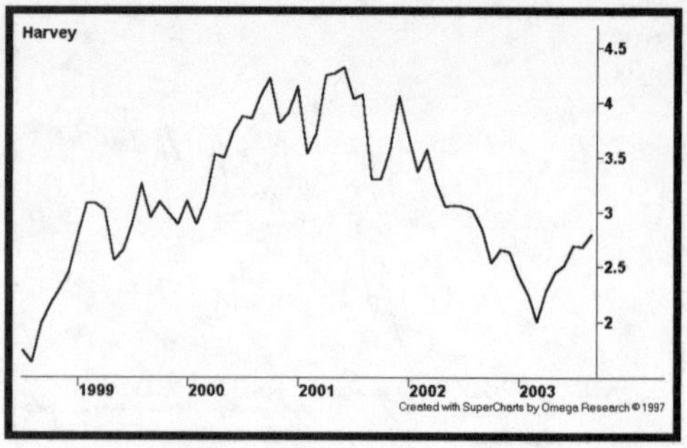

www.harveynorman.com.au

Harvey Norman operates a chain of 170 retail stores specialising in electrical and electronic goods, home appliances, furniture, flooring, carpets and manchester, throughout Australia and New Zealand. Many of the stores are independently held as part of a franchise operation, from which Harvey Norman receives income for advisory and advertising services. It also receives rental income from property investments, from its own stores and from the provision of finance to franchisees and customers. It has bought controlling stakes in Rebel Sport and in the Singapore retailer Pertama, and is expanding into Europe.

Latest Business Results (June 2003, Full Year)

The company recorded another strong rise in revenues and profits. Total group sales from all stores, both company-owned and franchised, rose 14% to $3.17 billion. During the year, nine new stores or complexes were opened in Australia, one small lighting store was closed, and the flagship Harvey Norman store in Slovenia was opened in Ljubljana. Six retail stores or complexes were opened in New Zealand. At June 2003 the group property portfolio was valued at $771.7 million, up from $659.9 million a year earlier.

Outlook

Harvey Norman continues to drive ahead. Domestically, consumer spending remains firm, and the company believes it is set to ride an enormous boom in demand for digital video and audio home entertainment products. It is also developing a new franchised retail concept known as Mega Flooring Depot, selling carpets, general floor coverings, rugs and timber flooring. The majority-owned Rebel Sport is achieving superb growth. After a sluggish start, the Singapore stores have turned the corner into profit, and the company is looking at expansion opportunities. New Zealand too shows good potential, with stores there performing well. The company has also launched itself in Ireland, with its initial two stores opening in August and September 2003. Nevertheless, Harvey Norman's once high-flying shares have become volatile at times, on concerns that the company's period of consistent high growth might have come to an end.

HVN Year to 30 June	2002	2003
Revenues ($mn)	1,121.9	1,379.1
Asia (%)	30	26
Franchising & corporate (%)	23	21
Retail - Rebel Sport (%)	21	21
Retail - New Zealand (%)	14	18
Non-franchised retail (%)	6	9
Property investments (%)	5	5
EBIT ($mn)	209.6	256.7
EBIT margin (%)	18.7	18.6
Gross margin (%)	24.8	25.9
Operating profit before tax ($mn)	189.4	233.3
Profit after tax ($mn)	128.3	151.0
Earnings per share (¢)	12.3	14.3
Cashflow per share (¢)	17.9	20.6
Dividend (¢)	4.5	5
Percentage franked	100	100
Net tangible assets per share ($)	0.75	0.90
Interest cover (times)	10.4	11.0
Return on equity (%)	18.2	17.0
Debt-to-equity ratio (%)	33.4	37.7
Current ratio	1.6	1.8

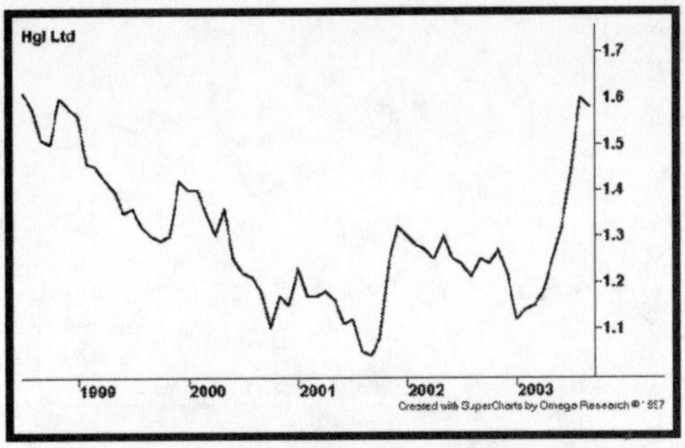

www.hgl.com.au

HGL Limited

Share price ($)	1.44
12-month high ($)	1.47
12-month low ($)	1.07
Market capitalisation ($mn)	68.5
Price-to-NTA-per-share ratio	1.4
5-year share price return (% p.a.)	8.4

Sector: Industrials	Company	Sector
Price-earnings ratio (times)	8.4	12.1
Dividend yield (%)	8.3	3.9

HGL is a small diversified investment group that specialises in acquiring and rejuvenating underperforming niche businesses. Generally, these businesses are partially owned by their management or other industry experts. The company divides its many subsidiaries into four main divisions: information technology, industrial abrasives, optical and fabrics. A fifth division, investment banking, is responsible for strategic investments in listed and unlisted companies and property.

Latest Business Results (March 2003, Half Year)

Sales and profits fell. However, this largely reflected timing issues. HGL's operations include the buying and selling of assets, and the March 2002 half included the sale of its 50% holding in GMA Garnet, with a pre-tax profit of $5.8 million, and a revaluation of its then 8% stake (now 6%) in boutique fund manager Hunter Hall International. Earnings (before tax and interest) from continuing operating business actually jumped 78% to $4.4 million, with sales revenues up 17% to $40 million. Much of the gain came in the company's information technology division, with sales up 35% to $18 million and a big jump in profits.

Outlook

In December 2002, HGL acquired 28% of MMC Asset Management, an Adelaide boutique funds manager, for $1.9 million. In April 2003, it acquired Sydney Point-of-Sale, a distributor of price ticketing and shelf management systems, for $7 million. In July 2003, it bought BLC Cosmetics, the distributor of Thalgo natural beauty and skin care products, for $9 million. As a result, it sees annual after-tax profit rising to $4.6 million, before the profit on asset sales. It expects to make a profit of $4.5 million during the September 2003 half from the sale of strategic investments made in two listed companies, Sabre Group and Lemarne, and it is actively seeking further acquisitions.

HNG Year to 30 September	2001	2002
Revenues ($mn)	88.1	83.9
EBIT ($mn)	10.6	14.6
EBIT margin (%)	12.0	17.4
Operating profit before tax ($mn)	9.6	14.4
Profit after tax ($mn)	6.1	8.0
Earnings per share (¢)	13.2	17.2
Cashflow per share (¢)	24.9	25.8
Dividend (¢)	10.25	12
Percentage franked	37	0
Interest cover (times)	11.1	75.9
Return on equity (%)	14.0	17.7
Half Year to 31 March	**2002**	**2003**
Revenues ($mn)	43.9	39.5
Operating profit before tax ($mn)	11.4	2.9
Profit after tax ($mn)	6.3	2.0
Earnings per share (¢)	13.6	4.3
Dividend (¢)	6	4.2
Percentage franked	0	100
Net tangible assets per share ($)	0.97	1.00
Debt-to-equity ratio (%)	–	–
Current ratio	4.1	4.0

Hills Industries Limited

Share price ($)	4.00	
12-month high ($)	4.00	
12-month low ($)	2.94	
Market capitalisation ($mn)	542.2	
Price-to-NTA-per-share ratio	3.4	
5-year share price return (% p.a.)	22.8	
Sector: Industrials	**Company**	**Sector**
Price-earnings ratio (times)	19.3	12.1
Dividend yield (%)	5.3	3.9

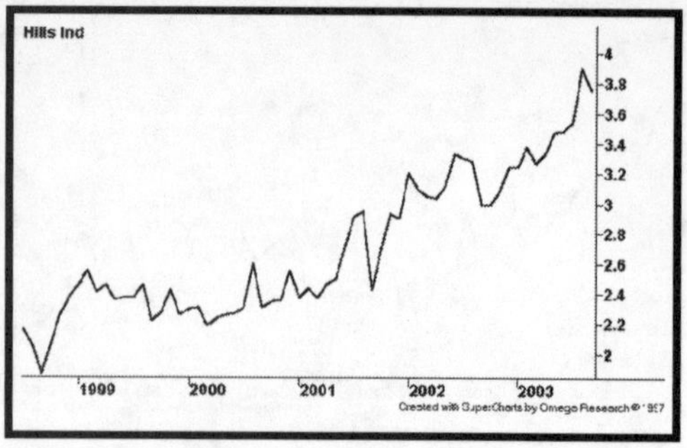

www.hills.com.au

Adelaide-based Hills, founded in 1946, is famous for its clothes hoists. However, it also manufactures a diverse range of other products, including garden equipment, outdoor play apparatus, industrial tubing, metal spectacle frames, closed circuit TV systems, satellite dishes, security alarms and television antennas. It owns 45% of the listed metal products manufacturer Korvest.

Latest Business Results (June 2003, Full Year)

Revenues and profits were both up strongly, in another good year for the company. Once again, the building and industrial products division was the primary contributor, with revenues up 26% and profits (before interest and tax) rising 62%. As in the previous year, the Orrcon structural tubing and the Fielders steel roofing businesses enjoyed strong business, as did Korvest. The home and hardware products division saw sales up 10%, but with only a marginal gain in profits, as the Freudenberg Household Products joint venture in the UK incurred a loss. In the electronics division, sales and profits both edged down, due mainly to a sharp decline in demand for home security systems.

Outlook

Hills has become a major beneficiary of the strength in the domestic construction industry, with profits for its building and industrial products division soaring 168% over two years. In the same period, home and hardware profit has risen just 2% and electronics profit is down 2%. The challenge for the company is to maintain growth should the construction cycle move into a downturn, and it continues to restructure its building products businesses, with cost-cutting moves, new marketing initiatives and new products that it believes will sustain profits. It is launching a major publicity campaign for its hardware and electronics products, with the aim of raising the profile of the Hills brand. The key product in the campaign is the Hills Home Hub system, a structured cabling product that enables new home buyers to cost-effectively access modular security, television, DVD, sound, lighting and telephone control systems. It sees great potential in its new K-Care acquisition, which makes disability and rehabilitation equipment.

HIL Year to 30 June	2002	2003
Revenues ($mn)	580.3	660.6
Building & industrial (%)	45	50
Home & hardware (%)	26	25
Electronics (%)	28	24
EBIT ($mn)	43.5	54.2
EBIT margin (%)	7.5	8.2
Gross margin (%)	33.1	34.0
Operating profit before tax ($mn)	39.2	49.8
Profit after tax ($mn)	23.9	27.2
Earnings per share (¢)	19.4	20.7
Cashflow per share (¢)	30.5	34.5
Dividend (¢)	20	21
Percentage franked	100	100
Net tangible assets per share ($)	1.03	1.17
Interest cover (times)	10.1	12.5
Return on equity (%)	18.4	17.5
Debt-to-equity ratio (%)	42.9	27.9
Current ratio	1.5	1.8

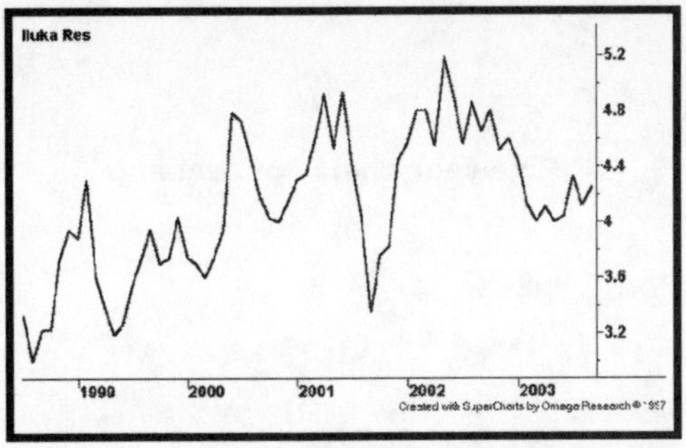

www.iluka.com

ILUKA RESOURCES LIMITED

Share price ($)	4.33
12-month high ($)	4.90
12-month low ($)	3.69
Market capitalisation ($mn)	1,003.4
Price-to-NTA-per-share ratio	1.2
5-year share price return (% p.a.)	11.1

Sector: Materials	Company	Sector
Price-earnings ratio (times)	8.9	16.0
Dividend yield (%)	5.1	2.9

Perth-based Iluka is the world's second-largest producer and processor of titanium minerals – used in paint pigments and other protective coatings – and the world's largest miner and processor of zircon, which is used in ceramics and refractories. It also has a coal mining joint venture. It has production and processing operations in Australia and the US, and extensive mineral exploration activities in several countries. It owns half the equity of the publicly listed Consolidated Rutile.

LATEST BUSINESS RESULTS (JUNE 2003, HALF YEAR)

Improved operational efficiencies, higher production and the sale of non-core assets were insufficient to offset the impact of lower sales revenues, a $3.9 million writedown relating to the revaluation of inventory in the US and higher depreciation charges and tax expenses, and the after-tax profit was down. The decrease in revenues reflected the divestiture during 2002 of its Koba Tin business, and lower mineral sands sales. Mineral sands revenues from Western Australian operations fell 8% to $263 million, which was partially offset by a 20% jump in US sales revenues to $50 million. However, US operations recorded a loss. Coal sales rose 4% to $16 million.

OUTLOOK

The short-term outlook seems positive, with production and demand continuing to rise, and operational improvements evident in both Western Australia and the US, where profitability is starting to turn around. However, the 2003 full-year profit remains quite dependent on currency rate trends and the company says it anticipates an after-tax profit figure of $80 million to $90 million. Longer term, the company has a series of initiatives in place designed to ensure continued growth. It is proceeding with its $190 million Murray Basin mineral sands project in Victoria, with the first production expected late in 2005. It has also received permission to start work on another major mineral sands project in South Georgia, with full production expected around mid 2004.

ILU Year to 31 December	2001	2002
Revenues ($mn)	900.8	894.5
EBIT ($mn)	88.4	128.4
EBIT margin (%)	9.8	14.4
Operating profit before tax ($mn)	63.0	102.1
Profit after tax ($mn)	63.7	109.0
Earnings per share (¢)	29.3	48.6
Cashflow per share (¢)	81.5	92.0
Dividend (¢)	22	22
Percentage franked	9	9
Interest cover (times)	3.5	4.9
Return on equity (%)	9.3	14.4
Half Year to 30 June	**2002**	**2003**
Revenues ($mn)	443.4	388.5
Operating profit before tax ($mn)	35.7	40.0
Profit after tax ($mn)	41.1	36.7
Earnings per share (¢)	18.9	15.8
Dividend (¢)	10	10
Percentage franked	20	92
Net tangible assets per share ($)	3.72	3.63
Debt-to-equity ratio (%)	51.0	43.5
Current ratio	1.6	2.2

Incitec Pivot Limited

Share price ($)	15.52	
12-month high ($)	15.60	
12-month low ($)	14.00	
Market capitalisation ($mn)	903.4	
Price-to-NTA-per-share ratio	2.6	
5-year share price return (% p.a.)	–	
Sector: Materials	**Company**	**Sector**
Price-earnings ratio (times)	31.4	16.0
Dividend yield (%)	2.4	2.9

Five-year chart not available

www.incitecpivot.com.au

Fertiliser manufacturer and distributor Incitec has merged with one of its rivals, Pivot, to make a new company that was formally launched in June 2003. Both Incitec and Pivot have histories that date back more than 80 years, and the new company will be a major force in the rural economy, with manufacturing facilities in Queensland, Victoria and New South Wales, major distribution facilities throughout the eastern seaboard of Australia, and expected annual production of around three million tonnes. Incitec's former parent, Orica, owns 70% of the new company, and much of the balance is held by the farming community.

Latest Business Results (March 2003, Half Year)

The latest available complete results are the full-year figures – to September 2002 – for Incitec, which are shown in the table on this page. However, in merger documents presented to the stock exchange, the new company issued various details of half-year performance to March 2003. In that period, Incitec had sales of $254 million and a profit (before tax and interest) of $1.7 million. Pivot had sales of $164 million and a profit of $9.7 million. Both companies reported that they were hurt by the ongoing drought conditions in many parts of Australia, with their sales down 13% to 15% from the March 2002 half. Based on figures in the merger documents, the merged company in March 2003 had a nominal debt-to-equity ratio of 28% and net tangible assets of approximately $6 per share.

Outlook

Pivot has traditionally been strong in the southeast of Australia and in Tasmania, while Incitec's strength has been in northern NSW and Queensland. The new company becomes the dominant force in the Australian fertiliser industry, with an expected 50% national market share, and more than 70% of the eastern seaboard market. Annual sales revenues of approximately $1 billion are forecast. Merger costs of some $79 million include mainly staff redundancies and asset writedowns, and the company has said it expects $30 million in annual efficiency benefits by the end of the 2004 year. Incitec Pivot shares seem unlikely to be very liquid.

IPL Year to 30 September	2001	2002
Revenues ($mn)	982.5	950.2
EBIT ($mn)	128.1	97.7
EBIT margin (%)	13.0	10.3
Operating profit before tax ($mn)	121.2	97.1
Profit after tax ($mn)	69.3	65.1
Earnings per share (¢)	53.5	49.4
Cashflow per share (¢)	80.7	77.3
Dividend (¢)	28	37
Percentage franked	100	100
Interest cover (times)	18.4	170.8
Return on equity (%)	19.2	16.4
Net tangible assets per share ($)	2.48	3.07
Debt-to-equity ratio (%)	–	–
Current ratio	1.8	2.1

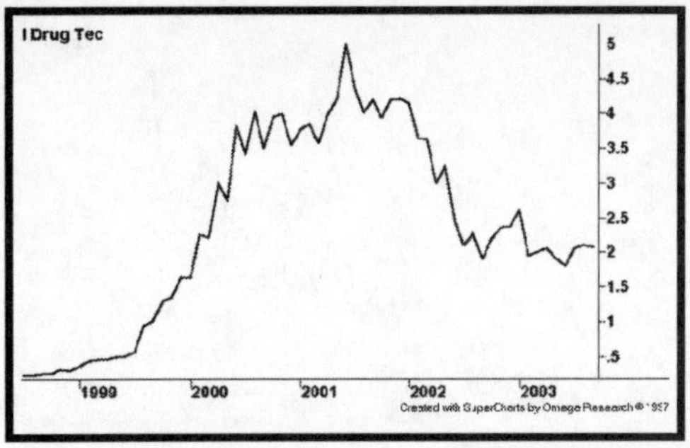

www.idtaus.com.au

Institute of Drug Technology Australia Ltd

Share price ($)	2.33	
12-month high ($)	3.03	
12-month low ($)	1.66	
Market capitalisation ($mn)	97.1	
Price-to-NTA-per-share ratio	4.1	
5-year share price return (% p.a.)	47.2	
Sector: Health Care	**Company**	**Sector**
Price-earnings ratio (times)	23.6	40.6
Dividend yield (%)	2.6	2.9

The Melbourne-based Institute of Drug Technology Australia (IDT), established in 1975, is a small but well-regarded developer and manufacturer of active pharmaceutical ingredients (APIs) for local and international companies. It also provides technical consulting and clinical trial services to the pharmaceuticals, chemical and biotechnology industries. In addition, it operates a research and development business for clients.

Latest Business Results (June 2003, Full Year)

The company just barely managed to achieve its ninth straight profit increase, despite strong revenues growth. There was a solid contribution to sales from the previous year's acquisition of the Adelaide-based CMAX clinical trials unit, and revenues from several of IDT's manufactured products also grew during the year as a result of increased demand. However, downward pressure on prices for some generic products contributed to a reduction of revenue from this source. Also, fee for service activity from the Australian biotechnology and small pharmaceutical sector was significantly reduced during the year due to a steady reduction in investment capital and research funds. The company also suffered from downward pressure on pricing for some generic drugs, together with the final costs associated with fully integrating the CMAX business into its operations.

Outlook

IDT has established a strong reputation internationally for the manufacture of APIs, and this provides around half its turnover. Much of this business is based on 10-year contracts, thus providing a very stable revenues stream. The company has a particular specialty in producing components for anti-cancer drugs. This has been reflected in the powerful acceleration in recent years of profits and the company's share price, particularly evident since the company's laboratory and production facilities were licensed by the US Food and Drug Administration for the manufacture of APIs. The CMAX acquisition places IDT in a strong position to attract significant new drug development contracts with local and overseas clients. Advanced new manufacturing facilities are due to commence operations by the end of the 2003. The company reports that the level of enquiry for its services continues to be strong, though much future growth depends on levels of funding available from government and the private sector.

IDT Year to 30 June	2002	2003
Revenues ($mn)	20.9	25.5
EBIT ($mn)	5.9	6.0
EBIT margin (%)	28.3	23.5
Gross margin (%)	63.6	70.8
Operating profit before tax ($mn)	5.9	6.0
Profit after tax ($mn)	4.2	4.2
Earnings per share (¢)	9.9	9.9
Cashflow per share (¢)	14.1	15.0
Dividend (¢)	5	6
Percentage franked	100	100
Net tangible assets per share ($)	0.54	0.57
Interest cover (times)	–	–
Return on equity (%)	19.3	17.0
Debt-to-equity ratio (%)	–	–
Current ratio	1.8	3.4

K&S Corporation Limited

Share price ($)	3.60	
12-month high ($)	3.64	
12-month low ($)	2.31	
Market capitalisation ($mn)	108.0	
Price-to-NTA-per-share ratio	2.0	
5-year share price return (% p.a.)	31.8	
Sector: Industrials	**Company**	**Sector**
Price-earnings ratio (times)	9.8	12.1
Dividend yield (%)	4.4	3.9

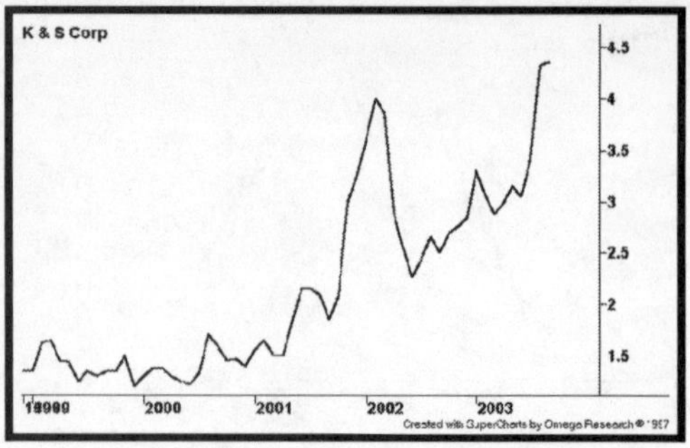

www.ksgroup.com.au

Based in Mt Gambier, and with a history stretching back more than 55 years, K&S is one of Australia's leading transport, warehousing and logistics companies, with a strategy directed towards large national contracts. It controls one of the largest company-owned fleets in Australia, as well as owning over 160,000 square metres of warehousing and a large range of rail and sea containers. It operates through four divisions: K&S Freighters is involved in road, rail and coastal sea forwarding in support of full and break-bulk loads; K&S Integrated Distribution handles warehousing, storage and local distribution; K&S Agencies manages Ampol fuel distribution throughout regions of South Australia and Victoria; and K&S (NZ) provides full truckload and break bulk distribution throughout New Zealand. The company chairman, Allan Scott, owns more than 60% of the equity.

Latest Business Results (June 2003, Full Year)

In an excellent year for its business, K&S saw a solid increase in sales revenues and profits. The core transport business helped generate a significant increase in revenue streams, with particular strength in the paper, steel, aluminium and timber industries. In October 2002 the company entered the New Zealand market to transport lumber products for Fletcher Challenge Forests, and this business generated revenues of $6.7 million. There was also a strong contribution from a new PaperlinX contract. However, the warehousing business remained in the red.

Outlook

K&S appears to have overcome the turmoil that hit the company early in 2002 when it emerged that a senior employee had apparently lost more than $20 million of company money through gambling. This matter has gone before the courts, with the company hopeful of recovering at least something. With its business now booming, the company has started a $10 million fleet upgrade program. It is also looking for acquisition opportunities, and it believes that further growth will come through aggressive contract tendering for new business. The New Zealand operation has given the company a base from which to grow, and it is actively seeking new business. The company's warehousing operation is expected to move into profit during the June 2004 year.

KSC Year to 30 June	2002	2003
Revenues ($mn)	267.3	293.3
EBIT ($mn)	15.2	17.9
EBIT margin (%)	5.7	6.1
Gross margin (%)	10.9	14.6
Operating profit before tax ($mn)	12.0	15.3
Profit after tax ($mn)	8.8	11.1
Earnings per share (¢)	29.5	36.9
Cashflow per share (¢)	66.9	75.7
Dividend (¢)	11.5	16
Percentage franked	100	100
Net tangible assets per share ($)	1.54	1.84
Interest cover (times)	4.7	6.9
Return on equity (%)	17.0	20.2
Debt-to-equity ratio (%)	101.5	39.9
Current ratio	1.0	1.0

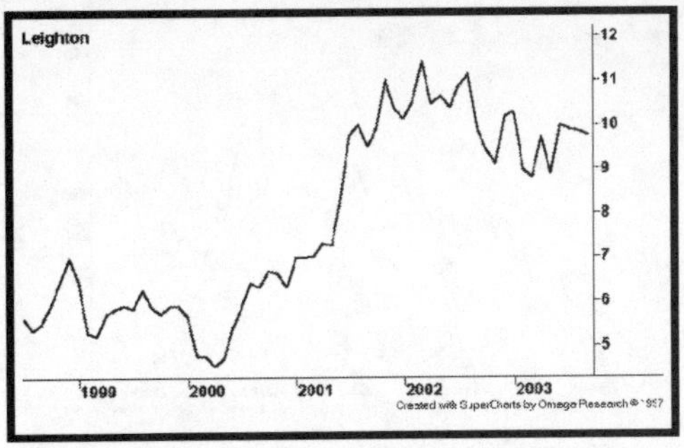

www.leighton.com.au

LEIGHTON HOLDINGS LIMITED

Share price ($)	9.75	
12-month high ($)	11.35	
12-month low ($)	8.52	
Market capitalisation ($mn)	2,652.2	
Price-to-NTA-per-share ratio	3.2	
5-year share price return (% p.a.)	18.2	
Sector: Industrials	**Company**	**Sector**
Price-earnings ratio (times)	18.9	12.1
Dividend yield (%)	4.5	3.9

Founded in 1949, Leighton is Australia's largest project development and contracting group. It incorporates Leighton Contractors, Thiess Contractors, Leighton Asia, Leighton Properties and John Holland, and employs more than 10,000 people at sites around the Asia-Pacific region and in South America. The German construction company Hochtief owns 51% of Leighton's shares.

LATEST BUSINESS RESULTS (JUNE 2003, FULL YEAR)

Despite a buoyant construction environment, profits fell, with the company hit by a $40 million writedown of its investment in the failed cable company Nextgen Networks. The mining and resources sector was the largest contributor to business, with revenues jumping 52% and work in hand up 23%, thanks especially to contract coalmining work by Thiess. The rail sector lay behind a strong contribution from engineering and infrastructure, with Thiess starting construction on the Epping–Chatswood section of the Parramatta Rail Link in Sydney and John Holland ahead of schedule on the Alice Springs–Darwin railway line. In June 2003, Leighton had work in hand of $9.7 billion, up from $8.4 billion a year earlier, including the finalisation of the Western Sydney Orbital and the Central Reclamation project in Hong Kong. A total of $1.1 billion in mining contracts helped boost the figure. However, the company's order book was hurt by the collapse of the $1.7 billion Australian Magnesium Corporation project at Stanwell, Queensland, for which Leighton was contractor.

OUTLOOK

Leighton is forecasting a continuing high level of order inflow, with projects on the horizon that include the $800 million Lane Cove Tunnel in Sydney and the $1.8 billion Mitcham–Frankston freeway in Melbourne, and it expects revenues and profits to rise in the 2003–04 year. For the time being it does not see many major new projects coming from Asia. The company has net cash holdings of more than $380 million, and is thought to be interested in a major acquisition – the government's Australian Submarine Corporation is a possibility – or in pursuing some major infrastructure developments. In mid 2003, considerable speculation arose about the future of Leighton, with news that its parent, Hochtief, is for sale.

LEI Year to 30 June	2002	2003
Revenues ($mn)	4,979.6	4,848.5
Mining & resources (%)	27	36
Engineering & infrastructure (%)	36	34
Building & property (%)	22	19
Telecommunications (%)	11	8
EBIT ($mn)	225.0	222.2
EBIT margin (%)	4.5	4.6
Operating profit before tax ($mn)	233.7	222.5
Profit after tax ($mn)	169.2	140.0
Earnings per share (¢)	63.1	51.7
Cashflow per share (¢)	182.5	169.2
Dividend (¢)	42	44
Percentage franked	70	100
Net tangible assets per share ($)	2.81	3.06
Interest cover (times)	–	–
Return on equity (%)	22.1	17.0
Debt-to-equity ratio (%)	–	–

Macquarie Bank Limited

Share price ($)	31.95	
12-month high ($)	32.18	
12-month low ($)	18.75	
Market capitalisation ($mn)	6,707.9	
Price-to-NTA-per-share ratio	3.0	
5-year share price return (% p.a.)	23.7	
Sector: Financials	**Company**	**Sector**
Price-earnings ratio (times)	19.4	16.2
Dividend yield (%)	2.9	4.5

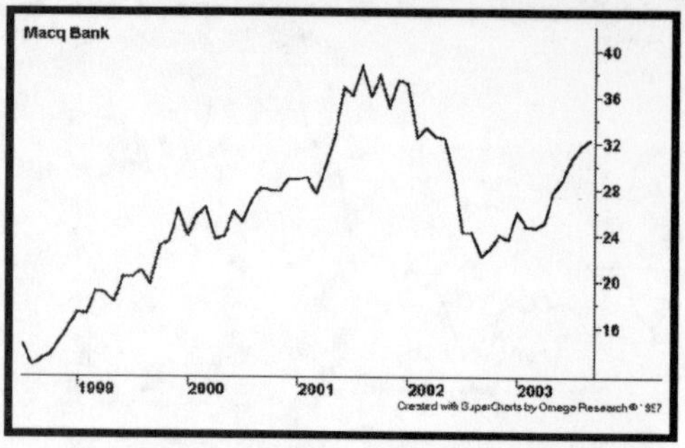

www.macquarie.com.au

Macquarie, established in 1969 as Hill Samuel Australia, a subsidiary of a British merchant bank, is now Australia's leading locally owned investment bank. Its business is divided into six broad operating groups: investment banking, treasury and commodities, equity markets, banking and property, funds management and financial services. It has activities in 18 countries, including strategic alliances with companies in China, Korea, Japan, Malaysia, the US and South Africa.

Latest Business Results (March 2003, Full Year)

Profits rose again in a strong result achieved at a time of turbulent world financial markets. The core investment banking group continued to perform well, with its performance marginally up. The group maintained its position as a world leader in project and other structured financings, overcoming a relative dearth of new underwriting opportunities. The treasury and commodities group had another strong year, with every division achieving a record or near-record result, driven by increased market share and product and market diversity. The banking and property group posted its fifth consecutive record profit. Property funds under management jumped 50% to $7.2 billion. The equity markets group overcame adverse trading conditions to post a rise in profits. The funds management group's contribution was broadly flat, despite the contraction of the overall Australian funds management industry. After posting two years of losses, the financial services group moved into profit, thanks to continued growth in client numbers and revenues.

Outlook

Macquarie has become a global financial powerhouse, and when markets are strong it has the potential to realise high profits. The star is the investment banking business, which accounts for around half of the company's profit. It has developed a particular expertise in infrastructure investment, and advises governments and financial institutions around the world, as well as managing its own specialist funds. Another area of particular expertise is the equity warrants market, which can be extremely profitable in the right market conditions. Despite previous concerns about its direction and growth, Macquarie has indicated that it expects March 2004 profits to continue to expand, with particularly strong performances likely from investment banking and wealth management operations.

MBL Year to 31 March	2002	2003
Operating income ($mn)	1,600.0	1,890.0
Net interest income ($mn)	219.0	247.0
Operating expenses ($mn)	1,245.0	1,430.0
Operating profit before tax ($mn)	355.0	460.0
Profit after tax ($mn)	250.0	333.0
Earnings per share (¢)	132.6	164.8
Dividend (¢)	93	93
Percentage franked	70	87
Non-interest income to total income (%)	86.3	86.9
Net tangible assets per share ($)	10.18	10.69
Cost-to-income ratio (%)	77.8	75.7
Return on equity (%)	14.9	15.8
Return on assets (%)	0.9	1.1

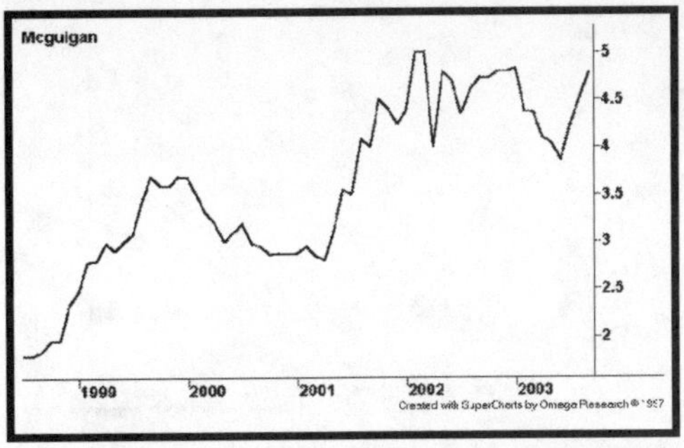

www.mcguiganwines.com.au

McGuigan Simeon Wines Limited

Share price ($)	4.65
12-month high ($)	5.10
12-month low ($)	3.69
Market capitalisation ($mn)	457.3
Price-to-NTA-per-share ratio	2.1
5-year share price return (% p.a.)	25.5

Sector: Consumer Staples	Company	Sector
Price-earnings ratio (times)	13.9	17.9
Dividend yield (%)	4.3	3.6

McGuigan Simeon Wines was formed from the merger in 2002 of Brian McGuigan Wines with Simeon Wines. It is now Australia's third-largest listed winery, with vineyards in many premium viticulture regions. Its labels include the Harvest range and the Black Label range. It is also Australia's largest seller of bulk wine and it develops and manages vineyards. Exports are more than 40% of sales.

Latest Business Results (June 2003, Full Year)

The merger between Brian McGuigan and Simeon was completed on 21 June 2002, and a direct comparison of the June 2003 result with the June 2002 Brian McGuigan result, as presented in the table on this page, only partially illustrates the company's progress. Therefore, the company has prepared a pro forma profit and loss account for the merged company for June 2002, to make comparisons more meaningful. On this basis, sales revenues were up 25% and the after-tax profit jumped 27%. Domestically, bottled sales of $45.9 million were up 13%, reflecting increasing gains through the company's own national distribution network, as well as new supply relationships and marketing and branding improvements. However, bulk sales fell 17% to $82.6 million, due to the poor vintage, and also the redirection of product to bottled sales. Bulk wine exports grew 103%, with bottled wine exports up 106%. American sales grew 300%, those to New Zealand 106% and to the UK 47%.

Outlook

Thanks to the merger, McGuigan Simeon has become one of Australia's most efficient producers of wines at various price points, and in the midst of a price war in the industry it has been able to post some impressive gains in sales and profits. It is buying Miranda Wines, Australia's eighth-largest winery, for $25.5 million. Miranda is particularly strong in cask wine, and the acquisition gives McGuigan an immediate presence in this market segment, which represents 45% of domestic wine sales by volume. It also broadens the company's grape-buying and production base, and provides access to new domestic and export customers. Thanks to new alliances, McGuigan Simeon is realising very strong growth in sales to Britain and the US.

MGW Year to 30 June	2002	2003
Revenues ($mn)	100.5	290.5
Bulk wine & grapes (%)	17	42
Bottled wine (%)	67	29
Bulk in bottle (%)	0	18
Vineyard development (%)	16	10
EBIT ($mn)	17.7	56.1
EBIT margin (%)	17.6	19.3
Gross margin (%)	24.9	15.7
Operating profit before tax ($mn)	16.5	46.1
Profit after tax ($mn)	11.5	32.2
Earnings per share (¢)	25.9	33.3
Cashflow per share (¢)	27.4	44.3
Dividend (¢)	15	20
Percentage franked	100	100
Net tangible assets per share ($)	1.84	2.19
Interest cover (times)	14.8	5.6
Return on equity (%)	8.4	13.0
Debt-to-equity ratio (%)	54.9	65.4
Current ratio	1.7	2.4

McPherson's Limited

Share price ($)	3.77	
12-month high ($)	3.90	
12-month low ($)	1.94	
Market capitalisation ($mn)	201.1	
Price-to-NTA-per-share ratio	5.5	
5-year share price return (% p.a.)	40.9	
Sector: Industrials	**Company**	**Sector**
Price-earnings ratio (times)	13.0	12.1
Dividend yield (%)	4.0	3.9

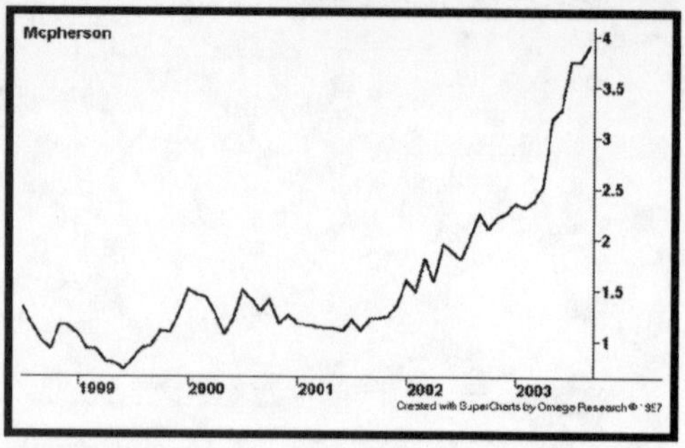

www.mcphersons.com.au

Melbourne-based McPherson's, established in 1860, operates in three broad areas. Its housewares division markets a wide range of kitchenware products, both within Australasia and internationally. Brand names include Wiltshire, Strachan, Grosvenor, Rodd and Crown Glassware. The Australasian business has a third of the kitchen knife and flatware cutlery markets. Overseas, trading as Richardson Sheffield and Regent-Sheffield, the company holds around 30% of the British and Canadian kitchen knife markets and 5% in the US. The company's second business is commercial printing. It is one of Australia's leading printers of books (including this one) and its William Brooks division has a contract to produce 50% of Telstra's White and Yellow Page telephone directory requirements until June 2009. A third business, the distribution of hair care and beauty products, was launched in mid 2003 with the acquisition of Cork Asia Pacific.

Latest Business Results (June 2003, Full Year)

A strong contribution from its housewares business gave McPherson's an excellent profit result, despite a lacklustre printing operation and a slight dip in sales revenues. Housewares profits (before tax and interest) surged 76%, thanks to productivity improvements, the deletion of low-margin lines and strict control of expenses. A particularly good profit came from the company's Richardson Sheffield business in the UK, after several years of losses. However, the printing business saw profits down 15%, with excess capacity in the domestic printing industry resulting in pricing and profit margin pressures.

Outlook

McPherson's has two major businesses – kitchen cutlery and printing – that offer only modest scope for good growth. Thus, the company in July 2003 acquired, for approximately $101 million, Cork Asia Pacific, which sells a wide range of consumer products to pharmacies and other retailers throughout the Asia-Pacific region. Key product ranges include beauty and hair care accessories, impulse merchandising, baby care accessories and home health products. Cork also manages the supply and recycling of garment hangers to major retailers in Australia. The company believes the acquisition will eventually generate synergies of some $6 million per year, as Cork's business is integrated with the McPherson's housewares operation.

MCP Year to 30 June	2002	2003
Revenues ($mn)	253.0	248.7
Housewares (%)	53	52
Printing (%)	47	48
EBIT ($mn)	17.5	20.7
EBIT margin (%)	6.9	8.3
Operating profit before tax ($mn)	13.1	16.6
Profit after tax ($mn)	9.6	11.8
Earnings per share (¢)	24.6	29.1
Cashflow per share (¢)	43.3	43.4
Dividend (¢)	12	15
Percentage franked	100	100
Net tangible assets per share ($)	0.43	0.69
Interest cover (times)	4.0	5.1
Return on equity (%)	20.1	21.0
Debt-to-equity ratio (%)	112.7	68.6
Current ratio	2.4	2.4

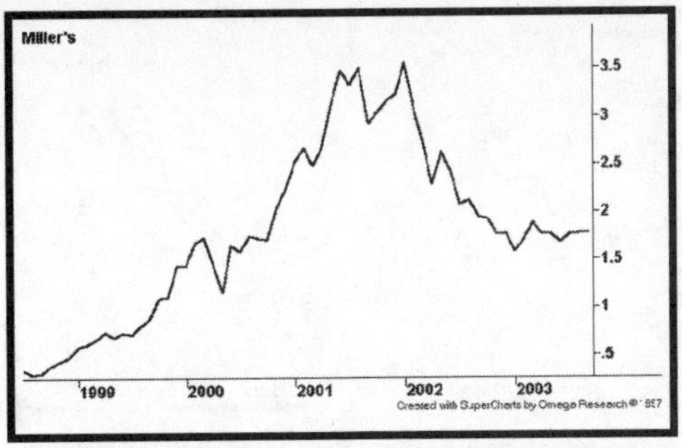

www.millersretail.com.au

Miller's Retail Limited

Share price ($)	1.78
12-month high ($)	2.31
12-month low ($)	1.52
Market capitalisation ($mn)	430.3
Price-to-NTA-per-share ratio	4.8
5-year share price return (% p.a.)	45.3

Sector: Consumer Discretion.	Company	Sector
Price-earnings ratio (times)	13.7	20.2
Dividend yield (%)	5.3	3.7

Sydney-based Miller's is a fast-growing retailer, operating in two broad market segments: its discount variety group manages a national chain of 338 discount variety stores under the names Crazy Clark's, Go-Lo and Chickenfeed; and its apparel group operates 678 specialty apparel stores with the names Miller's Fashion Club, Katies, 1626, Crossroads and Silhouette. The company's Miller's Retail Club customer loyalty program has more than two million members.

Latest Business Results (June 2003, Full Year)

Sales were up, but tighter margins squeezed profits. The company was also affected by the cost of merging its Go-Lo and Crazy Clark's businesses. Apparel sales were up 7% and discount variety sales increased by 10%. On a same-store basis, apparel maintained the momentum started in the latter half of the previous financial year, with growth of 1.1% for the year. However, on a same-store basis, discount variety store sales dipped 0.9%, though still an improvement on the previous year's 3.7% decline in sales. The company opened 109 new stores during the year and closed 59.

Outlook

Miller's has grown extremely rapidly over several years through a string of acquisitions, notably the Katies chain of women's apparel stores formerly operated by Coles Myer. The company is still in the process of bedding down all these new businesses into its operations, and expects further synergies and productivity benefits. However, at the same time, it faces very strong competition from rivals such as Target, Kmart and Big W. The company has established a research and development function to review new retail concepts, with several new formats currently being tested. The newly introduced Kidswear range has had a slow start, but sales picked up during winter. A menswear range will be trialled at 15 Crossroads stores, and the company also expects to launch sales of footwear and manchester. Miller's has a target for same-store sales growth in the June 2004 year of around 3%, though management admits some margin sacrifice might be necessary to achieve this goal. The present sales margin (earnings before interest, tax and amortisation, as a percentage of sales) of 6% is one of the highest among chain store retailers.

MRL Year to 30 June	2002	2003
Revenues ($mn)	963.6	1,049.7
Discount variety (%)	59	60
Apparel (%)	41	40
EBIT ($mn)	55.9	55.6
EBIT margin (%)	5.8	5.3
Gross margin (%)	42.7	43.7
Operating profit before tax ($mn)	48.1	45.8
Profit after tax ($mn)	31.7	30.5
Earnings per share (¢)	14.2	13.0
Cashflow per share (¢)	24.5	23.7
Dividend (¢)	8.5	9.5
Percentage franked	100	100
Net tangible assets per share ($)	0.25	0.37
Interest cover (times)	7.2	5.7
Return on equity (%)	23.5	15.1
Debt-to-equity ratio (%)	50.9	55.1
Current ratio	1.2	1.3

Monadelphous Group Limited

Share price ($)	4.20	
12-month high ($)	4.20	
12-month low ($)	2.49	
Market capitalisation ($mn)	80.5	
Price-to-NTA-per-share ratio	2.3	
5-year share price return (% p.a.)	19.0	
Sector: Industrials	**Company**	**Sector**
Price-earnings ratio (times)	11.0	12.1
Dividend yield (%)	6.0	3.9

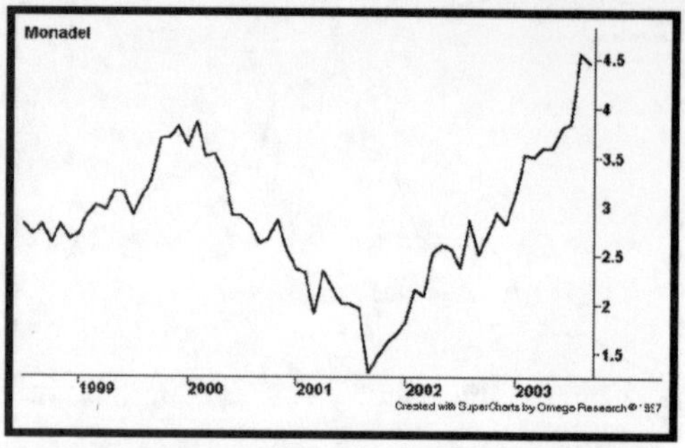

www.monadel.com.au

Perth-based Monadelphous is an engineering company that provides project management, construction, maintenance and support services to the mining, mineral processing and associated industries. It operates from branches at key mining and mineral processing centres throughout Australia. Although the mining sector has been the major focus of its work, it is becoming increasingly diversified, with growing involvement in the energy and government sectors.

Latest Business Results (June 2003, Full Year)

Sales revenues and profits soared, in an excellent result that the company termed two years' growth in one year. This came despite the placing into voluntary administration of a customer, Western Metals Zinc, which owed it $400,000. The company benefited from work on a number of major projects, including design and construction of alumina handling facilities for Queensland Alumina at the Gladstone alumina refinery, construction works for a major plant optimisation project for Alcan at the Gove alumina refinery in the Northern Territory, construction works associated with the Mt Arthur North Coal project for BHP Billiton in New South Wales, the provision of general services to the North West Shelf LNG4 expansion project for Woodside Energy at Karratha, Western Australia and the completion of deconstruction works associated with the HIsmelt steel project at Kwinana, Western Australia. The company announced that it was revising its dividend policy for the foreseeable future, increasing the dividend payout ratio to 60% to 70% of net profit, from 50% to 60% previously.

Outlook

As a small company, Monadelphous is starting to benefit disproportionately from increasing spending on resource development in Australia. It has already been awarded a string of contracts from BHP Billiton in relation to the expansion of iron ore facilities in Western Australia, and it is hopeful of winning work for the $3.8 billion Aldoga Aluminium project. Monadelphous has implemented a new upgraded management structure aimed at achieving long-term growth, with the particular aim of boosting its ability to undertake larger contracts and to penetrate industrial services markets in the eastern states. It is also in the process of closing down some of its less efficient fabrication and engineering workshops in regional areas of Australia.

MND Year to 30 June	2002	2003
Revenues ($mn)	154.7	243.7
EBIT ($mn)	6.8	10.1
EBIT margin (%)	4.4	4.1
Gross margin (%)	9.3	7.8
Operating profit before tax ($mn)	6.8	10.1
Profit after tax ($mn)	4.8	7.1
Earnings per share (¢)	26.0	38.2
Cashflow per share (¢)	54.1	66.5
Dividend (¢)	14	25
Percentage franked	100	100
Net tangible assets per share ($)	1.52	1.83
Interest cover (times)	–	–
Return on equity (%)	17.9	22.8
Debt-to-equity ratio (%)	–	–
Current ratio	1.4	1.5

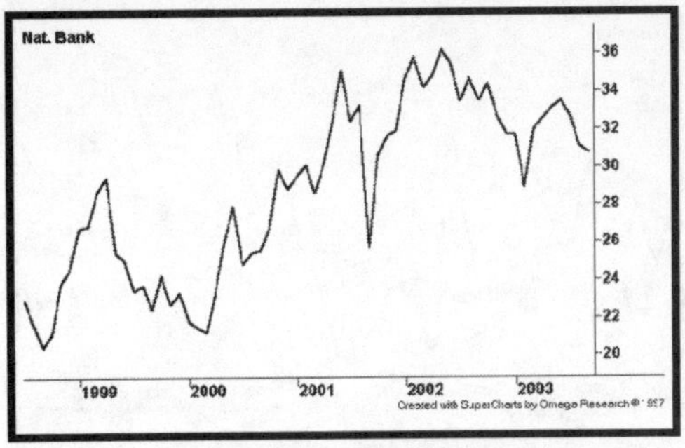

www.national.com.au

National Australia Bank Limited

Share price ($)	32.52
12-month high ($)	35.99
12-month low ($)	28.36
Market capitalisation ($mn)	49,259.8
Price-to-NTA-per-share ratio	2.2
5-year share price return (% p.a.)	13.6

Sector: Financials	Company	Sector
Price-earnings ratio (times)	13.3	16.2
Dividend yield (%)	4.5	4.5

The NAB, Australia's largest bank, is a world-class operation with a wide spread of financial activities. It owns the Clydesdale Bank, Yorkshire Bank and Northern Bank in Britain, as well as the National Irish Bank and the Bank of New Zealand. It also manages a major funds management operation, based on the MLC business that it bought from Lend Lease.

Latest Business Results (March 2003, Half Year)

Profits rose, in a pleasing turnaround after problems with its former HomeSide subsidiary – a US mortgage provider – helped force September 2002 full-year profits down. Australian business benefited from a 22% rise in home lending, though this came at the expense of lower interest margins. The bank realised an excellent performance from its New Zealand operations, with strong lending growth, higher interest margins and a sharp reduction in costs. However, British business was generally flat. The total value of Australian funds under management declined slightly to $65 billion, and there was a $205 million non-cash reduction in the valuation of the wealth management business.

Outlook

With some 30% of its profits deriving from its British and Irish businesses, NAB has sparked concern among investors that it might suffer similar problems to those experienced by AMP, and this has had an impact on the share price. The company has announced that it has confidence in its offshore assets, and is looking to expand its wealth management operations in Britain and elsewhere, believing these will be significant drivers of future growth. It also continues to work at trimming costs, under its Positioning for Growth program, with $195 million in annual cost savings already achieved, and a target of $370 million annually by September 2004. Its wide spread of activities makes NAB less vulnerable than most domestic rivals to a housing slowdown.

NAB Year to 30 September	2001	2002
Operating income ($mn)	11,493.0	11,870.0
Net interest income ($mn)	6,960.0	7,222.0
Operating expenses ($mn)	5,674.0	5,949.0
Operating profit before tax ($mn)	4,766.0	5,180.0
Profit after tax ($mn)	4,019.0	3,779.0
Earnings per share (¢)	261.1	244.0
Dividend (¢)	135	147
Percentage franked	100	95
Non-interest income to total income (%)	39.4	39.2
Cost-to-income ratio (%)	49.4	50.1
Return on equity (%)	17.9	16.2
Return on assets (%)	1.1	1.0
Half Year to 31 March	**2002**	**2003**
Operating income ($mn)	6,078.0	6,259.0
Operating profit before tax ($mn)	2,805.0	2,851.0
Profit after tax ($mn)	1,977.0	2,121.0
Earnings per share (¢)	127.1	139.2
Dividend (¢)	72	80
Percentage franked	100	100
Net tangible assets per share ($)	14.50	14.92

National Foods Limited

Share price ($)	3.80	
12-month high ($)	3.86	
12-month low ($)	3.07	
Market capitalisation ($mn)	1,119.3	
Price-to-NTA-per-share ratio	4.4	
5-year share price return (% p.a.)	14.6	
Sector: Consumer Staples	**Company**	**Sector**
Price-earnings ratio (times)	18.4	17.9
Dividend yield (%)	5.1	3.6

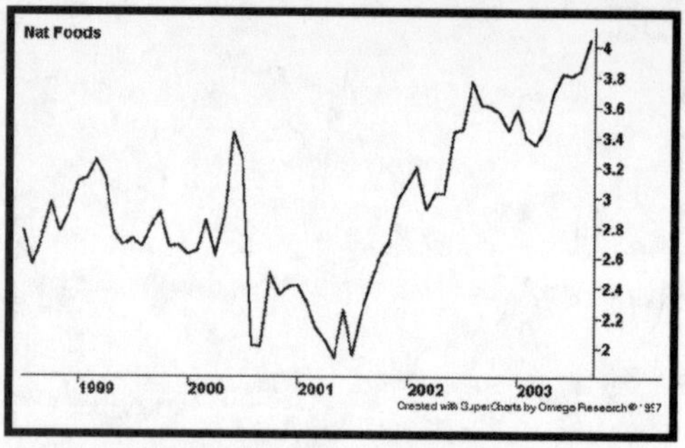

www.natfoods.com.au

National Foods, headquartered in Melbourne, was created in 1991 from the amalgamation of several dairy and food-related businesses, some with histories dating back to the 1880s. It is one of Australia's foodstuffs giants, specialising in milk and other dairy products. It is a market leader for many of its products, and Australia's only nationwide milk processor, with its Pura brand produced and marketed in all states. Other brands include Classic, Farmers Union, Masters, Big M, Yoplait, Fruche, Yogo and King Island Dairy. It holds the Yoplait franchise for several Asian countries, and is also a major cheese exporter.

Latest Business Results (June 2003, Full Year)

Profits continued to recover, after a sharp slump two years earlier when the company was hit by steep cuts in milk prices, forced on it by the giant supermarket chains. The two-year contract to supply house-brand milk to Woolworths stores nationwide – the largest food contract ever awarded in Australia – was successfully implemented during the year, and contributed to operational efficiency and earnings. There was also an impressive turnaround from King Island Dairy, acquired for $89 million in February 2002. From a small loss in June 2002, it moved to EBIT of $5.6 million in June 2003.

Outlook

Thanks to the tight grip now held by the supermarket chains on milk pricing, National Foods must continue to work at boosting productivity and cutting costs in order to maintain growth. It has already said it expects a further double-digit rise in sales and profits in the June 2004 year. It sees particular potential in high-margin gourmet foods. It is already a leading supplier of specialty cheeses – thanks to the King Island Dairy business – and of smoked salmon products, and it hopes for further bolt-on acquisitions in this business. It is also working to expand its activities in the 'impulse purchase' beverages market, such as fizzy drinks, juices and sports drinks, and has announced the purchase from Bonlac Foods of its ultra–heat treated flavoured milk plant. Though National Foods already has 50% of the flavoured milk market, the acquisition allows it to expand further into non-chilled drinks.

NFD Year to 30 June	2002	2003
Revenues ($mn)	1,096.3	1,225.0
EBIT ($mn)	81.1	93.4
EBIT margin (%)	7.4	7.6
Gross margin (%)	39.2	41.8
Operating profit before tax ($mn)	74.3	86.0
Profit after tax ($mn)	51.1	60.1
Earnings per share (¢)	17.9	20.6
Cashflow per share (¢)	32.0	35.3
Dividend (¢)	16.5	19.5
Percentage franked	100	100
Net tangible assets per share ($)	0.68	0.87
Interest cover (times)	12.0	12.5
Return on equity (%)	13.4	14.4
Debt-to-equity ratio (%)	22.9	7.1
Current ratio	0.6	0.8

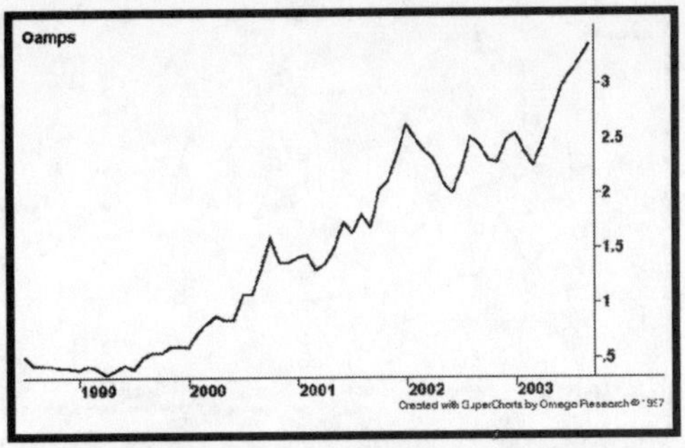

www.oamps.com.au

OAMPS Limited

Share price ($)	3.09	
12-month high ($)	3.82	
12-month low ($)	2.15	
Market capitalisation ($mn)	234.4	
Price-to-NTA-per-share ratio	7.3	
5-year share price return (% p.a.)	60.9	
Sector: Financials	**Company**	**Sector**
Price-earnings ratio (times)	12.2	16.2
Dividend yield (%)	5.5	4.5

Melbourne-based OAMPS, established in 1976 as the Oil Agents Mutual Provident Society, is one of Australia's largest insurance brokers and underwriters. It also operates in various other related businesses: its premium funding arm is a lending facility for clients, it has a funds management business, acts as trustee to superannuation funds and it provides clients with a range of other financial products, such as leasing facilities, warranty services and mortgage finance. It has a particular expertise in workers' compensation and occupational health and safety issues. It also operates an insurance broking and underwriting business in the United Kingdom, where it specialises in oil, tanker and hazardous goods risks.

Latest Business Results (June 2003, Full Year)

The company benefited from an upturn in the global insurance business, with another excellent result. There was a strong organic result as well as the full benefits of a string of acquisitions over the previous three years. The broking business saw net revenues, after underwriter payments, up 39%, with pre-tax profit (before eliminations) rocketing 72%. The Australian International Insurance underwriting business continued to benefit from a hardening of the markets, particularly within certain specialist niches in which it operates, and net revenues soared 46%, with profit up 77%. The small financial services business recorded excellent 49% revenue growth, though it barely broke even for the year. Premium funding revenue and profits edged up.

Outlook

OAMPS has already said that it sees profits expanding by at least a further 10% in the 2003–04 year. It hopes to achieve further organic growth by cross-selling to its client base, which it believes will allow it to achieve returns that are above the broking industry average. In particular, it wishes to place more emphasis on its financial services arm, which it sees as offering great potential. Another area that it believes has potential is corporate insurance broking, and it is strengthening its resources in this sector. It is also working to expand its premium funding operation, which involves using underwriting fees to finance insurance premium payments by its broking clients, and is a low-risk, high-margin business. It expects increased cost efficiencies from a new IT platform for its businesses.

OMP Year to 30 June	2002	2003
Revenues ($mn)	134.7	191.5
Underwriting (%)	59	60
Broking (%)	35	35
Financial services (%)	3	3
Premium funding (%)	3	2
EBIT ($mn)	13.3	23.5
EBIT margin (%)	9.9	12.3
Operating profit before tax ($mn)	17.4	27.4
Profit after tax ($mn)	11.5	18.1
Earnings per share (¢)	20.1	25.4
Cashflow per share (¢)	25.9	32.5
Dividend (¢)	20	17
Percentage franked	100	100
Net tangible assets per share ($)	0.45	0.42
Interest cover (times)	–	–
Return on equity (%)	19.0	19.5
Debt-to-equity ratio (%)	–	–
Current ratio	1.1	1.1

OPSM Group Limited

Share price ($)	3.80	
12-month high ($)	3.93	
12-month low ($)	3.00	
Market capitalisation ($mn)	515.2	
Price-to-NTA-per-share ratio	12.6	
5-year share price return (% p.a.)	8.1	
Sector: Health Care	**Company**	**Sector**
Price-earnings ratio (times)	21.0	40.6
Dividend yield (%)	1.4	2.9

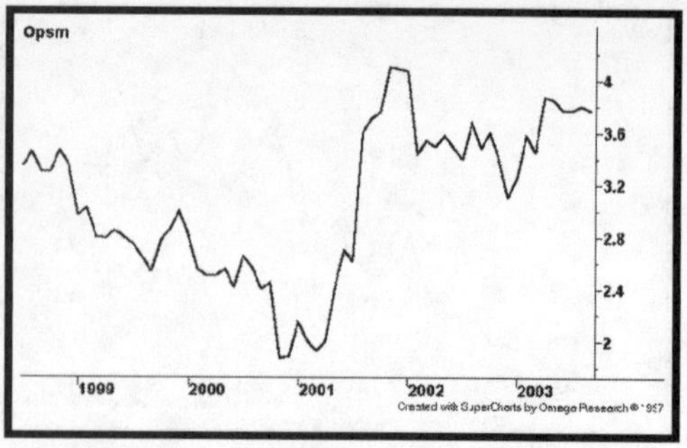

www.opsm.com.au

Sydney-based OPSM, established in 1932, is Australia's biggest manufacturer and retailer of prescription spectacles, with a third of the market. Its 471 Australian stores are divided into three groups – OPSM, Laubman & Pank and Budget Eyewear – each targeting a different market segment. The company is also the market leader in New Zealand, with 35 stores, and it has expanded into Asia where it has 76 stores in Hong Kong, 12 in Singapore and 13 in Malaysia. It has been the subject of a takeover bid by the Luxottica Group of Italy, which has become the majority shareholder.

Latest Business Results (June 2003, Full Year)

The company enjoyed strong sales growth, but the after-tax profit fell with a hit coming from the effects of the SARS virus in Asia. Domestic business was strong, with all three store groups reporting good increases in sales, although new point of sale technology and supply chain processes led to poor profits from Laubman & Pank. New management engineered a turnaround in New Zealand operations, with a 19% increase in revenues. However, the SARS outbreak caused a sharp drop in discretionary consumer spending in Hong Kong and Singapore, with a 14.5% decline in revenues and an estimated negative $4.5 million impact on pre-tax profits. The company also reported a significant item loss of $5.2 million, including the costs of responding to the Luxottica takeover bid. Group store numbers increased from 531 to 607.

Outlook

OPSM's future is tied up with the attempt by Luxottica to acquire the company. As this book was going to press, in September 2003, the Italian company held 83% of OPSM's equity – insufficient to move to full control – with several large institutional shareholders refusing to sell their stakes. Domestically, the company is working to integrate recent acquisitions. Substantial progress has been made on refocusing its supply chain management strategy. The new $12 million EyeBiz facility in Sydney was opened in August 2003, and will supply lenses for all eyewear sold in OPSM Group stores in Australia and New Zealand, with the aim of ensuring faster service to customers, a better quality product and reduced costs.

OPS Year to 30 June	2002	2003
Revenues ($mn)	415.4	482.6
EBIT ($mn)	31.6	35.3
EBIT margin (%)	7.6	7.3
Operating profit before tax ($mn)	29.3	32.8
Profit after tax ($mn)	25.2	24.3
Earnings per share (¢)	18.9	18.1
Cashflow per share (¢)	32.7	34.5
Dividend (¢)	14.5	5.5
Percentage franked	100	100
Net tangible assets per share ($)	0.55	0.30
Interest cover (times)	13.4	14.3
Return on equity (%)	21.5	19.9
Debt-to-equity ratio (%)	6.6	35.7
Current ratio	1.1	0.6

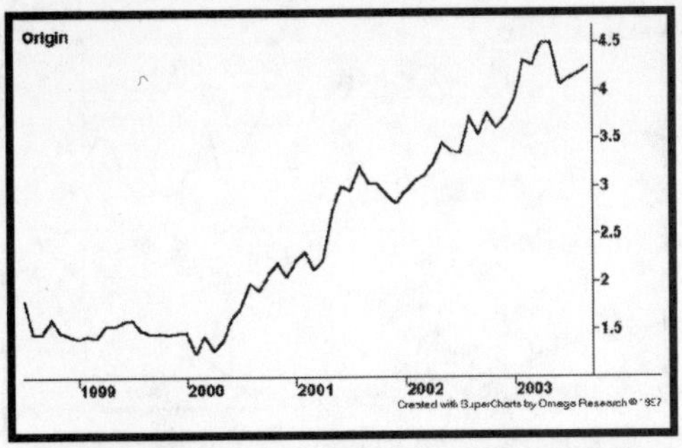

www.originenergy.com.au

Origin Energy Limited

Share price ($)	4.28	
12-month high ($)	4.54	
12-month low ($)	3.32	
Market capitalisation ($mn)	2,769.6	
Price-to-NTA-per-share ratio	2.9	
5-year share price return (% p.a.)	–	
Sector: Energy	**Company**	**Sector**
Price-earnings ratio (times)	17.2	11.0
Dividend yield (%)	2.3	2.8

Origin Energy, formerly the energy arm of the Boral Group, was demerged in 2000. Today it is one of Australia's leading energy companies, supplying natural gas, electricity and liquefied petroleum gas to more than two million business and residential customers in Australia, New Zealand and the Pacific. It operates under four core business units: exploration and production, retail, generation and networks. It owns 85% of the equity of Oil Company of Australia and 19% of the gas distributor Envestra.

Latest Business Results (June 2003, Full Year)

The mid 2002, $132 million acquisition of Victorian electricity supplier CitiPower caused a strong surge in revenues and profits. Energy retailing profits (before interest and tax) jumped 56% to $144 million, or more than half of total company earnings. By contrast, exploration and production profits were flat at $103 million, with higher oil prices, increased gas sales and three new Perth Basin oilfields all offset by the sale of Eromanga Basin oil assets in the previous year. The acquisition of the Mt Stuart Power Station in Townsville, Queensland, gave a 70% boost to generation division profits, to $26.5 million. The networks division recorded a 9% rise in profits, to $21 million, due mainly to higher fees and distributions from Envestra.

Outlook

The CitiPower acquisition means that energy retailing is now Origin's most profitable business, though short-term growth is expected to be only modest, with higher electricity purchasing costs offsetting any efficiency gains. But a significant increase in oil production from the Perth Basin and a full year's contribution from the Mt Stuart Power Station will be positive factors for the company. Origin has several major projects that should contribute to long-term growth. It is involved in the SEA Gas pipeline scheme, which will pump gas to Adelaide from Port Campbell in Victoria from early 2004. It is also part of the BassGas project, which is due to come on-stream in mid 2004, and could eventually supply 10% of Victoria's natural gas. And it is working with Oil Company of Australia on the development of coal seam gas in Queensland.

ORG Year to 30 June	2002	2003
Revenues ($mn)	2,389.2	3,326.5
EBIT ($mn)	230.7	295.3
EBIT margin (%)	9.7	8.9
Operating profit before tax ($mn)	187.9	246.6
Profit after tax ($mn)	128.7	162.0
Earnings per share (¢)	20.2	24.8
Cashflow per share (¢)	47.5	54.9
Dividend (¢)	5	10
Percentage franked	100	40
Net tangible assets per share ($)	1.48	1.48
Interest cover (times)	5.4	6.1
Return on equity (%)	8.8	9.7
Debt-to-equity ratio (%)	38.9	40.9
Current ratio	1.1	1.2

Pacific Hydro Limited

Share price ($)	3.67	
12-month high ($)	4.00	
12-month low ($)	2.69	
Market capitalisation ($mn)	476.0	
Price-to-NTA-per-share ratio	2.5	
5-year share price return (% p.a.)	38.0	
Sector: Utilities	**Company**	**Sector**
Price-earnings ratio (times)	16.7	15.2
Dividend yield (%)	1.4	4.6

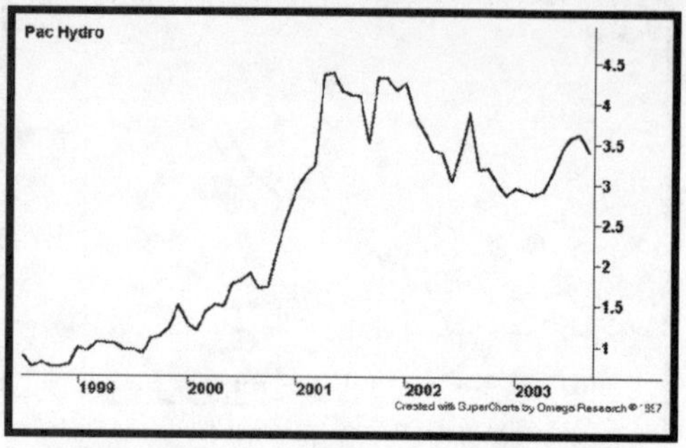

www.pacifichydro.com.au

Melbourne-based Pacific Hydro is a niche power producer dedicated to the development and operation of renewable energy generation projects. It has become a leader in hydro-electric power generation, and operates three facilities in Victoria and the Ord River project in the Kimberley region of Western Australia, which supplies power to local towns and to the operations of Argyle Diamonds. It also operates Australia's largest wind energy projects, at Challicum Hills and at Codrington, both in Victoria. It holds a 50% interest in the US$150 million Bakun River hydro project in the Philippines. American Electric Power, the largest generator of electricity in the United States, holds 19% of Pacific Hydro's equity.

Latest Business Results (June 2003, Full Year)

Pre-tax profit fell, hurt by lower hydro revenues – due to the drought – and the impact of a stronger dollar on the translation of earnings from the Philippines. But a substantially lower tax expense meant after-tax profits were up. Returns from the Philippines rose substantially, more than offsetting the sale in the previous year of the company's New Zealand power generation assets.

Outlook

Pacific Hydro's steady growth and its status as a green energy company have been strong incentives for the shares. It has a string of new projects under development or in the planning stage, and the company's generating capacity has the potential to increase three- or four-fold by 2006. The Challicum Hills wind farm – now Australia's largest – began power generation in July 2003. The $270 million Portland project, also in Victoria, has received planning approval and is in the final development stages. Due for completion in 2005, it will be one of the world's largest wind farm projects. Other wind projects are in South Australia and Western Australia. In the Philippines, the Bakun supplemental water project is expected to boost output there by 50% by 2005. The company's first two hydro stations in Fiji, being built with the Fiji Electrical Authority, are due for completion in early 2004. The company is also ready to start work on a major hydro project in Chile.

PHY Year to 30 June	2002	2003
Revenues ($mn)	63.5	68.9
EBIT ($mn)	32.1	29.9
EBIT margin (%)	50.6	43.5
Operating profit before tax ($mn)	29.9	29.4
Profit after tax ($mn)	26.8	28.4
Earnings per share (¢)	20.9	22.0
Cashflow per share (¢)	24.2	25.5
Dividend (¢)	3	5
Percentage franked	0	0
Net tangible assets per share ($)	1.34	1.49
Interest cover (times)	14.3	55.3
Return on equity (%)	16.1	14.6
Debt-to-equity ratio (%)	–	14.5
Current ratio	2.6	1.0

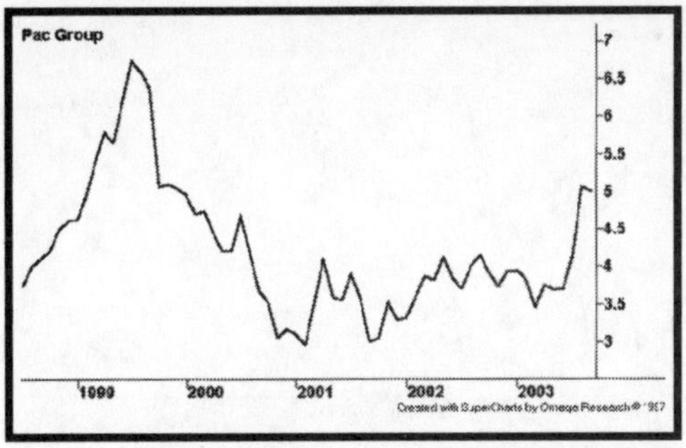

www.pacifica.com.au

Pacifica Group Limited

Share price ($)	4.80
12-month high ($)	4.84
12-month low ($)	3.30
Market capitalisation ($mn)	661.7
Price-to-NTA-per-share ratio	2.4
5-year share price return (% p.a.)	8.7

Sector: Consumer Discretion.	Company	Sector
Price-earnings ratio (times)	15.7	20.2
Dividend yield (%)	4.2	3.7

Melbourne-based Pacifica is a major manufacturer of vehicle components, selling its innovative clutch and braking systems to automobile makers around the world, and with overseas production facilities in America, Malaysia and Thailand. It is also a manufacturer of metal products for the construction industry, although it is working to divest itself of this business. In August 2003, it acquired the Italian drum brake manufacturer Automotive Products Italia.

Latest Business Results (June 2003, Half Year)

Profits rose again, thanks to a buoyant domestic auto industry and the company's ongoing cost-cutting efforts. The gains would have been higher but for the impact of the stronger dollar. Reduced revenues reflected the sale of the company's Webforge subsidiary, which made metal products for the construction industry. The company enjoyed notable success in North America, with increased sales and market share – despite a flat overall market – thanks to its exposure to the booming sports utility vehicle market and also because of increased production from its South Carolina plant. However, Asian sales and profits were down.

Outlook

Pacifica's business is geared to international vehicle demand, which remains resilient. In particular, on the basis of contracts already signed, it sees firm growth in 2004. The $60-million acquisition of Automotive Products Italia – which is a major supplier to Fiat, Ford and Nissan in Europe, and which has licences in Turkey, Japan and Brazil – is expected to boost company sales by 10%. It also helps Pacifica to diversify, to establish a solid base in Europe and to move more strongly into the small car sector. The company is negotiating the sale of Melwire and its remaining construction subsidiaries, and has expressed interest in further acquisitions in the automotive parts industry.

PBB Year to 31 December	2001	2002
Revenues ($mn)	1,133.8	1,077.3
Automotive (%)	75	87
Construction products (%)	15	13
Plastics (%)	6	0
EBIT ($mn)	83.9	92.3
EBIT margin (%)	7.4	8.6
Gross margin (%)	14.6	15.9
Operating profit before tax ($mn)	62.7	77.0
Profit after tax ($mn)	33.3	44.3
Earnings per share (¢)	22.2	30.5
Cashflow per share (¢)	66.9	71.8
Dividend (¢)	8.5	20
Percentage franked	81	82
Interest cover (times)	4.0	6.0
Return on equity (%)	10.0	14.6
Half Year to 30 June	**2002**	**2003**
Revenues ($mn)	553.1	469.0
Operating profit before tax ($mn)	39.4	46.3
Profit after tax ($mn)	21.8	24.0
Earnings per share (¢)	14.7	20.7
Dividend (¢)	9	10
Percentage franked	60	100
Net tangible assets per share ($)	2.08	1.98
Debt-to-equity ratio (%)	38.7	33.1
Current ratio	1.2	1.3

PaperlinX Limited

Share price ($)	5.09	
12-month high ($)	5.38	
12-month low ($)	4.42	
Market capitalisation ($mn)	2,089.8	
Price-to-NTA-per-share ratio	1.5	
5-year share price return (% p.a.)	–	
Sector: Materials	**Company**	**Sector**
Price-earnings ratio (times)	13.9	16.0
Dividend yield (%)	5.4	2.9

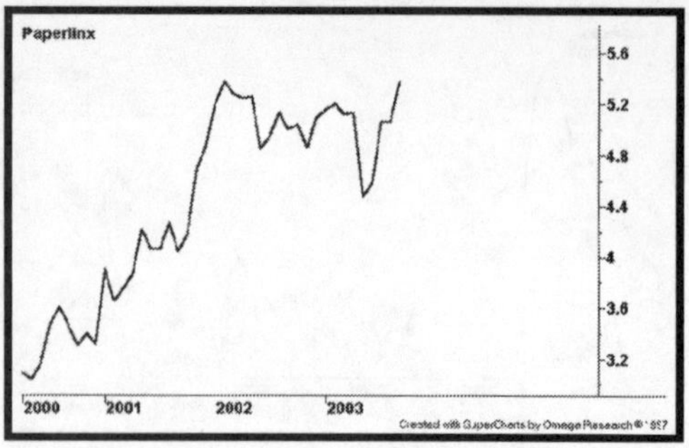

www.paperlinx.com.au

Melbourne-based PaperlinX came into being in 2000 when paper and packaging giant Amcor demerged its businesses into two separate companies. Today it is a leading Australian manufacturer of communication papers and packaging papers – Amcor being the main customer for the latter – with four plants in Victoria, NSW and Tasmania. It is also a major international paper merchant and distributor, and more than 60% of revenues derive from its overseas activities, mainly in North America and Europe.

Latest Business Results (June 2003, Full Year)

Profits were up in a generally flat paper market, thanks mainly to the contribution of PaperlinX's new British acquisition, The Paper Company. As a result, the merchanting and paper trading division saw sales up 34% and profits (before interest and tax) soar 65%. Otherwise, business was hurt by increased competition. In particular, the strong Australian dollar resulted in cheaper imported papers and reduced export earnings. Sales revenues for the communication papers division dipped 5%, with profits down 20%. Packaging papers saw revenues slightly down too, though profits rose a healthy 25%, thanks to some higher prices paid by Amcor.

Outlook

Though paper manufacturing comprises only about a quarter of PaperlinX's sales, it is responsible for more than 60% of company profits, and one problem for the company is achieving growth, given its dominance of the domestic market. Thus, it is working to expand its global paper merchanting operations, aiming to become a major participant with significant economies of scale, though recognising that this is a business where margins are thin and competition and risk can be high. It is finalising the $1.3 billion acquisition of the trading arm of the Dutch paper merchant Buhrmann, and this will make PaperlinX the world's third-largest paper merchant. However, paper demand is quite dependent on trends in the economy, and the company is finding that mediocre economic conditions in many countries are limiting sales. Domestically, it could benefit from an easing of pulp prices. It is also undertaking a major cost-reduction program.

PPX Year to 30 June	2002	2003
Revenues ($mn)	2,968.6	3,628.1
Merchanting & paper trading (%)	62	72
Communication papers (%)	23	19
Packaging papers (%)	8	7
EBIT ($mn)	215.1	233.2
EBIT margin (%)	7.2	6.4
Gross margin (%)	21.0	21.1
Operating profit before tax ($mn)	176.9	190.4
Profit after tax ($mn)	123.0	132.1
Earnings per share (¢)	37.9	36.6
Cashflow per share (¢)	61.9	59.4
Dividend (¢)	27	27.5
Percentage franked	87	60
Net tangible assets per share ($)	3.23	3.40
Interest cover (times)	5.6	5.4
Return on equity (%)	10.3	9.2
Debt-to-equity ratio (%)	27.3	8.8
Current ratio	2.0	2.8

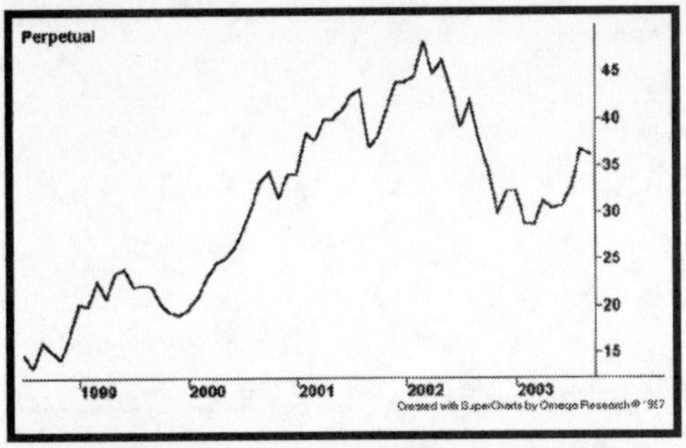

www.perpetual.com.au

Perpetual Trustees Australia Limited

Share price ($)	37.50
12-month high ($)	43.00
12-month low ($)	25.10
Market capitalisation ($mn)	1,413.8
Price-to-NTA-per-share ratio	6.1
5-year share price return (% p.a.)	23.1

Sector: Financials	Company	Sector
Price-earnings ratio (times)	20.8	16.2
Dividend yield (%)	2.9	4.5

Sydney-based Perpetual was established in 1885 and is now a dynamic financial services company. It is involved in trustee operations, funds management, estate administration, charitable planning, property management, financial planning and tax consulting. With the Australian Stock Exchange it operates the share registry business ASX Perpetual Registrars.

Latest Business Results (June 2003, Full Year)

In a difficult operating environment, Perpetual posted an excellent result. This came despite a fall in funds under management from $19.4 billion to $17.4 billion, following the departure of the company's star fund manager Peter Morgan. Institutional funds dropped from $6 billion to $2.2 billion. However, retail funds – much more profitable than institutional – grew from $13.4 billion to $15.2 billion. Despite weak equity markets, Personal Financial Services achieved revenues of $65.6 million, comparable to the previous year, and it added some $760 million in gross new fund inflows. Corporate Trust had another strong year, with revenues increasing from $36.6 million to $41.9 million. Securitisation funds under administration grew 36% to $71.2 billion. However, ASX Perpetual Registrars was adversely affected by subdued trading conditions, despite a 12% increase in revenues. Perpetual's share of the joint venture's net loss was $0.6 million.

Outlook

Perpetual's success over several years in transforming itself from a stodgy provider of traditional trustee services into a diversified financial services company has generated powerful profits and a soaring share price. But its latest growth came at the expense of a sharp cut in staff numbers during the year, and the company has said that a competitive business environment could force further redundancies. It is also looking for ways to improve its underperforming international funds, and it hopes to bring more partners into its ASX Perpetual Registrars venture. Its flagship Industrial Share Fund continues its strong performance, having achieved a positive return each year for 21 consecutive years. The company has built up substantial cash reserves, and has the financial capacity to pursue organic growth and also to make acquisitions, as a springboard for continued future expansion.

PPT Year to 30 June	2002	2003
Revenues ($mn)	244.1	265.0
EBIT ($mn)	82.1	93.4
EBIT margin (%)	33.6	35.2
Operating profit before tax ($mn)	83.7	96.1
Profit after tax ($mn)	58.7	68.2
Earnings per share (¢)	155.3	180.6
Cashflow per share (¢)	193.7	217.8
Dividend (¢)	110	110
Percentage franked	100	100
Net tangible assets per share ($)	5.21	6.13
Interest cover (times)	–	–
Return on equity (%)	23.9	25.1
Debt-to-equity ratio (%)	–	–
Current ratio	1.5	2.0

Peter Lehmann Wines Limited

Share price ($)	3.43	
12-month high ($)	4.11	
12-month low ($)	2.81	
Market capitalisation ($mn)	128.0	
Price-to-NTA-per-share ratio	2.6	
5-year share price return (% p.a.)	18.1	
Sector: Consumer Staples	**Company**	**Sector**
Price-earnings ratio (times)	23.6	17.9
Dividend yield (%)	2.6	3.6

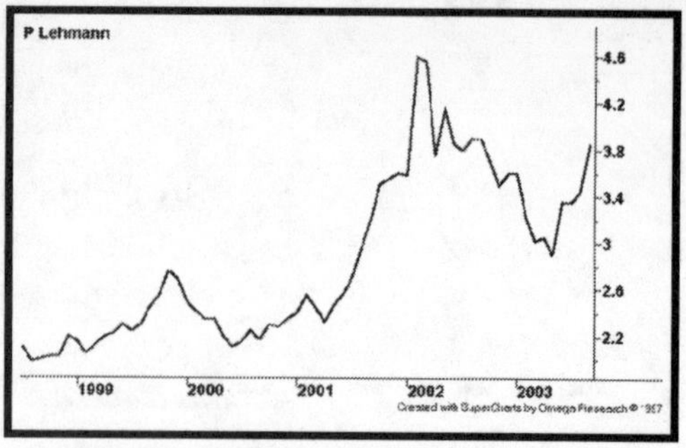

www.peterlehmannwines.com.au

Peter Lehmann Wines, based in South Australia's Barossa Valley region and founded in 1979, is one of Australia's medium-sized, quality winemakers. Wines are sold under the Peter Lehmann and Clancy's labels. It also crushes grapes and makes wines for other wineries. It operates a distribution company in Europe, marketing its own wines and those of several other wineries. The Hess Group, a family-owned Swiss group of enterprises with wine businesses in several countries, has made a takeover bid for the company.

Latest Business Results (June 2003, Full Year)

The company's profit growth came grinding to a halt. Sales revenues were up, but discounting by major rivals and an oversupply of wine in some markets led to a sharp decline in earnings, with all regions down. Domestic sales edged up, but profits fell, as the competitive market knocked margins. Overseas sales were about half the total, with Britain again by far the main destination. However, though British volumes rose 10%, sales revenues fell 4%, reflecting the impact of competition. Sales to continental Europe soared 63% on a volume basis, with revenues up 46%. Distribution problems led to a drop in North American sales and profits.

Outlook

The company's founder, Peter Lehmann, has announced his support of the takeover bid by the Hess Group, and has sold them a third of his 16% holding. He has said he wishes to stop his company being acquired by liquor conglomerate Allied Domecq, which has lifted its own holding to about 15%, and is viewed as stalking the winemaker. The company believes markets are improving, following a period of fierce discounting, and it expects good sales and profit growth in the June 2004 year. In particular, it views continental Europe as offering excellent opportunities for continued expansion. It hopes a new distribution agreement with the Hess Group will help it overcome problems with its US distribution. However, overseas markets remain highly competitive, with the dollar's strength another negative. It has completed a major investment program, giving it the capacity to process 20,000 tonnes of premium fruit. In 2003, its total crush was 14,302 tonnes.

PLW Year to 30 June	2002	2003
Revenues ($mn)	44.8	46.1
EBIT ($mn)	10.6	9.0
EBIT margin (%)	23.6	19.6
Gross margin (%)	41.2	41.7
Operating profit before tax ($mn)	9.9	7.7
Profit after tax ($mn)	6.9	5.4
Earnings per share (¢)	19.0	14.5
Cashflow per share (¢)	22.6	18.5
Dividend (¢)	11	9
Percentage franked	100	100
Net tangible assets per share ($)	1.19	1.30
Interest cover (times)	14.9	6.7
Return on equity (%)	17.5	11.7
Debt-to-equity ratio (%)	43.9	62.3
Current ratio	2.2	2.9

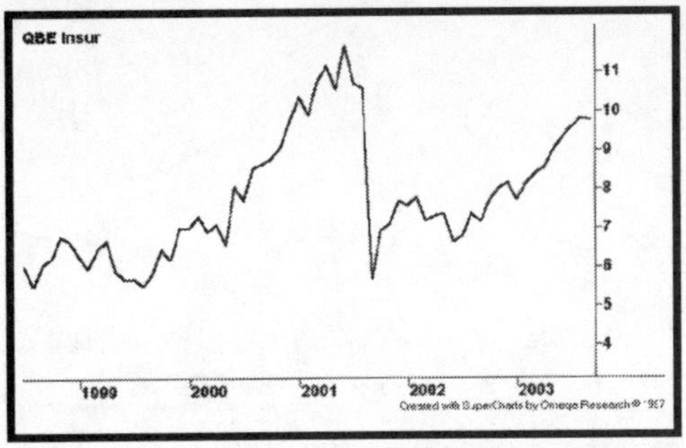

www.qbe.com.au

QBE Insurance Group Limited

Share price ($)	9.88
12-month high ($)	10.05
12-month low ($)	6.78
Market capitalisation ($mn)	6,230.9
Price-to-NTA-per-share ratio	2.4
5-year share price return (% p.a.)	14.6

Sector: Financials	**Company**	**Sector**
Price-earnings ratio (times)	21.4	16.2
Dividend yield (%)	3.5	4.5

QBE – founded as North Queensland Insurance Company in 1886 – is one of Australia's best-regarded insurance companies, specialising in general insurance and reinsurance. It has expanded globally, with more than 200 offices in 43 countries, and over two-thirds of its business comes from abroad, particularly from Europe.

Latest Business Results (June 2003, Half Year)

Profits more than doubled in a result that sent the share price soaring – though this was in part due to net realised and unrealised after-tax gains on equities of $7 million, compared to losses of $60 million for the June 2002 period. But insurance profit was $259 million, compared with $160 million a year before. Despite the stronger Australian dollar, gross written premium was up 11%, to $4.8 billion. Growth was assisted by strong premium rate increases across most classes of business, and was consistent throughout most of the company's main regions of operations, though it was hurt by the stronger dollar. The ratio of claims to premiums fell from 99% to 96%. Net investment income for the half year was $189 million compared with $97 million for the June 2002 period, with improved equity markets offsetting lower interest yields and the effect of translating overseas income to the stronger Australian dollar.

Outlook

In the wake of the September 11 tragedy, the global insurance industry has been undergoing a period of intense rationalisation, with many companies finding the environment too tough for them to survive. QBE has been using this period to toughen up. It has divested itself of large amounts of low-margin business, in order to concentrate on its strengths. In particular, it has used this period to raise premiums, and this has been a key factor in its profit performance. The company believes it will achieve at least $8.5 billion of gross written premium for 2003, as its businesses benefit from favourable insurance market conditions and from significantly higher rates of customer retention. It plans more premium rate increases, and forecasts a further 10% growth in net earned premium for 2004, depending on currency movements. It is reducing its already-low exposure to equities, and is preparing for an interest-rate rise.

QBE Year to 31 December	**2001**	**2002**
Net earned premium ($mn)	4,634.0	5,642.0
Operating profit before tax ($mn)	262.0	311.0
Profit after tax ($mn)	227.0	277.0
Earnings per share (¢)	48.1	46.2
Dividend (¢)	30	35
Percentage franked	21	12
Return on equity (%)	10.5	9.9
Half Year to 30 June	**2002**	**2003**
Net earned premium ($mn)	2,679.0	3,083.0
Operating profit before tax ($mn)	124.0	313.0
Profit after tax ($mn)	115.0	241.0
Earnings per share (¢)	17.5	37.3
Dividend (¢)	16.5	20
Percentage franked	12	15
Net tangible assets per share ($)	3.72	4.09
Debt-to-equity ratio (%)	13.2	22.9
Current ratio	1.4	1.4

Rebel Sport Limited

Share price ($)	2.45	
12-month high ($)	2.50	
12-month low ($)	1.86	
Market capitalisation ($mn)	185.5	
Price-to-NTA-per-share ratio	2.8	
5-year share price return (% p.a.)	28.2	
Sector: Consumer Discretion.	**Company**	**Sector**
Price-earnings ratio (times)	11.3	20.2
Dividend yield (%)	2.4	3.7

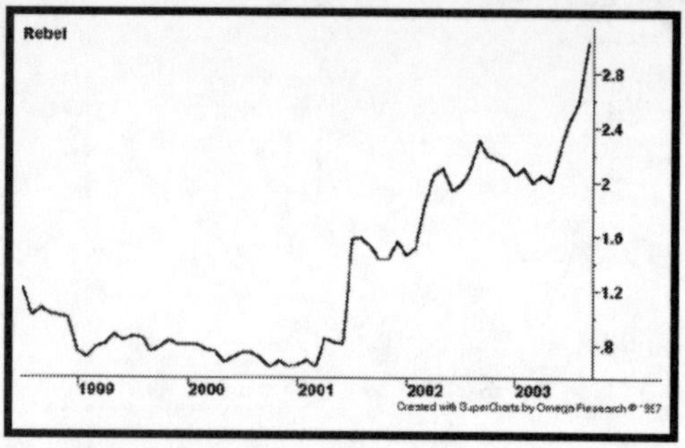

www.rebelsport.com.au

Rebel Sport, one of Australia's leading sporting goods retailers, began trading as a single store in Sydney's west in 1985. It has grown into a large chain of retail outlets across Australia and New Zealand. The New Zealand stores are operated as part of a master franchise agreement with the Briscoes retail housewares group. It has also bought the small Glue chain of 'athleisure' stores, which sell fashionable sporting and leisure wear. Following a takeover bid in 2001, Harvey Norman Holdings now owns a majority of Rebel Sport's equity.

Latest Business Results (June 2003, Full Year)

In a challenging year, Rebel reported a superb result, with profits more than doubling, thanks to a series of restructuring initiatives that have been put in place since the Harvey Norman takeover. Rebel Sport has changed its accounting time, and the June 2002 results are for a 15-month period. On a normalised 12-month basis, sales revenues were up 13.6%. Sales revenues from like-for-like stores increased by 7.3%. The company opened six new Rebel Sport stores, to bring the total to 50. It also opened one new Glue store, bringing that total to four.

Outlook

Rebel Sport is involved in a major overhaul of its operations that has led to an impressive restructuring of its finances with profits surging and its bank borrowings falling to minimal levels. It has divested power to its store managers, including profit-sharing schemes, with greatly enhanced shop efficiency, and it has changed some of its suppliers. It is also working to revitalise its product offerings to better meet changing customer needs. It is trialling a new apparel, footwear and accessory concept, themed around the mountain, hiking and outdoor brands. It is also introducing its own 'home brand' items, as well as some top-end exclusive products. Rebel now believes it has in place a strong platform for future growth, and it anticipates opening a further 15 to 20 stores over the next three years. It sees opportunities arising from the Rugby World Cup and the 2004 Olympic Games. After a period of challenge, the Glue retail business is starting to realise its potential.

REB Year to 28 June*	2002	2003
Revenues ($mn)	296.8	276.9
EBIT ($mn)	13.1	23.5
EBIT margin (%)	4.4	8.5
Gross margin (%)	36.2	35.9
Operating profit before tax ($mn)	10.6	23.2
Profit after tax ($mn)	8.1	16.3
Earnings per share (¢)	9.9**	21.8
Cashflow per share (¢)	24.7**	35.1
Dividend (¢)	1	6
Percentage franked	100	100
Net tangible assets per share ($)	0.68	0.88
Interest cover (times)	5.4	77.4
Return on equity (%)	16.9**	27.9
Debt-to-equity ratio (%)	16.4	–
Current ratio	1.7	1.9

** 15 months to 30 June 2002.*
*** Annualised.*

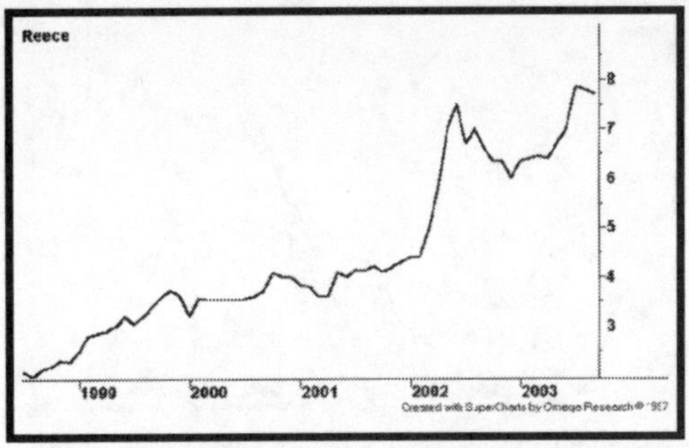

www.reece.com.au

REECE AUSTRALIA LIMITED

Share price ($)	8.38
12-month high ($)	8.85
12-month low ($)	5.95
Market capitalisation ($mn)	835.6
Price-to-NTA-per-share ratio	3.5
5-year share price return (% p.a.)	34.9

Sector: Industrials	Company	Sector
Price-earnings ratio (times)	17.9	12.1
Dividend yield (%)	2.5	3.9

Melbourne-based hardware wholesaler Reece Australia traces its origins back to 1919, when Harold Reece started selling plumbing supplies from the back of a truck. It has gradually expanded from its Victorian roots, with notable growth coming from the acquisition of the Plumbing World and Bridglands chains. Today it is one of the country's leading suppliers of plumbing products, with more than 190 stores and showrooms nationwide. It also operates a National Training Centre in Melbourne, for plumbers wishing to enhance their technical and business skills.

LATEST BUSINESS RESULTS (JUNE 2003, FULL YEAR)

The home construction boom and growing strength in the home renovations sector delivered a further boost to Reece's profits. The company also benefited from continuing internally generated efficiencies and from the opening of 18 new shops.

OUTLOOK

Reece is a conservatively managed company that occupies a central position in the hardware supply business. It sells mainly to plumbers and builders, though it does have some retail business as well. Heavily geared to the housing cycle, it will be affected by any downturn, especially as its products are used quite early in the home construction phase. The company itself has said that it expects a domestic slowdown in new housing and unit development during the 2003–04 year. It is also affected by the moves of competitors like Bunnings and Danks to boost their plumbing businesses, and its margins edged down in the June 2003 year. It is noteworthy that on a half-yearly basis, the company's profits have not grown since the June 2002 half. However, with no debt and nearly $45 million in cash reserves, it is looking to expand both by acquisition and through opening new shops. As it continues to build up cash, it may also opt for some kind of capital return to shareholders. It has launched a series of specialised stores and services to meet evolving needs, including Reece Irrigation for the landscape and agricultural supply industries, Reece Projects for larger residential developments, Reece Gas for customers working with domestic and commercial gas appliances and evaporative cooling systems, and Reecedesign for architects and interior designers.

REH Year to 30 June	2002	2003
Revenues ($mn)	636.7	740.2
EBIT ($mn)	60.1	66.6
EBIT margin (%)	9.4	9.0
Gross margin (%)	25.2	25.9
Operating profit before tax ($mn)	61.5	67.7
Profit after tax ($mn)	42.5	46.7
Earnings per share (¢)	42.6	46.9
Cashflow per share (¢)	51.2	56.2
Dividend (¢)	17	21
Percentage franked	100	100
Net tangible assets per share ($)	2.03	2.42
Interest cover (times)	–	–
Return on equity (%)	22.4	21.0
Debt-to-equity ratio (%)	–	–
Current ratio	1.8	2.0

Ridley Corporation Limited

Share price ($)	1.67	
12-month high ($)	1.67	
12-month low ($)	1.26	
Market capitalisation ($mn)	442.8	
Price-to-NTA-per-share ratio	1.7	
5-year share price return (% p.a.)	10.5	
Sector: Consumer Staples	**Company**	**Sector**
Price-earnings ratio (times)	11.9	17.9
Dividend yield (%)	3.4	3.6

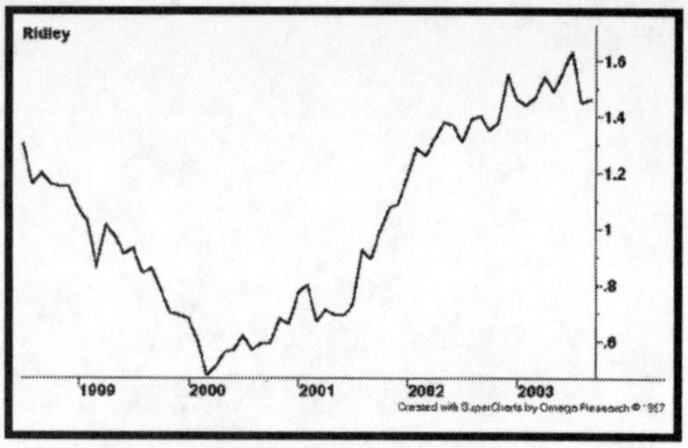

www.ridley.com.au

Sydney-based Ridley is a global producer of animal feed and salt, operating through three business divisions: Ridley Agriproducts is Australia's largest stockfeed producer, with several major brands and 23 manufacturing sites across the country; Cheetham Salt is the largest producer of domestic and refined salt in Australia and New Zealand; and Ridley Inc. is the sixth-largest producer of animal feed products in North America, serving customers in the US, Western Canada and Ontario. Ridley Inc's operations include 26 mills in the US and 15 in Canada.

Latest Business Results (June 2003, Full Year)

Continued improvements in the Australian agriproducts and salt divisions – reflecting growing demand and the company's major restructuring efforts of recent years – were offset by weaker earnings in Ridley Inc., which took a $2 million after-tax hit from the stronger dollar. The company was also hurt by difficult market conditions in the second half, including some lower producer prices, and drought conditions in some markets. These conditions not only reduced the demand for feed but resulted in the decision by Ridley to increase provisions for doubtful debts as some customers' financial positions deteriorated. The Cotswold Swine Genetics division recorded a $9.7 million pre-tax loss – similar to its loss of the previous year – and the company treated as a significant item an after-tax $5.9 million writedown of the carrying value of this business.

Outlook

The company sees the softer market conditions that prevailed throughout the second half of the June 2003 year in the animal nutrition businesses as continuing until at least the end of the calendar year, with particular weakness in the North American swine sector. The strength of the dollar will also hurt earnings. However, Ridley could benefit from a recovering domestic rural environment, as well as from its financial restructuring, which continues to deliver cost efficiencies. Its Cheetham Salt business delivers very high margins, and continues to grow domestically, and the company is experiencing strong demand from Japan. In July 2003, Ridley announced that, after heavy losses, it was negotiating the sale of its Cotswold Swine Genetics business.

RIC Year to 30 June	2002	2003
Revenues ($mn)	1,408.3	1,410.9
US feeds (%)	41	39
Agriproducts (%)	34	39
Canada feeds (%)	16	15
Salt (%)	5	5
EBIT ($mn)	77.1	71.3
EBIT margin (%)	5.5	5.1
Gross margin (%)	15.2	15.1
Operating profit before tax ($mn)	59.3	58.3
Profit after tax ($mn)	32.2	37.2
Earnings per share (¢)	13.1	14.0
Cashflow per share (¢)	25.6	24.9
Dividend (¢)	4.5	5.75
Percentage franked	100	100
Net tangible assets per share ($)	0.90	0.98
Interest cover (times)	4.3	5.5
Return on equity (%)	11.1	12.0
Debt-to-equity ratio (%)	54.9	41.2
Current ratio	1.2	1.7

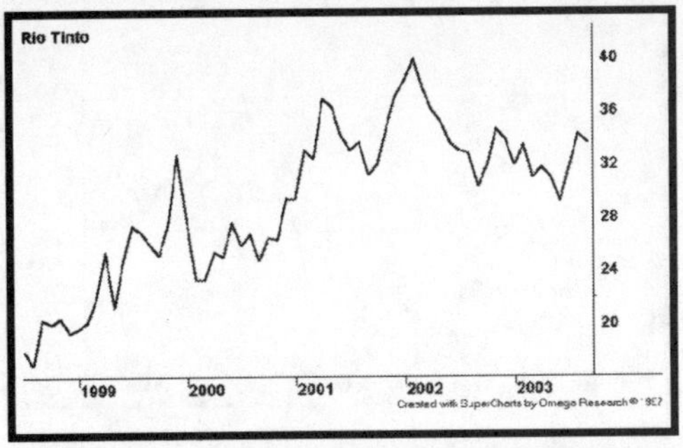

www.riotinto.com

Rio Tinto Limited

Share price ($)	33.12	
12-month high ($)	35.45	
12-month low ($)	27.99	
Market capitalisation ($mn)	16,458.3	
Price-to-NTA-per-share ratio	4.0	
5-year share price return (% p.a.)	14.5	
Sector: Materials	**Company**	**Sector**
Price-earnings ratio (times)	16.2	16.0
Dividend yield (%)	3.2	2.9

British-based Rio Tinto, one of the world's largest mining companies, retains its ASX presence in a dual-listing structure, and continues to pay franked dividends to Australian shareholders. Australian subsidiaries include Coal & Allied Industries, and it has a big stake in Papua New Guinea's Lihir Gold. Among its major products, it mines copper, gold, industrial minerals, iron ore, diamonds and coal and is a large aluminium producer.

Latest Business Results (June 2003, Half Year)

The strong Australian dollar forced Rio Tinto's profits down again, in a result that was worse than most forecasts. The company's energy businesses were hit especially hard, with profits falling in half – due especially to Chinese and Indonesian competition for coal sales – while aluminium and industrial minerals earnings also dropped sharply. But a 44% jump in Chinese demand pushed iron ore profits higher, with copper and diamonds also buoyant. According to the company, higher world prices lifted company profits by US$87 million, but this was more than offset by currency movements, which slashed profits by US$152 million.

Outlook

Rio Tinto is heavily geared to commodities prices and to economic conditions in the industrialised countries and in China. It expects trends in China to have a growing impact on global prices. In particular, it sees demand and prices rising strongly for products that China imports, notably iron ore, copper and alumina. On the other hand, it is being hurt by extreme price weakness in products – especially coal – for which China is a big exporter. In response to Chinese demand, Rio Tinto is advancing by two years its plans to boost annual output at the West Angelas iron ore mine in Western Australia to 20 million tonnes, and it is conducting a feasibility study on a 50% boost to iron ore production at Hammersley. A new 26-year alumina supply agreement underpins the first stage of subsidiary Comalco's new alumina refinery, which is scheduled to begin shipments in 2005.

RIO Year to 31 December	2001	2002
Revenues ($mn)	20,187.0	19,945.0
EBIT ($mn)	5,712.0	4,727.0
EBIT margin (%)	28,295.4	23.7
Operating profit before tax ($mn)	5,217.0	4,430.0
Profit after tax ($mn)	3,213.0	2,818.0
Earnings per share (¢)	233.3	204.6
Cashflow per share (¢)	363.8	332.2
Dividend (¢)	115.27	105.93
Percentage franked	100	100
Interest cover (times)	11.5	15.9
Return on equity (%)	25.3	23.5
Half Year to 30 June	**2002**	**2003**
Revenues ($mn)	9,523.0	9,054.0
Operating profit before tax ($mn)	2,105.0	1,569.0
Profit after tax ($mn)	1,317.0	1,044.0
Earnings per share (¢)	95.7	75.8
Dividend (¢)	54.06	45.02
Percentage franked	100	100
Net tangible assets per share ($)	8.72	8.31
Debt-to-equity ratio (%)	76.2	66.1
Current ratio	0.9	1.0

The Rock Building Society Limited

Share price ($)	3.40	
12-month high ($)	3.58	
12-month low ($)	2.85	
Market capitalisation ($mn)	52.8	
Price-to-NTA-per-share ratio	2.3	
5-year share price return (% p.a.)	14.7	
Sector: Financials	**Company**	**Sector**
Price-earnings ratio (times)	13.7	16.2
Dividend yield (%)	5.4	4.5

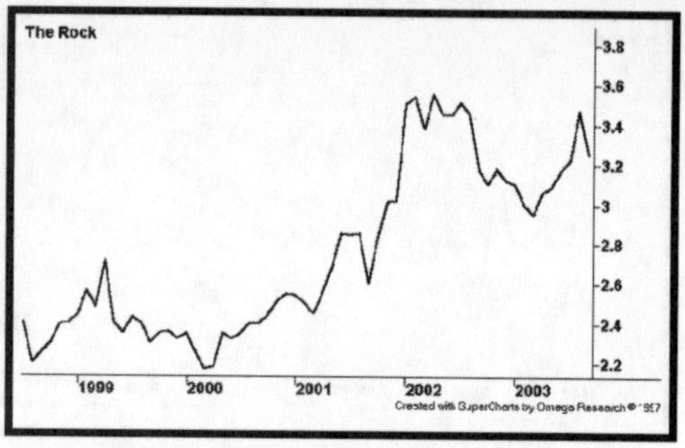

www.therock.com.au

The Rock Building Society was established in 1967 and is based in Rockhampton. Its main role has been to take retail deposits and provide housing finance for Queensland residents, and it is the leading home lender in central Queensland. It also has a strong presence in the south of the state and a growing business in NSW and Victoria.

Latest Business Results (June 2003, Full Year)

Despite its high gearing to the ongoing housing boom, the Rock Building Society reported a decline in profits, as a result of its efforts to diversify away from its dependence on home mortgages. In particular, it has been working to move into insurance broking and financial planning, and to reinforce its presence interstate, and the result was a sharp increase in costs, with the cost-to-income ratio rising above 70%, one of the highest of all the listed financial institutions. There were new loan approvals of $325 million, with the loan portfolio growing by 13% to $876 million. Retail deposits were up 18%, with a significant impact from mortgage offset accounts and the launch of a cash management account product. Term deposit funds grew as investors sought a safe haven from volatile sharemarkets. New insurance business rose 42%.

Outlook

The Rock sees much future growth potential from its major thrust into insurance broking and financial planning, despite heavy initial costs, and it has established new branch operations in Cairns and Melbourne for this purpose. In particular, it aims to attract new customers through offering higher levels of service than rival institutions. It eventually intends to establish boutique retail financial outlets, including online facilities, in many other regions, offering a full range of services. It is also strengthening its business banking operations, including the launch of a personalised business banking service in Rockhampton. With third-party mortgage originators the principle source of new home loan business, the company is being forced to devote additional resources to client retention, in order to limit 'churning', as brokers increasingly encourage borrowers to refinance their loans.

ROK Year to 30 June	2002	2003
Operating income ($mn)	18.3	20.2
Net interest income ($mn)	8.1	7.4
Operating expenses ($mn)	12.3	14.7
Operating profit before tax ($mn)	6.0	5.6
Profit after tax ($mn)	4.2	3.9
Earnings per share (¢)	30.4	24.9
Dividend (¢)	18	18.5
Percentage franked	100	100
Non-interest income to total income (%)	55.8	63.6
Net tangible assets per share ($)	1.76	1.51
Cost-to-income ratio (%)	67.0	72.7
Return on equity (%)	16.7	16.2
Return on assets (%)	1.2	1.0

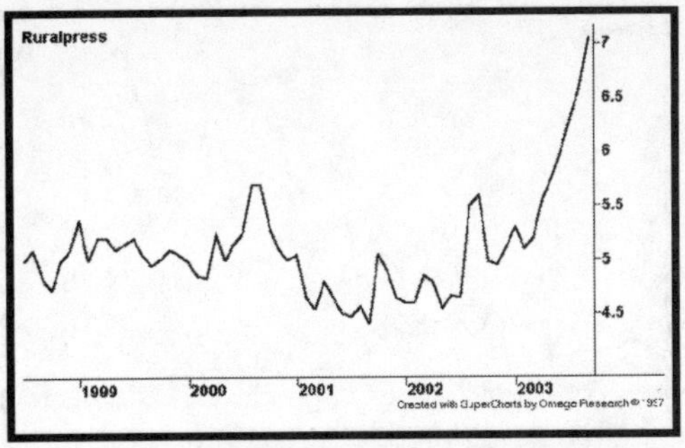

www.ruralpress.com.au

Rural Press Limited

Share price ($)	6.20	
12-month high ($)	6.34	
12-month low ($)	4.30	
Market capitalisation ($mn)	740.0	
Price-to-NTA-per-share ratio	125.9	
5-year share price return (% p.a.)	12.9	
Sector: Consumer Discretion.	**Company**	**Sector**
Price-earnings ratio (times)	10.5	20.2
Dividend yield (%)	3.8	3.7

NSW-based Rural Press was established in 1911, and is today one of the world's leading agricultural publishers, with specialist newspapers and magazines in Australia, America and New Zealand. It also manages a string of regional newspapers – including *The Canberra Times* – throughout Australia. In addition, it operates printing businesses in all Australian states, and it owns Star Broadcasting Network, which operates six radio stations in South Australia and Queensland. The Fairfax family own more than 50% of the equity.

Latest Business Results (June 2003, Full Year)

Prolonged drought conditions could not stop Rural Press from achieving strong gains in sales revenues and profits. The company's booming domestic publishing and printing businesses saw revenues up 11% and profit (before interest and tax) soaring 24%. Agricultural publications actually saw revenues down 5%, but this was more than offset by the strength of most regional publications. Advertising levels in the real estate and motor vehicle categories were particularly strong. New publications acquired in Bendigo and Horsham in July 2002 provided positive contributions. Revenues and profits for the US magazine publishing business fell due to a combination of sluggish market conditions, the discontinuation of some low-margin custom publishing activities and the strong dollar. The radio business remained in the red.

Outlook

Rural Press has been working to diversify its earnings base, and domestic agricultural publishing is now only about 15% of total earnings. The lifting of the drought looks set to revive this side of its business. The company continues to look for further publishing acquisitions. The printing business is seeing growing demand for four-colour reproduction, while continued improvements in technology allow for further gains in operating margins. A new Ballarat print site, launched in August 2003, will enhance this division's business. US publishing operates in a highly competitive environment, and the company is hoping for a recovery in the US economy to stimulate activities. Rural Press has moved to take 100% ownership of its radio business – previously it held just half the equity – and it believes this will help it effect a turnaround in profits. The company is also interested in further radio station acquisitions.

RUP Year to 30 June	2002	2003
Revenues ($mn)	435.9	463.8
EBIT ($mn)	90.7	109.0
EBIT margin (%)	20.8	23.5
Operating profit before tax ($mn)	82.2	101.7
Profit after tax ($mn)	53.7	68.4
Earnings per share (¢)	46.9	58.9
Cashflow per share (¢)	60.6	71.7
Dividend (¢)	15.4	23.6
Percentage franked	100	100
Net tangible assets per share ($)	0.01	0.05
Interest cover (times)	10.7	14.8
Return on equity (%)	10.7	11.3
Debt-to-equity ratio (%)	18.4	19.5
Current ratio	1.2	1.3

St George Bank Limited

Share price ($)	21.28	
12-month high ($)	21.97	
12-month low ($)	16.60	
Market capitalisation ($mn)	10,758.8	
Price-to-NTA-per-share ratio	4.2	
5-year share price return (% p.a.)	19.8	
Sector: Financials	**Company**	**Sector**
Price-earnings ratio (times)	18.6	16.2
Dividend yield (%)	3.8	4.5

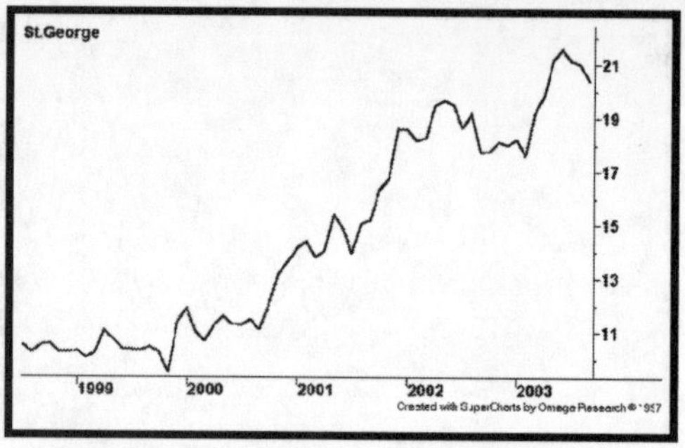

www.stgeorge.com.au

Sydney-based St George has grown from a series of mergers and acquisitions to become Australia's fifth-largest retail bank. It has its business centred in South Australia (where it is number one, thanks to its acquisition of BankSA) and in NSW. It also owns the master trust business Sealcorp, and it is advancing into New Zealand.

Latest Business Results (March 2003, Half Year)

Profits rose strongly in another excellent result. Net interest income was up 10% and non-interest income 9%, while operating expenses rose only 2%. Outstanding home loans grew 10% to $38.5 billion, thanks in particular to increased business sourced through the third-party mortgage broker market. Retail deposits reached nearly $32 billion, an increase of 16%. Managed fund assets of $17.7 billion were marginally down on the figure of a year before.

Outlook

Restrictions on acquiring St George ended in July 2002, and the shares have been caught up in speculation of a takeover bid by one of the big four banks. But so far this has not eventuated. With a high proportion of home loans in its business, St George has been enjoying high profit growth and it has achieved success in driving down costs. Its return on equity is high and its cost-to-income ratio is among the lowest of all the banks. Through the Even Better Bank program, annual cost savings of $28 million were achieved during the March 2003 half year, with a 2003 full year target of $60 million, and $80 million in 2004. It is concerned about its relatively low cross-sell ratio, and is working to introduce new products for its retail customer base. St George began a banking alliance with Foodstuffs, New Zealand's largest supermarket retailer, in 2003, and is looking for opportunities to expand further in Victoria and Queensland. St George Bank believes it can achieve double-digit profit growth in 2004 and 2005.

SGB Year to 30 September	2001	2002
Operating income ($mn)	1,925.0	2,185.0
Net interest income ($mn)	1,235.0	1,333.0
Operating expenses ($mn)	1,085.0	1,247.0
Operating profit before tax ($mn)	711.0	834.0
Profit after tax ($mn)	445.0	563.0
Earnings per share (¢)	95.2	114.2
Dividend (¢)	65	80
Percentage franked	100	100
Non-interest income to total income (%)	35.8	39.0
Cost-to-income ratio (%)	56.4	57.1
Return on equity (%)	13.5	16.6
Return on assets (%)	0.9	1.1
Half Year to 31 March	**2002**	**2003**
Operating income ($mn)	1,059.0	1,159.0
Operating profit before tax ($mn)	410.0	484.0
Profit after tax ($mn)	274.0	325.0
Earnings per share (¢)	55.9	59.5
Dividend (¢)	38	45
Percentage franked	100	100
Net tangible assets per share ($)	3.99	5.03

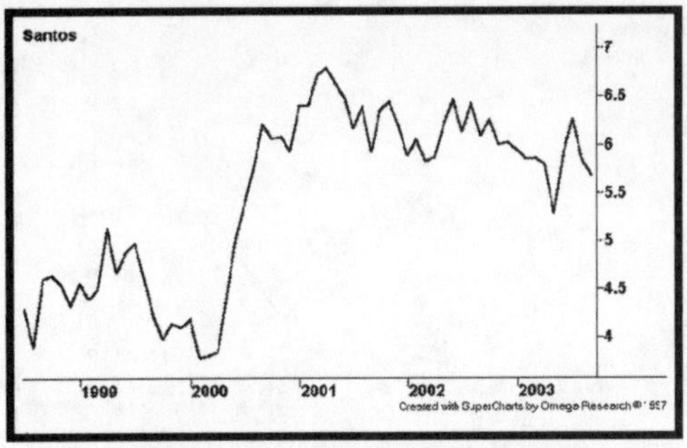

www.santos.com.au

Santos Limited

Share price ($)	6.07
12-month high ($)	6.51
12-month low ($)	5.18
Market capitalisation ($mn)	3,529.1
Price-to-NTA-per-share ratio	1.2
5-year share price return (% p.a.)	10.2

Sector: Energy	Company	Sector
Price-earnings ratio (times)	10.9	11.0
Dividend yield (%)	4.9	2.8

Adelaide-based Santos, established in 1954, is one of Australia's leading independent producers of oil and gas. Most of its output is from the Cooper/Eromanga Basins in central Australia, though it has interests in other parts of Australia, as well as in the US, Indonesia and Papua New Guinea. It is Australia's largest gas producer, supplying natural gas to all mainland states and territories. It is a substantial shareholder in Magellan Petroleum.

Latest Business Results (June 2003, Half Year)

Profits only edged up, despite a buoyant global energy market. With $34 million of exploration writedowns factored in, the after-tax profit actually fell nearly 17%. Production dipped 3%, and production costs were down 4% to $131 million. Sales volumes decreased by 0.8 million barrels of oil equivalent (boe) to 26.5 million boe. The company's cost of sales rose by $28 million to $445 million through higher Petroleum Resources Rent Tax and higher depletion. However, higher average oil and gas prices boosted revenues.

Outlook

Santos is partially captive to fluctuating energy prices. It has said that each US$1 per barrel change in the oil price would affect its second-half after-tax profit by around A$6 million, while a US$1 per thousand cubic feet change in the US gas price would have a similar impact. It has already announced that it anticipates 2003 production of 54 to 55 million boe, compared to 57 million in 2002. However, it expects good results during 2004 and 2005 from its large-scale exploration program and two new projects, Bayu-Undan in the Timor Sea (Santos's share 10.6%) and Mutineer Exeter in Western Australia (33.4%). The last project in particular, coming on-stream in mid 2005, is expected to give a big lift to Santos. The company has declared its intention to undertake more high-risk/high-reward exploration, and is particularly active in the Otway and Sorell Basins between Victoria and Tasmania.

STO Year to 31 December	2001	2002
Revenues ($mn)	1,459.7	1,478.4
EBIT ($mn)	681.0	535.5
EBIT margin (%)	46.7	36.2
Gross margin (%)	73.7	72.0
Operating profit before tax ($mn)	627.6	493.3
Profit after tax ($mn)	445.9	322.1
Earnings per share (¢)	72.9	55.5
Cashflow per share (¢)	141.7	136.2
Dividend (¢)	30	30
Percentage franked	100	100
Interest cover (times)	12.8	12.7
Return on equity (%)	17.7	11.5
Half Year to 30 June	**2002**	**2003**
Revenues ($mn)	673.1	716.0
Operating profit before tax ($mn)	243.2	252.0
Profit after tax ($mn)	166.3	170.0
Earnings per share (¢)	24.8	22.3
Dividend (¢)	15	15
Percentage franked	100	100
Net tangible assets per share ($)	4.77	5.10
Debt-to-equity ratio (%)	45.0	33.9
Current ratio	0.7	1.1

SDI Limited

Share price ($)	7.00
12-month high ($)	7.30
12-month low ($)	3.35
Market capitalisation ($mn)	163.3
Price-to-NTA-per-share ratio	10.2
5-year share price return (% p.a.)	102.0

Sector: Health Care	Company	Sector
Price-earnings ratio (times)	30.0	40.6
Dividend yield (%)	1.1	2.9

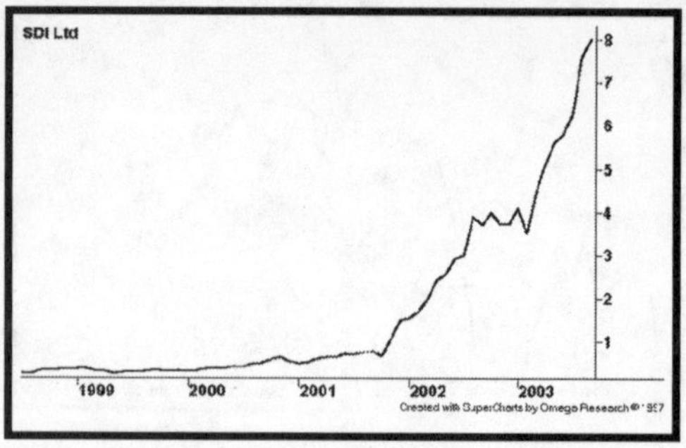

www.sdi.com.au

Melbourne-based SDI (formerly Southern Dental Industries), founded in 1972, develops and manufactures specialist dental restorative materials. It has two major product groups: alloy materials for fillings; and aesthetic materials, such as composites, adhesives, sealants and tooth whitening systems. More than 90% of sales are overseas, mainly in Europe, North America and South America. All the company's manufacturing is done in Melbourne, and it has offices and warehouses in Cologne, Chicago and Sao Paulo. The company founder, Jeffery Cheetham, and his family, own half of SDI's equity.

Latest Business Results (June 2003, Full Year)

For the fourth straight year SDI recorded after-tax profit growth of more than 35%, as global demand continues to swell for its products. In local currencies, sales in North America increased by 14.7%, in South America by 13.6% and in Europe by 18.8%. However, the stronger Australian dollar limited the total consolidated sales increase to 7.2%. Export sales represented 93% of the total.

Outlook

SDI has established a firm position in the Australian market for its products, and despite the company's small size it is also among the top 10 worldwide. It has an estimated 60% of the Australian market for amalgams and 10% globally, and lesser shares for other products. It devotes a high percentage of revenues to research and development work, with a dozen scientists, and has been successful in receiving government grants for this, with the result that it has started to release a steady stream of new products. It is achieving significant success with its new Pola tooth whitening system. Tooth whitening has become a $1 billion market in the US, with rapid growth and very high margins. SDI also sees strong indications that demand will exceed forecasts for its Riva new-generation glass ionomer cement restorative material that chemically binds silicon-cured fillings. The company is also seeing continuing double-digit growth in demand for its traditional amalgams and dental filling alloys. SDI is a conservatively managed company, with low levels of debt. Currency fluctuations have the potential to upset the company's earnings, though it engages in a degree of hedging.

SDI Year to 30 June	2002	2003
Revenues ($mn)	34.2	36.7
EBIT ($mn)	5.9	8.1
EBIT margin (%)	17.3	22.0
Gross margin (%)	62.4	65.9
Operating profit before tax ($mn)	5.6	7.8
Profit after tax ($mn)	4.0	5.5
Earnings per share (¢)	17.2	23.3
Cashflow per share (¢)	22.6	29.5
Dividend (¢)	5.0	7.5
Percentage franked	100	100
Net tangible assets per share ($)	0.51	0.69
Interest cover (times)	22.1	34.0
Return on equity (%)	24.6	27.5
Debt-to-equity ratio (%)	14.5	14.7
Current ratio	2.5	2.8

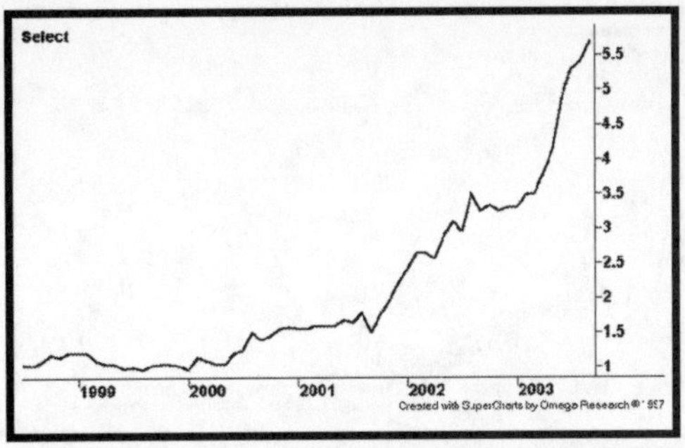

www.selectharvests.com.au

Select Harvests Limited

Share price ($)	5.45	
12-month high ($)	5.54	
12-month low ($)	3.04	
Market capitalisation ($mn)	192.6	
Price-to-NTA-per-share ratio	5.0	
5-year share price return (% p.a.)	46.5	
Sector: Consumer Staples	**Company**	**Sector**
Price-earnings ratio (times)	17.4	17.9
Dividend yield (%)	3.4	3.6

Melbourne-based Select Harvests is Australia's biggest almond grower and processor. As well as its own almond orchards, in Victoria's Sunraysia district, it has a thriving business managing orchards owned by external investors. In addition, it operates the Lucky Candy and Munch Nuts businesses, which involves the processing, packing and marketing of edible nuts, dried fruits and seeds. It also manufactures a range of pesticides. In mid 2003 it acquired the Meriram group of health food companies.

Latest Business Results (June 2003, Full Year)

Select Harvests continued to reap the benefits of its massive transformation program, with another strong rise in sales and profits, boosted by expanding global demand for almonds and by a 20% rise in average world prices. However, the key factor was the company's moves into managing orchards for external investors. This business saw profit (before interest and tax) up more than 50% to $6.1 million. Profits from the company's own orchards rose 22% to $7.3 million. However, profits were down on the company's food manufacturing and marketing activities, hit by the costs of consolidating production facilities. The drought led to a profit decline for the small pesticides business.

Outlook

In five years Select Harvests' almond acreage – company owned or under management – has grown from 2,100 acres to 10,000 acres, making it among the five largest almond growers in the world. Almond production in the June 2003 year of 2,800 tonnes – up from 1,900 tonnes in June 1998 – is set to rise sharply as new plantings mature. This is occurring as the health benefits of almonds are leading to a strong rise in global demand and prices are coming off cyclical lows. The company itself forecasts that reduced crops in the US and Spain mean that 2003–04 demand may exceed supply. It has consolidated its food-manufacturing operations at a state-of-the-art processing facility in Melbourne, and is now achieving efficiency gains. It believes its acquisition of the Meriram group of companies – manufacturers of a range of health foods, cooking ingredients and breakfast cereals – will provide some synergy benefits and entry into a fast-growing sector of the food business.

SHV Year to 30 June	2002	2003
Revenues ($mn)	78.3	81.0
Processing & marketing (%)	60	63
Management services (%)	17	20
Almond orchards (%)	18	11
Pesticide products (%)	5	5
EBIT ($mn)	14.7	17.4
EBIT margin (%)	18.8	21.5
Gross margin (%)	27.7	32.2
Operating profit before tax ($mn)	12.8	16.1
Profit after tax ($mn)	8.6	11.0
Earnings per share (¢)	25.4	31.3
Cashflow per share (¢)	36.7	42.6
Dividend (¢)	13.5	18.5
Percentage franked	100	100
Net tangible assets per share ($)	0.77	1.08
Interest cover (times)	7.6	13.3
Return on equity (%)	18.7	20.1
Debt-to-equity ratio (%)	38.8	14.5
Current ratio	1.3	1.6

Sims Group Limited

Share price ($)	10.18	
12-month high ($)	10.35	
12-month low ($)	6.41	
Market capitalisation ($mn)	957.1	
Price-to-NTA-per-share ratio	2.8	
5-year share price return (% p.a.)	18.2	
Sector: Materials	**Company**	**Sector**
Price-earnings ratio (times)	12.4	16.0
Dividend yield (%)	5.3	2.9

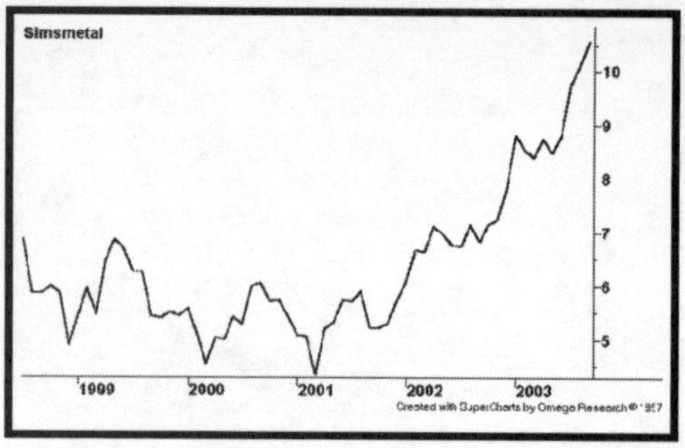

www.simsmetal.com.au

Sydney-based Sims, formerly called Simsmetal, was founded in 1917, and is today Australia's largest metals recycler. It has become the world's largest producer of ferrous scrap metal, used in steel making, and a leading producer of non-ferrous scrap, particularly copper and aluminium. Some 60% of revenues and profits come from overseas operations, primarily in America, Britain and New Zealand.

Latest Business Results (June 2003, Full Year)

Improved ferrous metals prices and a strong focus on cost efficiencies delivered Sims a booming result. Total volumes handled of 5.14 million tonnes represented just a marginal rise from the previous year, but higher prices led to a 12% boost to sales revenues and a 55% jump in profits. A focus on operational efficiencies led to record shredder production and shredder non-ferrous recovery revenues, and the company also benefited from the rationalisation or disposal of underperforming business units – notably its loss-making Southern Californian business – and the launch of its new recycling solutions division, which was profitable in its maiden year of operations. The shredding of ferrous raw material, and the recovery of the non-ferrous content of it, continued to be the main profit contributor, accounting for more than 75% of profit.

Outlook

Sims is working to mitigate the effects of fluctuating prices on its business, although there are limits to this. It is also hurt by the strong dollar, and has already announced that it sees its 2003–04 results little changed from 2002–03, though much depends on ferrous metals prices, which have been firm. Growing competition domestically from Smorgon Steel is another negative for its business. But it is a beneficiary of strongly growing steel demand in China. It also sees great potential for its new recycling solutions division, which has been set up to help companies meet increasingly stringent regulations in Europe and America concerning the need to recycle scrap electronics products and white goods such as refrigerators. With $70 million in net cash, Sims is ready to make a major acquisition to enhance its operations, though if something suitable does not present itself it may opt for some kind of capital return to shareholders.

SMS Year to 30 June	2002	2003
Revenues ($mn)	1,409.2	1,579.7
EBIT ($mn)	76.6	114.2
EBIT margin (%)	5.4	7.2
Operating profit before tax ($mn)	71.2	112.0
Profit after tax ($mn)	48.5	75.0
Earnings per share (¢)	54.0	82.2
Cashflow per share (¢)	96.4	122.5
Dividend (¢)	36	54
Percentage franked	100	73
Net tangible assets per share ($)	2.91	3.69
Interest cover (times)	14.1	51.9
Return on equity (%)	15.0	20.4
Debt-to-equity ratio (%)	6.7	–
Current ratio	1.8	1.9

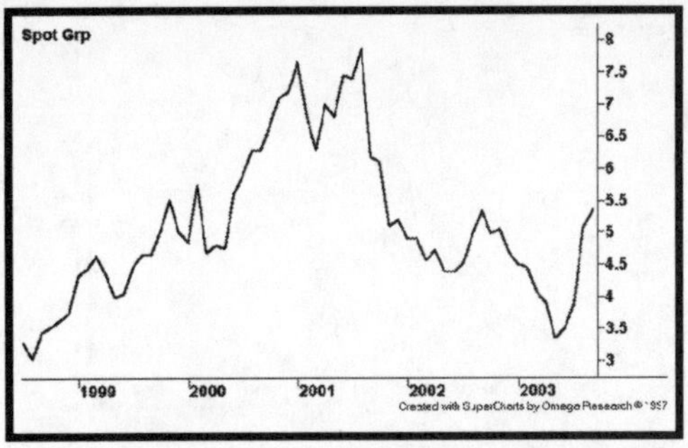

www.spotless.com.au

SPOTLESS GROUP LIMITED

Share price ($)	4.68	
12-month high ($)	5.45	
12-month low ($)	3.23	
Market capitalisation ($mn)	1,039.5	
Price-to-NTA-per-share ratio	–	
5-year share price return (% p.a.)	14.2	
Sector: Industrials	**Company**	**Sector**
Price-earnings ratio (times)	18.7	12.1
Dividend yield (%)	4.9	3.9

Melbourne-based Spotless started in the 1940s as a dry-cleaning and laundry operation, and incorporates two businesses. The first of these, Support Services (formerly Spotless Services), provides a wide range of integrated services – including catering, cleaning, maintenance and uniform supply – to more than 20,000 organisations throughout Australia and New Zealand. The company's other business, Retailer Services (formerly Spotless Plastics), is an international supplier of clothes-hanger handling and display systems to retailers and garment manufacturers. It operates in the US, Australia, New Zealand, Hong Kong and Turkey.

LATEST BUSINESS RESULTS (JUNE 2003, FULL YEAR)

The company enjoyed a big profit increase, although some $14 million of this derived from an unrealised foreign exchange gain. Without this, the after-tax profit would have been up by about 15%. The best result came from New Zealand, with revenues up 16% and profits up 20% – thanks in part to a favourable currency rate, but also to good business in food services, property services and laundry business. Australian business was generally firm, with profits up nearly 11% and good growth from newer business and from the hospital pharmaceutical products distributor Clifford Hallam. However, the company's US subsidiary fell into the red, having been engaged in relief work around the World Trade Center in the previous year. The Retailer Services business had a mixed year, with higher revenues in local currencies generally offset by the firmer dollar, but it was still able to post an excellent 11% gain in profit.

OUTLOOK

Currency fluctuations are masking the growth of the company's Retailer Services operations, where it is achieving good growth and very high margins. Though making up just 16% of total company sales, this business delivers more than 40% of profit. The company has acquired the Braitrim clothes-hanger business in the UK, and is restructuring this with the aim of boosting efficiencies, as well as using it to expand European operations. The other promising area for Spotless is New Zealand, which provides 12% of total company sales but 19% of profit, with business continuing to grow strongly. In Australia, the company sees continuing good potential from government outsourcing work.

SPT Year to 30 June	2002	2003
Revenues ($mn)	2,179.1	2,359.6
Support services (%)	82	84
Retailer services (%)	18	16
EBIT ($mn)	92.3	109.3
EBIT margin (%)	4.2	4.6
Gross margin (%)	61.4	59.5
Operating profit before tax ($mn)	66.2	83.9
Profit after tax ($mn)	32.4	51.6
Earnings per share (¢)	15.9	25.0
Cashflow per share (¢)	48.6	58.2
Dividend (¢)	22	23
Percentage franked	100	100
Net tangible assets per share ($)	–	–
Interest cover (times)	3.5	4.3
Return on equity (%)	7.1	10.5
Debt-to-equity ratio (%)	71.7	61.0
Current ratio	1.2	1.1

STW Communications Group Limited

Share price ($)	3.27
12-month high ($)	3.29
12-month low ($)	2.40
Market capitalisation ($mn)	496.0
Price-to-NTA-per-share ratio	2.9
5-year share price return (% p.a.)	34.9

Sector: Consumer Discretion.	Company	Sector
Price-earnings ratio (times)	19.4	20.2
Dividend yield (%)	3.8	3.7

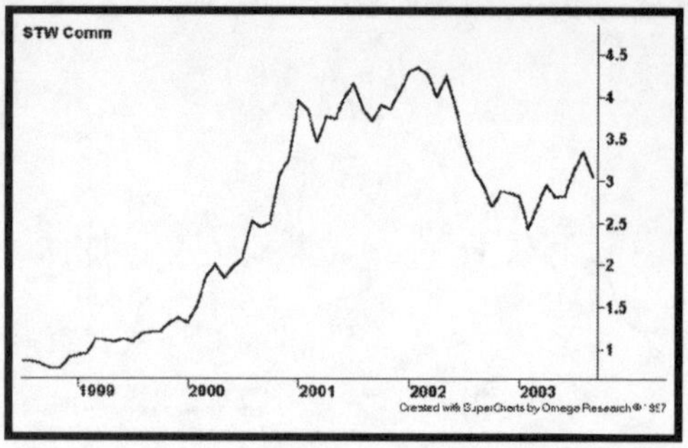

www.singo.com.au

Sydney-based STW Communications Group, formerly called Singleton Group, was founded by entrepreneur John Singleton, who is the largest shareholder. It is a holding company, owning two-thirds of Singleton Ogilvy & Mather Holdings as well as a 49% interest in the Australian and New Zealand operations of the advertising company J. Walter Thompson and a 20% stake in Indonesia's third-largest television network, PT Surya Citra Televisi (known as SCTV). It also owns around 40 smaller businesses in such fields as internet design and marketing, ethnic advertising, public relations and direct marketing.

Latest Business Results (June 2003, Half Year)

Revenues and profits were up in a recovering advertising environment. The core advertising and communications business saw after-tax profit up 17% to $8.6 million, including excellent growth from many affiliated companies. However, the media division recorded a 9% profit decline, to $2.4 million. This business comprises the company's Indonesian television interests, and was hurt by adverse currency exchange movements and lower program ratings and advertising revenues.

Outlook

STW retains a string of blue chip domestic and international clients, and this underpins its business. Thanks to its many small associated companies, it is increasingly able to offer customers a 'one-stop shop' strategy. The company has already said that it expects Australian and New Zealand operations to provide profit growth in 2003 of 15% to 20% over 2002. However, despite a recovery in the advertising business, competition remains strong, and for long-term growth STW believes it needs further acquisitions. It bought interests in four companies in the June 2003 half, and since then has acquired more, including a 49% stake in Western Australia's largest agency, The Brand Agency. STW sees good potential for its SCTV business in Indonesia despite disappointing first-half results. This company has undergone a management shake-up and is expecting a significantly improved second half.

SGN Year to 31 December	2001	2002
Revenues ($mn)	81.5	122.5
EBIT ($mn)	25.9	37.9
EBIT margin (%)	31.8	30.9
Operating profit before tax ($mn)	25.6	37.9
Profit after tax ($mn)	17.5	25.3
Earnings per share (¢)	13.0	16.8
Dividend (¢)	7.3	12.5
Percentage franked	100	100
Interest cover (times)	89.1	2525.8
Return on equity (%)	23.1	19.0
Half Year to 30 June	**2002**	**2003**
Revenues ($mn)	55.1	60.8
Operating profit before tax ($mn)	14.8	16.4
Profit after tax ($mn)	10.0	11.0
Earnings per share (¢)	6.7	7.2
Dividend (¢)	3.4	4.3
Percentage franked	100	100
Net tangible assets per share ($)	1.15	1.14
Debt-to-equity ratio (%)	–	–
Current ratio	1.1	1.7

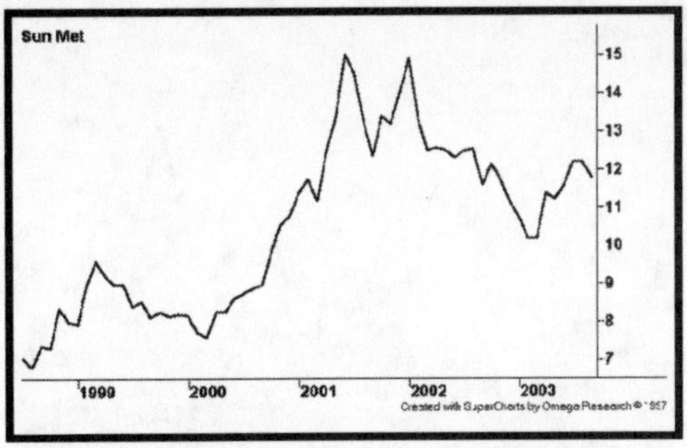

www.suncorp.com.au

Suncorp-Metway Limited

Share price ($)	12.00	
12-month high ($)	13.25	
12-month low ($)	9.12	
Market capitalisation ($mn)	6,502.5	
Price-to-NTA-per-share ratio	2.4	
5-year share price return (% p.a.)	11.6	
Sector: Financials	**Company**	**Sector**
Price-earnings ratio (times)	16.5	16.2
Dividend yield (%)	4.7	4.5

Brisbane-based Suncorp-Metway, Queensland's largest company, was formed from the merger of Metway Bank, the Queensland Industry Development Corporation and the insurance company Suncorp. It divides its businesses into three core areas – banking, insurance and wealth management. It is Australia's sixth-largest bank and second-largest general insurance company – the latter under the GIO brand – with some 3.8 million customers.

Latest Business Results (June 2003, Full Year)

A surge in second-half business, following a lacklustre first half, handed Suncorp a strong gain in profits. Insurance was the key, with the general insurance arm more than doubling its pre-tax profit, to $233 million, driven by premium growth, up 12% to $2 billion, and operating expenses down 4%. Banking profit rose nearly 9% to $318 million. Lending grew 11% to more than $25 billion, led by commercial lending, though housing loan growth was weaker than that of many rivals. In a difficult environment for the funds management business, wealth management operations delivered a $41 million profit, down from $58 million a year before.

Outlook

Suncorp-Metway has unveiled a five-year strategy designed to achieve maximum benefits from its three core businesses of banking, insurance and wealth management. Despite a product cross-selling ratio that is higher than for other banks, it believes it can sell still more of its products to its large customer base. It sees business banking – in which it lags rivals – as offering significant growth potential, particularly in the areas of small business, property and agribusiness. In retail banking it is renewing its focus on core products, while streamlining its home loans process, in an attempt to win back lost market share. It plans more aggressive marketing of its insurance products, with a particular focus on the corporate property market, which it believes offers strong growth prospects. The company plans to strengthen its wealth management arm by increasing from 8% to 10% over three years this business's penetration among Suncorp's existing banking customers. It also plans a new emphasis on pre-retirees and the youth market. It hopes to boost funds under management through an increased focus on gaining wholesale mandates.

SUN Year to 30 June	2002	2003
Operating income ($mn)	3,500.0	4,022.0
Net interest income ($mn)	550.0	592.0
Operating expenses ($mn)	2,996.0	3,361.0
Operating profit before tax ($mn)	405.0	550.0
Profit after tax ($mn)	311.0	384.0
Earnings per share (¢)	60.5	72.7
Dividend (¢)	54	56
Percentage franked	100	100
Non-interest income to total income (%)	84.3	85.3
Net tangible assets per share ($)	4.30	4.90
Cost-to-income ratio (%)	85.6	83.6
Return on equity (%)	10.3	11.0
Return on assets (%)	1.0	1.0

Sydney Aquarium Limited

Share price ($)	4.65	
12-month high ($)	4.90	
12-month low ($)	4.00	
Market capitalisation ($mn)	105.3	
Price-to-NTA-per-share ratio	5.2	
5-year share price return (% p.a.)	9.5	
Sector: Consumer Discretion.	**Company**	**Sector**
Price-earnings ratio (times)	16.7	20.2
Dividend yield (%)	5.8	3.7

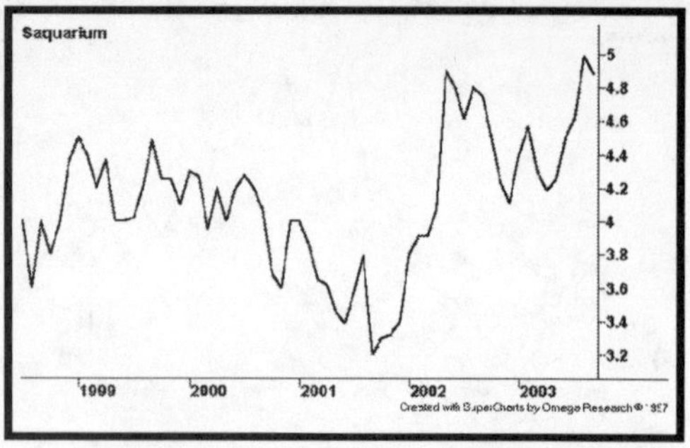

www.sydneyaquarium.com.au

The Sydney Aquarium at Darling Harbour is one of Australia's most popular tourist attractions, and includes the $14 million Great Barrier Reef Oceanarium and the Shark Bite cafe. The company also owns and operates the long-established Oceanworld Manly.

Latest Business Results (June 2003, Full Year)

In a sluggish tourism environment – hit by the Bali bombing, the war in Iraq, the SARS outbreak and tension on the Korean Peninsula – Sydney Aquarium saw its revenues and profits down. However, the decline was only minor, which was viewed as evidence of the strength of the company's operations. Visitor numbers of 1.19 million were down nearly 6% from the previous year's record level. Overseas visitors (58% of the total) were down 9%, and local visitors (34% of the total) were down 2%. However, there was a rise in interstate visitor numbers, reflecting increased marketing activity, and some evidence of destination switching to domestic holidays from overseas. The average visitor spend was up around 1%, due to higher admission receipts. Average food and beverage sales were down, but this was offset by higher demand for retail souvenir products. Oceanworld Manly saw revenues up 23% to $1.45 million, and this business moved from the red into the black.

Outlook

Sydney Aquarium is a key attraction for international visitors to Australia, and it is quite dependent on global tourism trends. As long as Australia remains popular with overseas tourists it can expect good business. However, to enjoy strong growth it needs new attractions, and it has announced the development of 'Australia's Animal World', a $29 million modern fauna park also at Darling Harbour. It is still waiting for official approval of this project, and does not foresee it opening until at least 2005. The company bought Oceanworld Manly as a defensive move, to stop it becoming a major rival to its own business, and for some years this operation struggled. However, the introduction of a shark dive experience in November 2002 – along with new activities including functions, birthday parties and corporate team-building – has led to a major turnaround in business.

SAQ Year to 30 June	2002	2003
Revenues ($mn)	24.5	23.6
EBIT ($mn)	9.2	9.1
EBIT margin (%)	37.5	38.5
Gross margin (%)	58.8	58.6
Operating profit before tax ($mn)	8.7	8.4
Profit after tax ($mn)	6.2	6.0
Earnings per share (¢)	28.8	27.8
Cashflow per share (¢)	41.4	36.8
Dividend (¢)	28	27
Percentage franked	100	100
Net tangible assets per share ($)	0.74	0.89
Interest cover (times)	21.0	14.0
Return on equity (%)	39.1	34.0
Debt-to-equity ratio (%)	38.8	47.0
Current ratio	0.2	0.4

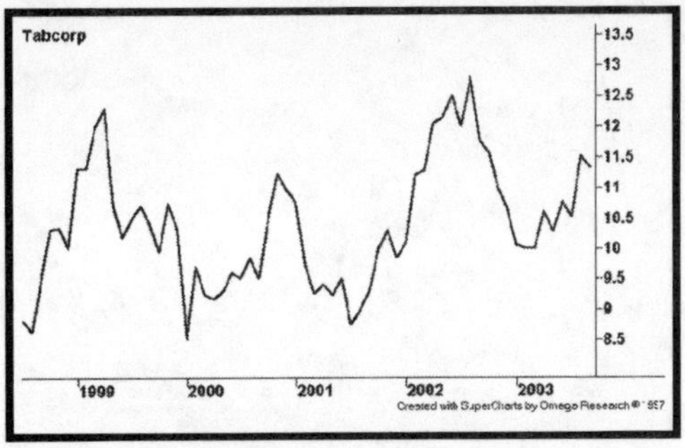

www.tabcorp.com.au

Tabcorp Holdings Limited

Share price ($)	11.40	
12-month high ($)	13.00	
12-month low ($)	9.50	
Market capitalisation ($mn)	4,167.3	
Price-to-NTA-per-share ratio	–	
5-year share price return (% p.a.)	9.1	
Sector: Consumer Discretion.	**Company**	**Sector**
Price-earnings ratio (times)	15.5	20.2
Dividend yield (%)	5.9	3.7

Tabcorp was established in 1994 with the privatisation of Victoria's TAB operations. It has the sole licence to conduct off-course totalisators in Victoria, on horse and greyhound racing events. It also has licences to operate gaming machines and conduct keno games in clubs and hotels in Victoria. It acquired Sydney's Star City casino in 1999, and is in merger discussions with Queensland's Jupiters casino operation.

Latest Business Results (June 2003, Full Year)

Tabcorp's long run of strong growth finally came to a halt, with a decline in revenues and just a modest increase in profit. The key factor was the introduction of smoking bans in Victorian gaming venues from September 2002, resulting in reduced patronage. Gaming revenues declined by 13% in the second half of the year relative to the prior corresponding period, and division profits fell 10% for the year. By contrast, wagering revenues rose 4%, with profits up 12%, supported by a strong Spring Carnival and growth from provincial and interstate racing. Star City revenues were up 3% and profits grew by 12%, with a good performance from table games and strong non-gaming (hotel and entertainment) revenues.

Outlook

The planned merger with Jupiters – expected from mid November 2003, subject to government and regulatory body approvals – will transform Tabcorp. As well as offering considerable synergies, it will make the company Australia's largest gambling and entertainment group, operating approximately 18,000 gaming machines, with four casino and hotel facilities in Queensland and New South Wales, wagering and sports betting operations in Victoria, keno operations on the east coast of Australia, gaming machine monitoring operations in Victoria and Queensland, the AWA game machine servicing business and an international monitoring, gaming and totalisator sales business. However, the challenge of realising the integration of the two companies could initially put pressure on profits. Tabcorp believes it is addressing the issue of reduced gaming room patronage with enhanced amenities for smokers at its Tabaret venues. It is also making major refurbishments, introducing new games and boosting the number of one-cent machines.

TAH Year to 30 June	2002	2003
Revenues ($mn)	1,933.1	1,900.7
Gaming (%)	47	45
Star City (%)	32	33
Wagering (%)	21	22
EBIT ($mn)	432.9	435.4
EBIT margin (%)	22.4	22.9
Operating profit before tax ($mn)	381.0	387.0
Profit after tax ($mn)	259.3	263.1
Earnings per share (¢)	69.5	73.5
Cashflow per share (¢)	98.1	102.9
Dividend (¢)	63	67
Percentage franked	100	100
Net tangible assets per share ($)	–	–
Interest cover (times)	8.3	9.0
Return on equity (%)	20.6	20.3
Debt-to-equity ratio (%)	50.9	49.0
Current ratio	0.4	0.2

Telstra Corporation Limited

Share price ($)	4.74	
12-month high ($)	5.08	
12-month low ($)	3.92	
Market capitalisation ($mn)	60,482.0	
Price-to-NTA-per-share ratio	5.0	
5-year share price return (% p.a.)	-0.3	
Sector: Telecom. Services	**Company**	**Sector**
Price-earnings ratio (times)	17.8	17.2
Dividend yield (%)	5.1	4.5

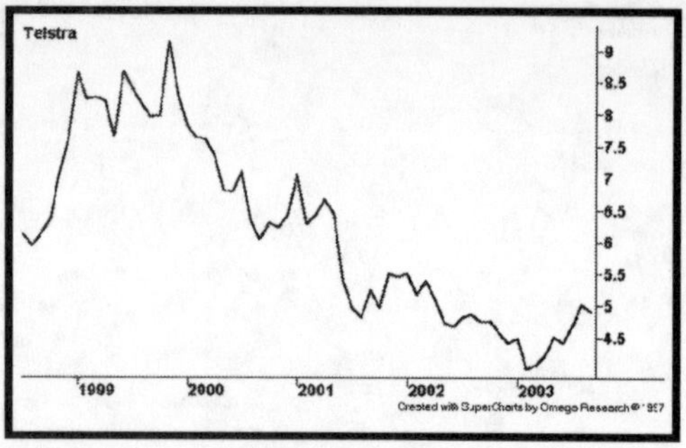

telstra.com

Telstra, still 50.1% owned by the federal government, is Australia's dominant telecommunications company, with a 60% to 65% market share. It provides local, long-distance and international telephone services, along with mobile communications, data and internet services and telephone directories. It owns 50% of the Foxtel pay television service and it has a strategic alliance with Hong Kong telecommunications giant PCCW.

Latest Business Results (June 2003, Full Year)

Profits fell to their lowest level in five years, though a key factor was a $965 million writeoff of the investment in the Reach Ltd telecommunications joint venture operation with PCCW in Asia. The company reported that on a normalised basis the after-tax profit actually rose about 6%. Revenues were generally flat for the company's basic telephone businesses, with customers increasingly taking advantage of the company's various discounted-rate initiatives, or moving to cheaper alternatives. However, there was continuing growth for mobile phone operations and internet activities.

Outlook

After several years of unsteadiness in its operations – partly from intense competition in the telecommunications market, and partly from its expensive ventures into Asia – Telstra believes its businesses have now stabilised, and that it is on the path to renewed growth. In particular, its mobile phone base is increasing and Asian businesses are turning the corner into profit. However, it is difficult to see how the company might expand rapidly. It sees broadband internet as offering great scope, and plans to spend $1 billion over five years on its broadband network, with the aim of doubling its customer base. The company is also planning a major cost-cutting program, aimed at reducing annual expenses by $600 million to $800-million within three years. It is known to be interested in a media acquisition, to provide content to its broadband and mobile services. Telstra shares are widely held, and the company has announced a share buyback scheme that could boost their value. There is much speculation about whether the government will succeed in its aim to place its 50.1% shareholding on the market.

TLS Year to 30 June	2002	2003
Revenues ($mn)	20,196.0	20,495.0
General telephone services (%)	39	39
Mobiles (%)	19	18
Data & internet (%)	14	14
EBIT ($mn)	6,216.0	5,723.0
EBIT margin (%)	30.8	27.9
Operating profit before tax ($mn)	5,446.0	4,928.0
Profit after tax ($mn)	3,661.0	3,429.0
Earnings per share (¢)	28.5	26.6
Cashflow per share (¢)	53.8	53.4
Dividend (¢)	22	24
Percentage franked	100	100
Net tangible assets per share ($)	0.83	0.95
Interest cover (times)	8.1	7.2
Return on equity (%)	26.8	23.2
Debt-to-equity ratio (%)	94.3	73.0
Current ratio	0.8	1.0

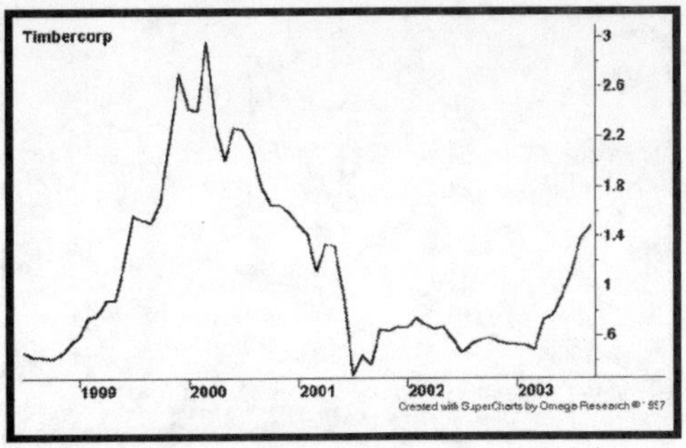

www.timbercorp.com.au

Timbercorp Limited

Share price ($)	1.31	
12-month high ($)	1.36	
12-month low ($)	0.46	
Market capitalisation ($mn)	284.2	
Price-to-NTA-per-share ratio	1.4	
5-year share price return (% p.a.)	30.6	
Sector: Materials	**Company**	**Sector**
Price-earnings ratio (times)	11.8	16.0
Dividend yield (%)	1.9	2.9

Timbercorp, based in Melbourne, is a prominent agribusiness company. It promotes plantation projects for outside investors, provides finance and manages the properties, receiving annuity-style fees for its services. The investments are intended for long-term investors, and offer the promise of substantial tax benefits, along with potentially high returns. The company's primary plantations are 74,000 hectares of blue gums in the Green Triangle region of Victoria–South Australia and in Western Australia. It also manages a 2,100 hectare olive tree plantation – one of the largest in the world – in central Victoria. With Select Harvests it has moved into the almond orchard business, with plantings of more than 2,460 hectares. It owns more than 11% of the equity of Select Harvests.

Latest Business Results (March 2003, Half Year)

Timbercorp has changed its financial year-end from June to September, and the latest results are the interim figures to March 2003. However, the company has not released any March 2002 comparative data. The latest available full-year results are to June 2002. For the six months to March 2003 the company reported that annuity-style income continued to grow strongly, at $33.2 million for the half year, with an EBIT contribution of $13.3 million. New business revenue for the period was $4.5 million.

Outlook

Timbercorp's shares have been recovering after being hurt by negative sentiment that followed an Australian Taxation Office crackdown on certain agricultural investment schemes. It is driving ahead with a series of growth initiatives. It has announced plans to merge its forestry assets with those of Futuris to create Australia's leading hardwood plantation company, which will manage plantations exceeding 167,000 hectares. It is also creating a new agricultural trust with Chiquita Brands South Pacific to invest in citrus orchards and vineyards. The company has already forecast that September 2003 profits will be significantly up on those of the June 2002 year.

TIM Year to 30 June*	2001	2002
Revenues ($mn)	102.2	97.2
EBIT ($mn)	38.2	43.8
EBIT margin (%)	37.3	45.0
Operating profit before tax ($mn)	37.8	37.9
Profit after tax ($mn)	25.4	22.8
Earnings per share (¢)	12.9	11.1
Cashflow per share (¢)	14.0	13.1
Dividend (¢)	4	2.5
Percentage franked	100	100
Interest cover (times)	116.0	7.4
Return on equity (%)	21.6	13.8
Half Year to 31 March*		**2003**
Revenues ($mn)		37.1
Forestry (%)		40
Olives (%)		34
Almonds (%)		18
Operating profit before tax ($mn)		8.2
Profit after tax ($mn)		5.1
Earnings per share (¢)		1.5
Dividend (¢)		0
Percentage franked		–
Net tangible assets per share ($)		0.94
Debt-to-equity ratio (%)		54.2
Current ratio		1.0

** Timbercorp has changed its financial year-end from June to September.*

Toll Holdings Limited

Share price ($)	6.85	
12-month high ($)	8.82	
12-month low ($)	5.60	
Market capitalisation ($mn)	2,102.1	
Price-to-NTA-per-share ratio	4.1	
5-year share price return (% p.a.)	69.5	
Sector: Industrials	**Company**	**Sector**
Price-earnings ratio (times)	19.1	12.1
Dividend yield (%)	2.1	3.9

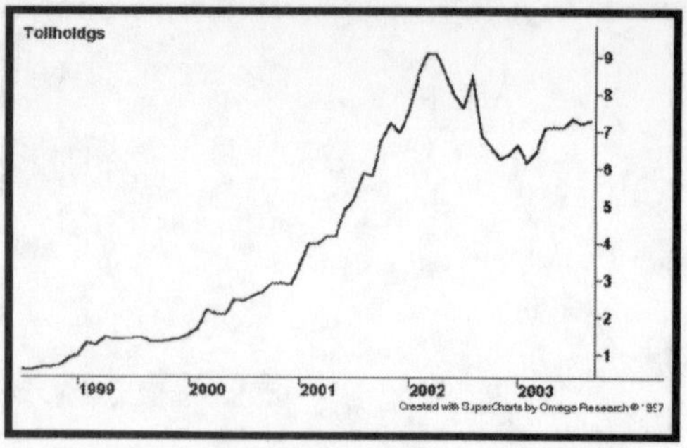

www.toll.com.au

Melbourne-based Toll Holdings was founded in Newcastle in 1888. It is today a giant transportation, warehousing and freight logistics company. It has one million square metres of warehouse space, it manages the ports of Geelong and Hastings and it has moved into rail freight, with the Pacific National joint venture with Patrick Corporation. Its four divisions are: Toll Logistics, which provides a wide range of transportation solutions for major customers; Toll Long Distance, which manages long-haul forwarding services; Toll North, which provides freight services in Queensland and the Northern Territory; and Toll Technologies, which manages e-commerce strategies.

Latest Business Results (June 2003, Full Year)

The strong economy and a continuing stream of acquisitions gave Toll Holdings a big increase in its revenues and profits. All major industry groups in which Toll operates were firm, with a very strong performance from the key food and beverage and the automotive sectors, and excellent growth from the resources sector. The company's port logistics operations experienced strong growth, and benefited from the full-year impact of the BHP stevedoring acquisition made in May 2002. Port operations in New Zealand performed ahead of expectations. In its first full year of operation, Pacific National performed ahead of plan to deliver Toll an after-tax profit of $28.3 million.

Outlook

Toll has become a transportation and logistics powerhouse, with rapidly growing businesses and, for a while, a surging share price. It has already forecast another record profit in 2003–04. It is working to transform the transportation of goods in Australia, through integrated high-tech road, rail, port and warehousing services. Its new Pacific National rail company – formerly the rail freight operations of the federal and NSW governments – is part of this strategy. With Australia's large rail freight infrastructure relatively underutilised, this business is seen as offering huge potential. Toll is also continually seeking new acquisitions in the highly fragmented Australian transportation industry. It is striving to become a force in New Zealand, with a growing business there and a takeover bid for train operator Tranz Rail Holdings.

TOL Year to 30 June	2002	2003
Revenues ($mn)	2,038.0	2,569.8
Long distance (%)	43	48
Logistics (%)	39	36
Toll North (%)	18	16
EBIT ($mn)	110.1	156.7
EBIT margin (%)	5.4	6.1
Operating profit before tax ($mn)	97.8	137.4
Profit after tax ($mn)	74.2	106.1
Earnings per share (¢)	27.9	35.9
Cashflow per share (¢)	47.7	61.9
Dividend (¢)	10.0	14.5
Percentage franked	100	100
Net tangible assets per share ($)	1.21	1.69
Interest cover (times)	9.0	8.1
Return on equity (%)	24.8	20.6
Debt-to-equity ratio (%)	81.6	41.7
Current ratio	1.0	1.0

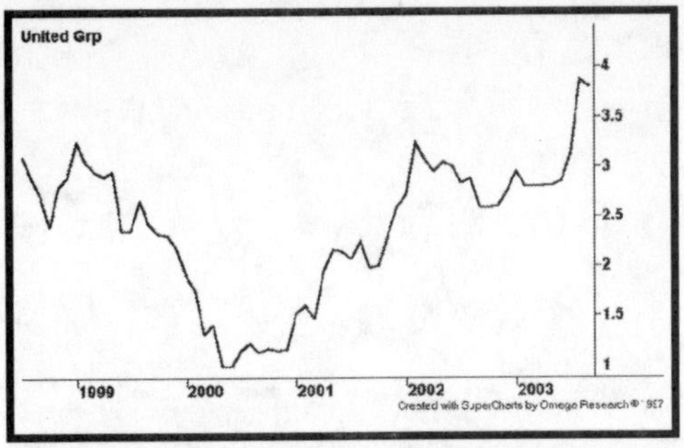

www.unitedgroup.com.au

United Group Limited

Share price ($)	3.36
12-month high ($)	3.38
12-month low ($)	2.38
Market capitalisation ($mn)	336.5
Price-to-NTA-per-share ratio	4.9
5-year share price return (% p.a.)	13.2

Sector: Industrials	Company	Sector
Price-earnings ratio (times)	14.0	12.1
Dividend yield (%)	4.2	3.9

Sydney-based United Group is one of Australia's leading engineering companies, with specialties in power supply, water and waste management, resources engineering, telecommunications and heavy haulage railways. It groups its activities into four businesses: United Goninan is a leader in railway manufacturing, maintenance and engineering; United KG is engaged in engineering, construction, facilities management and industrial maintenance businesses; United KFPW provides corporate property services; and United Gooder is a New Zealand engineering and construction business.

Latest Business Results (June 2003, Full Year)

Revenues and profits were up, driven partly by the United KFPW acquisition in October 2002, as well as by a bulging order book from the United Goninan business. There was also a strong turnaround in the profitability of United KG, which benefited from water, oil and gas projects in Queensland and Western Australia, and saw its margins improve from 2.1% to 5.2%. The small New Zealand operation realised strong growth in revenues, but with a disappointing profit performance. The company's order book doubled to $2.3 billion.

Outlook

United's business is booming, and it has said it expects a further double-digit increase in profits in 2003–04. United Goninan, Australia's largest provider of maintenance services to public and private railway operators, saw its order book double to $1.5 billion during 2002–03, driven mainly by $740 million of new passenger rail manufacturing contracts from NSW State Rail and the extension of the NSW MainTrain maintenance contract until 2009. There was also the expansion of the MTR Corporation contract for the $22 million refurbishment of 12 railcars to service the Penny's Bay Line in Hong Kong, and a $16 million contract with BHP Billiton to supply 120 iron ore wagons and 35 car bodies. The new United KFPW business – which acts as property manager and goods and services procurer for corporate clients – is seen as providing United with a significant new service that it can offer its existing client base, and United is seen as being keen to acquire further add-on businesses to enhance its operations.

UGL Year to 30 June	2002	2003
Revenues ($mn)	722.6	855.2
Service & maintenance (%)	54	49
Construction & fabrication (%)	37	40
Facilities management (%)	8	5
Property management (%)	0	5
EBIT ($mn)	26.4	37.0
EBIT margin (%)	3.7	4.3
Operating profit before tax ($mn)	22.0	31.0
Profit after tax ($mn)	16.3	21.9
Earnings per share (¢)	19.5	24.0
Cashflow per share (¢)	32.2	39.6
Dividend (¢)	10	14
Percentage franked	100	100
Net tangible assets per share ($)	1.05	0.69
Interest cover (times)	6.0	6.1
Return on equity (%)	13.8	15.1
Debt-to-equity ratio (%)	6.5	26.1
Current ratio	1.5	1.3

WADEPACK LIMITED

Share price ($)	1.63	
12-month high ($)	2.10	
12-month low ($)	1.22	
Market capitalisation ($mn)	51.2	
Price-to-NTA-per-share ratio	1.7	
5-year share price return (% p.a.)	27.5	
Sector: Industrials	**Company**	**Sector**
Price-earnings ratio (times)	6.8	12.1
Dividend yield (%)	3.1	3.9

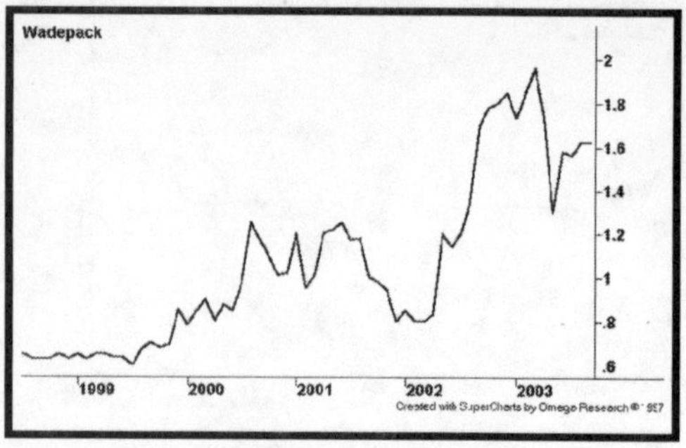

www.wadepack.com.au

Sydney-based Wadepack is a small, specialist printing and packaging company that was founded in 1947, and has grown through a series of mergers and acquisitions. Today it has activities in Sydney and Melbourne, though it recently closed its Brisbane operations. Its product range includes individual cartons, beverage baskets, display cartons, tissue boxes, window-faced cartons, blister cards and box and lid sets. Among its niche businesses, it supplies 80% of Australia's pharmaceutical companies with some of their packaging, it is a major supplier of CD packaging and promotional printing for the music industry, it prints around 80% of Australian takeaway popcorn packaging and it is a significant supplier of printed packaging for takeaway food company KFC.

LATEST BUSINESS RESULTS (JUNE 2003, HALF YEAR)

Revenues dipped and profits fell sharply, in distinct contrast to the December full-year results, when the company made large gains. Enhanced competition was one factor, along with reduced demand for certain products. Delays in commissioning new printing equipment also reportedly led to some business being lost. In addition, the company had to contend with rising selling and administration costs, primarily due to an increase in payroll following a two-year wage freeze.

WDP Year to 31 December	2001	2002
Revenues ($mn)	70.0	84.9
EBIT ($mn)	4.0	13.0
EBIT margin (%)	5.6	15.3
Gross margin (%)	18.3	25.3
Operating profit before tax ($mn)	2.5	11.1
Profit after tax ($mn)	1.6	7.6
Earnings per share (¢)	4.9	24.1
Cashflow per share (¢)	14.2	33.7
Dividend (¢)	3.5	5
Percentage franked	100	100
Interest cover (times)	2.8	7.0
Return on equity (%)	5.7	24.9
Half Year to 30 June	**2002**	**2003**
Revenues ($mn)	38.9	36.8
Operating profit before tax ($mn)	4.6	2.9
Profit after tax ($mn)	3.1	2.0
Earnings per share (¢)	9.9	6.3
Dividend (¢)	3.5	3.5
Percentage franked	100	100
Net tangible assets per share ($)	0.78	0.94
Debt-to-equity ratio (%)	74.1	55.0
Current ratio	1.8	1.4

OUTLOOK

Wadepack operates in a competitive environment that is dominated by giant and highly efficient companies such as Amcor, Visy and Carter Holt Harvey. As a result, it must be nimble to get business and maintain growth, and the company's profit record and share price performance have been volatile. The company believes it has successfully overcome problems with its new printing equipment, and that this will enhance productivity as well as provide new capacity. In August 2003, it announced the closure of its Brisbane facility, and it expects that this will reduce its cost base and pave the way for a long-term boost to margins.

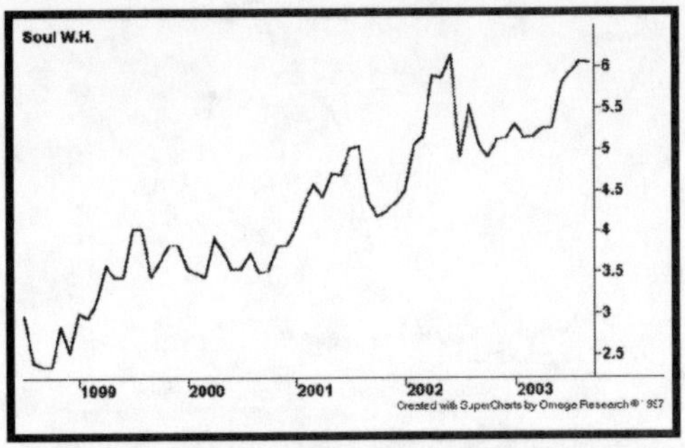

www.whsp.com.au

Washington H. Soul Pattinson & Company Ltd

Share price ($)	6.03
12-month high ($)	6.10
12-month low ($)	4.76
Market capitalisation ($mn)	1,408.0
Price-to-NTA-per-share ratio	2.3
5-year share price return (% p.a.)	24.3

Sector: Financials	Company	Sector
Price-earnings ratio (times)	19.8	16.2
Dividend yield (%)	2.3	4.5

With its origins as a Sydney pharmacy store, opened in 1872, and publicly listed for more than 100 years, Washington H. Soul Pattinson is today a diversified group. Its main businesses are: New Hope Corporation (69% owned), which has coal mining operations in Queensland and Indonesia; NBN Television is a Nine Network affiliate broadcasting to Newcastle and the Hunter Valley; SP Telecommunications (57% owned) provides telecommunications services to the Hunter Valley region; and Keith Harris (84% owned) manufactures juices and fragrances. The company also retains ownership of nine Sydney pharmacies, and it owns 22% of the equity in Australian Pharmaceutical Industries and 29% of nutritional supplement maker Clover Corporation. In a cross-shareholding arrangement designed to forestall takeovers, it owns nearly 50% of the equity of Brickworks, which in turn owns 41% of Soul Pattinson.

Latest Business Results (January 2003, Half Year)

In a good result, lower domestic production costs and higher prices led to an after-tax profit on coal of $14.6 million, up 59% from the January 2002 half, and despite a slightly reduced contribution from Indonesian operations. The company also benefited from its holding in Brickworks, which continued to see excellent business from the housing boom. There was a solid contribution from the company's investment portfolio. A weak advertising market saw reduced profits from NBN Television.

Outlook

The Brickworks takeover of Bristile could lead to significant cost reductions, though this business is threatened by a looming downturn in the booming housing cycle. New Hope Corporation has commenced coal production at New Acland in south-east Queensland, with expected annual output of two million tonnes. A turnaround in profitability for SP Telecommunications and Clover Corporation offers the prospect of future growth. Soul Pattinson is working to float its interest in New Hope Corporation.

SOL Year to 31 July	2001	2002
Revenues ($mn)	920.4	371.0
EBIT ($mn)	86.9	118.0
EBIT margin (%)	9.4	31.8
Operating profit before tax ($mn)	79.3	114.1
Profit after tax ($mn)	56.8	72.7
Earnings per share (¢)	23.8	30.5
Cashflow per share (¢)	40.6	41.8
Dividend (¢)	11.5	14
Percentage franked	100	100
Interest cover (times)	11.5	30.3
Return on equity (%)	9.3	11.1
Half Year to 31 January	**2002**	**2003**
Revenues ($mn)	169.3	179.8
Coal mining (%)	50	45
Media (%)	17	17
Pharmaceutical (%)	10	10
Operating profit before tax ($mn)	63.1	68.0
Profit after tax ($mn)	36.2	45.4
Earnings per share (¢)	15.2	19.0
Dividend (¢)	6	7
Percentage franked	100	100
Net tangible assets per share ($)	2.53	2.66
Debt-to-equity ratio (%)	24.2	21.7
Current ratio	2.0	1.4

Wesfarmers Limited

Share price ($)	28.11	
12-month high ($)	30.45	
12-month low ($)	21.73	
Market capitalisation ($mn)	10,554.3	
Price-to-NTA-per-share ratio	4.7	
5-year share price return (% p.a.)	23.6	
Sector: Industrials	**Company**	**Sector**
Price-earnings ratio (times)	19.7	12.1
Dividend yield (%)	4.5	3.9

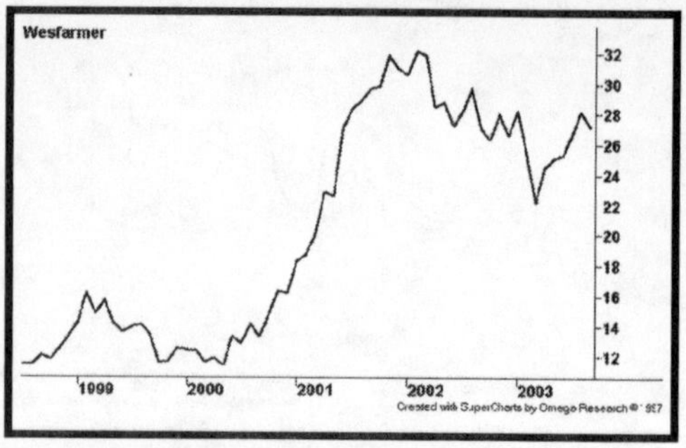

www.wesfarmers.com.au

Perth-based Wesfarmers, founded in 1914 as a farmers' co-operative, is a major force in rural business. It manufactures fertilisers and agricultural chemicals, and it operates the Bunnings and Hardwarehouse chains of hardware stores. It has forestry interests, is a coal miner and a supplier of liquefied petroleum gas (LPG). It is also engaged in numerous businesses related to livestock, wool, real estate and rural insurance and finance.

Latest Business Results (June 2003, Full Year)

Profits rose sharply again, in another impressive result. Once more the star was the booming hardware business, thanks in particular to a buoyant home renovation environment. Profits (before interest and tax) for this business were up 17%. Continuing drought conditions forced down revenues and profits for the rural services and insurance division, despite a record result from the Wesfarmers Federation Insurance unit. Energy division profits rose 10%, thanks to increased export sales volumes and higher selling prices for coal, and enhanced LPG margins. Industrial and safety distribution division profits soared 38%, driven by sales increases and cost savings resulting from logistics improvements and from the successful integration of the Atkins Carlyle, Protector and Alsafe businesses. Profits rose 7% for chemicals and fertilisers, thanks to increased efficiencies.

Outlook

Wesfarmers continues to ride the home renovation boom. It currently operates 116 warehouse hardware stores, and plans to open eight to twelve new ones each year, and is expanding to New Zealand. Rural businesses are also improving steadily with the lifting of the drought. Wesfarmers has acquired, for $320 million, the Australian and New Zealand insurance and associated businesses of Edward Lumley Holdings, and plans a major new insurance division. However, there are fears that energy operations will be hit by the strengthened Australian dollar and by lower coal prices. Wesfarmers has low debt levels and there is considerable speculation that it is looking for further major acquisitions, such as the $2.4 billion Dampier–Bunbury natural gas pipeline in Western Australia, or a transport infrastructure venture, in order to maintain its powerful growth record.

WES Year to 30 June	2002	2003
Revenues ($mn)	7,192.5	7,425.8
Hardware (%)	41	45
Rural services & insurance (%)	22	19
Industrial & safety distribution (%)	14	14
Energy (%)	13	14
Chemicals & fertilisers (%)	6	6
EBIT ($mn)	687.6	859.8
EBIT margin (%)	9.6	11.6
Gross margin (%)	27.0	28.5
Operating profit before tax ($mn)	607.3	788.6
Profit after tax ($mn)	413.9	538.2
Earnings per share (¢)	116.0	142.9
Cashflow per share (¢)	197.9	220.4
Dividend (¢)	111	127
Percentage franked	100	100
Net tangible assets per share ($)	4.79	5.95
Interest cover (times)	8.6	12.1
Return on equity (%)	16.6	15.0
Debt-to-equity ratio (%)	38.6	23.5
Current ratio	1.2	1.4

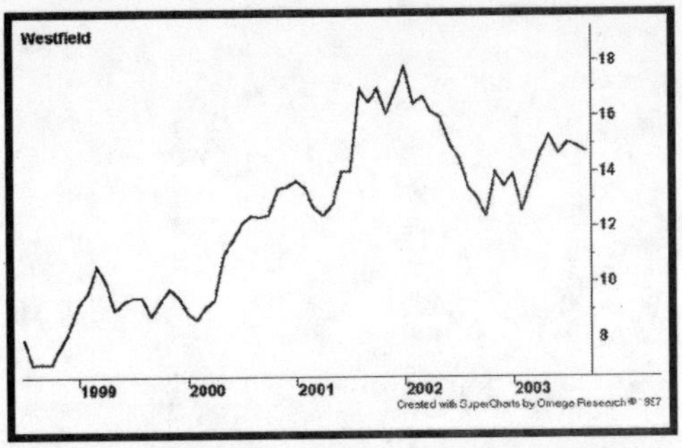

www.westfield.com.au

Westfield Holdings Limited

Share price ($)	15.02	
12-month high ($)	15.85	
12-month low ($)	12.04	
Market capitalisation ($mn)	8,455.2	
Price-to-NTA-per-share ratio	5.2	
5-year share price return (% p.a.)	17.2	
Sector: Financials	**Company**	**Sector**
Price-earnings ratio (times)	29.4	16.2
Dividend yield (%)	1.7	4.5

Westfield Holdings is one of the world's largest shopping centre companies. It has expertise in all aspects of shopping centres, acting as developer, architect, builder, property manager and funds manager. It is currently manager of a $31.7 billion portfolio of shopping centre assets – mainly owned by Westfield Trust and Westfield America Trust – that comprise over 8.7 million square metres of retail space and include 17,500 retail businesses in 115 shopping centres, in Australia, the United States, United Kingdom and New Zealand.

Latest Business Results (June 2003, Full Year)

A series of acquisitions by the Westfield group, notably the $4.8 billion Rodamco North America and the $1.5 billion Richard E. Jacobs portfolios of properties (owned by Westfield America Trust), contributed to another solid boost to Westfield's profits. Australian stores also performed well, with comparable specialty store sales up 6.5% for the year, and a figure of 2.3% for New Zealand. Occupancy levels remained in excess of 99.5%. During the year redevelopment projects valued at $290 million were completed in Australia and New Zealand. In the US, redevelopment projects valued at US$370 million were completed.

Outlook

The Westfield group continues to grow strongly, both organically and through acquisition, including the $1.9 billion purchase of the AMP Shopping Centre Trust. In Australia and New Zealand, as of June 2003, projects with a value of $2.4 billion were either under construction or in the advanced planning process, an increase of $540 million since June 2002. These included the major redevelopment of Westfield Bondi Junction, due to be completed in mid 2004. In the US, projects with a value of US$1.4 billion were either under construction or in the advanced planning process, up from US$515 million in June 2002. The company has received outline planning consent for three major British development projects totalling £780 million in value. Westfield has been considering the launch of a new specialist British property trust. Altogether, the company has reported that at June 2003 it had $6.4 billion worth of projects in the development pipeline, while future opportunities in excess of $5 billion had been identified.

WSF Year to 30 June	2002	2003
Revenues ($mn)	930.1	1,101.9
EBIT ($mn)	353.1	401.1
EBIT margin (%)	38.0	36.4
Operating profit before tax ($mn)	288.6	360.4
Profit after tax ($mn)	234.2	288.4
Earnings per share (¢)	42.1	51.1
Cashflow per share (¢)	46.4	54.8
Dividend (¢)	21.05	25.57
Percentage franked	48	45
Net tangible assets per share ($)	2.59	2.88
Interest cover (times)	5.5	9.9
Return on equity (%)	21.2	18.7
Debt-to-equity ratio (%)	77.1	57.5
Current ratio	1.0	1.0

Westpac Banking Corporation

Share price ($)	15.95	
12-month high ($)	17.14	
12-month low ($)	12.83	
Market capitalisation ($mn)	28,765.8	
Price-to-NTA-per-share ratio	2.9	
5-year share price return (% p.a.)	16.8	
Sector: Financials	**Company**	**Sector**
Price-earnings ratio (times)	13.2	16.2
Dividend yield (%)	4.4	4.5

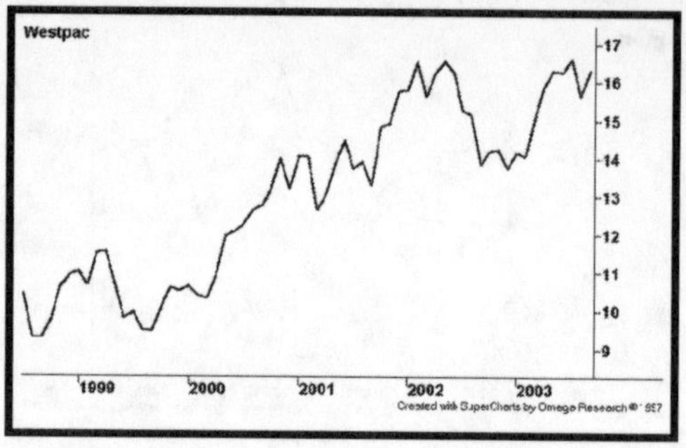

www.westpac.com.au

Westpac, which began trading in 1817 as the Bank of New South Wales, is one of Australia's big four banks, with interests in most areas of financial services. Around 15% of revenues and profit come from New Zealand, where Westpac Trust is the country's leading bank. It is moving strongly into wealth management, and has acquired BT Financial Group and Rothschild Australia Asset Management.

Latest Business Results (March 2003, Half Year)

Firm profit growth was again achieved, and without the benefit of Australian Guarantee Corporation earnings that were included in the 2002 first-half results. Excluding the impact of all acquisitions and divestments, the ongoing businesses boosted after-tax profit by 20%. The business and consumer banking group delivered 13% profit growth, driven by efficiency improvements and by a rise of 18% in outstanding home loans and 10% for business lending. Institutional banking earnings soared 64%, underpinned by good growth in customer business, improved financial market performances and reduced bad debts. New Zealand profit was up 46%. BT Financial Group earnings rose 10%.

Outlook

Westpac believes it can sustain profit growth even in the event of a housing downturn. It continues to boost productivity, with the cost-to-income ratio falling to 50.0% in March 2003, down from 52.8% a year before. Its target is annual revenue growth of 5% to 8%, while restricting expense growth to 2%. The BT operation experienced significant outflows in the wake of the acquisition, and though it has some $8 billion in funds under management, this is less than initial projections. However, the bank sees significant profit potential in the integration of the BT unit with its other wealth management businesses. Westpac has announced a new drive to gain market share in the small business sector, where it lags its rivals.

WBC Year to 30 September	2001	2002
Operating income ($mn)	6,737.0	7,263.0
Net interest income ($mn)	4,200.0	4,285.0
Operating expenses ($mn)	3,570.0	3,995.0
Operating profit before tax ($mn)	2,734.0	2,807.0
Profit after tax ($mn)	1,903.0	2,192.0
Earnings per share (¢)	105.7	121.0
Dividend (¢)	62	70
Percentage franked	100	100
Non-interest income to total income (%)	37.7	41.0
Cost-to-income ratio (%)	53.0	55.0
Return on equity (%)	20.1	21.8
Return on assets (%)	1.1	1.2
Half Year to 31 March	**2002**	**2003**
Operating income ($mn)	3,522.0	3,635.0
Operating profit before tax ($mn)	1,463.0	1,486.0
Profit after tax ($mn)	1,018.0	1,051.0
Earnings per share (¢)	54.8	56.0
Dividend (¢)	34	38
Percentage franked	100	100
Net tangible assets per share ($)	4.95	5.46

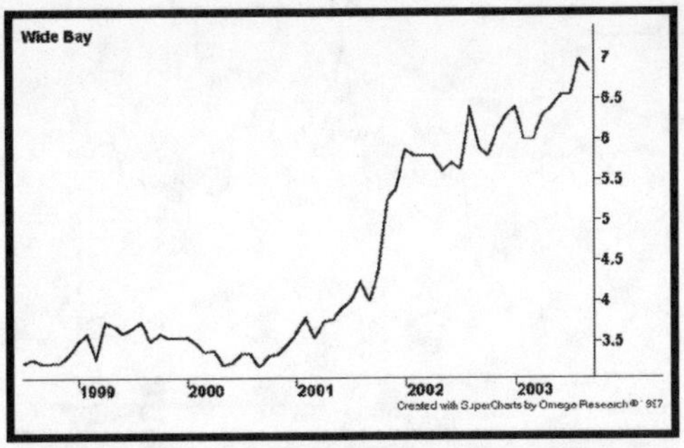

www.widebaycap.com.au

Wide Bay Capricorn Building Society Limited

Share price ($)	6.76	
12-month high ($)	6.81	
12-month low ($)	5.62	
Market capitalisation ($mn)	135.3	
Price-to-NTA-per-share ratio	1.7	
5-year share price return (% p.a.)	23.2	
Sector: Financials	**Company**	**Sector**
Price-earnings ratio (times)	14.9	16.2
Dividend yield (%)	4.7	4.5

Based in Bundaberg in Queensland, Wide Bay Capricorn Building Society was founded in 1979 from the merger of two smaller building societies. It is a leading provider of financial services in southeast and central Queensland, with a large network of branches. It has since merged with two more building societies to become one of Queensland's largest non-bank deposit-taking institutions. It operates a financial planning joint venture with Financial Technologies Securities. A 44%-owned subsidiary, Fincom is marketing automatic teller machine technology and software in Australia and abroad. It has expanded its lending base into Sydney, Melbourne and Adelaide.

Latest Business Results (June 2003, Full Year)

Continuing growth in home lending helped Wide Bay achieve higher revenues and profits, its fifth consecutive earnings increase. Loans approved for the year totalled $378 million, up nearly 24% from the previous year, with a 38% jump in the June 2003 half over the previous half. However, rising costs led to a small rise in the cost-to-income ratio. The company's captive lenders' mortgage insurer, Mortgage Risk Management, performed well, to show an after-tax surplus of nearly $1 million.

Outlook

The company experienced a high level of home loan 'churning' in the first half of the year – finance brokers trying to entice borrowers to refinance with another institution, in order to reap additional broking fees. This slowed the growth of Wide Bay's loan book during this period. However, a series of retention initiatives has led to an easing of this problem, as evidenced by the strong growth of lending in the second half of the year. Interstate operations continue to blossom, with Sydney, Melbourne and Adelaide all showing an increasing contribution to the loans book. The company is now working to install, by March 2004, an in-house electronic processing system for its home loan application processing, which is expected to provide significant cost savings. Mortgage Risk Management is expected to post strong profit growth in the June 2004 year.

WBB Year to 30 June	2002	2003
Operating income ($mn)	30.6	33.8
Net interest income ($mn)	23.8	24.8
Operating expenses ($mn)	18.2	20.5
Operating profit before tax ($mn)	12.4	13.3
Profit after tax ($mn)	8.8	9.2
Earnings per share (¢)	43.9	45.5
Dividend (¢)	32	32
Percentage franked	100	100
Non-interest income to total income (%)	22.1	26.8
Net tangible assets per share ($)	3.83	3.96
Cost-to-income ratio (%)	59.5	60.7
Return on equity (%)	14.8	11.7
Return on assets (%)	1.5	1.3

Woodside Petroleum Limited

Share price ($)	13.59	
12-month high ($)	13.84	
12-month low ($)	10.00	
Market capitalisation ($mn)	8,946.7	
Price-to-NTA-per-share ratio	4.5	
5-year share price return (% p.a.)	11.8	
Sector: Energy	**Company**	**Sector**
Price-earnings ratio (times)	12.4	11.0
Dividend yield (%)	2.9	2.8

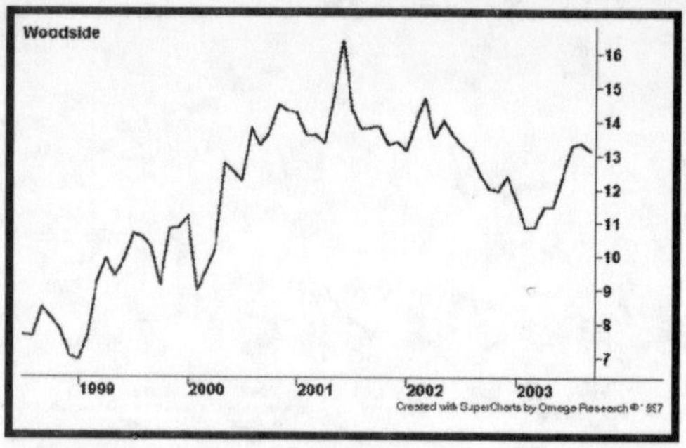

www.woodside.com.au

Perth-based Woodside, founded in 1954, is Australia's largest listed specialist energy company. Its major interest is the North West Shelf project off Western Australia, which supplies liquefied natural gas (LNG) for Japan, natural gas for the domestic market and liquefied petroleum gas (LPG), crude oil and condensate for international markets. Its oil fields include the Laminaria and Legendre projects, and it has exploration activities in several countries. Shell Australia owns 34% of Woodside's equity.

Latest Business Results (June 2003, Half Year)

Sales and profits were up. Production of 29.9 million barrels of oil equivalent was actually 3% down on the June 2002 half, but timing considerations meant that sales volumes rose 3%. Lower production, in line with expectations, from the Laminaria, Legendre and Cossack properties, was largely offset by an improved production performance from domestic gas, condensate and LNG. Domestic gas deliveries improved 23%, due to higher customer demand, while LNG production and sales increased 3%, thanks to high market demand. Condensate sales increased by 11%. The average realised sales price of A$46.49 per barrel of oil equivalent represented a 22% increase on the June 2002 half.

WPL Year to 31 December	2001	2002
Revenues ($mn)	2,398.3	2,240.6
EBIT ($mn)	1,257.6	1,109.1
EBIT margin (%)	52.4	49.5
Gross margin (%)	59.0	57.7
Operating profit before tax ($mn)	1,187.8	1,063.1
Profit after tax ($mn)	817.8	729.4
Earnings per share (¢)	122.7	109.4
Cashflow per share (¢)	174.2	150.8
Dividend (¢)	34	39
Percentage franked	100	100
Interest cover (times)	18.0	24.1
Return on equity (%)	35.1	29.9

Half Year to 30 June	2002	2003
Revenues ($mn)	977.0	1,118.6
Operating profit before tax ($mn)	314.0	436.8
Profit after tax ($mn)	197.1	272.2
Earnings per share (¢)	29.6	40.8
Dividend (¢)	16	21
Percentage franked	100	100
Net tangible assets per share ($)	4.13	3.00
Debt-to-equity ratio (%)	54.0	61.9
Current ratio	1.2	1.1

Outlook

Woodside has a 20-year supply agreement, starting from 1989, with eight Japanese electric power and gas companies to supply 7.5 million tonnes annually of LNG, and this underpins profits. Its business will receive a substantial boost from a $25 billion contract to supply China's Guangdong Province with three million tonnes of North West Shelf LNG annually for 25 years from 2005–06. Woodside has a 16.7% stake in this contract, and is in negotiation with its North West Shelf partners on a proposed $1.5 billion fifth LNG production train. Woodside has significant oil and gas interests in Mauritania, Algeria and the Timor Sea.

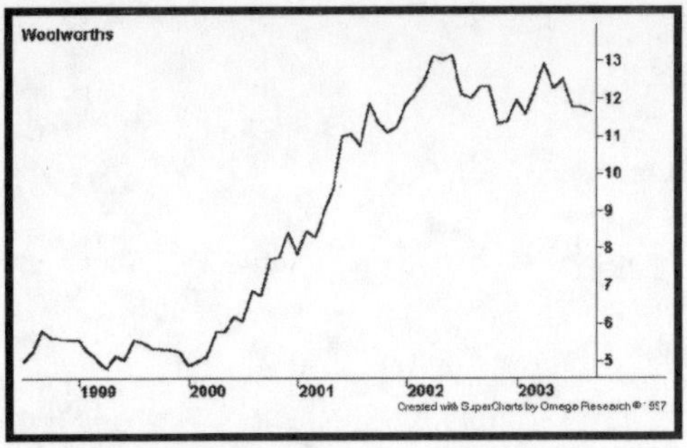

www.woolworths.com.au

Woolworths Limited

Share price ($)	11.85	
12-month high ($)	13.19	
12-month low ($)	10.64	
Market capitalisation ($mn)	12,178.7	
Price-to-NTA-per-share ratio	9.8	
5-year share price return (% p.a.)	18.8	
Sector: Consumer Staples	**Company**	**Sector**
Price-earnings ratio (times)	19.1	17.9
Dividend yield (%)	3.3	3.6

Woolworths, founded in Sydney in 1924, is one of Australia's retail giants, with around 10% of the total retail market and an estimated 28% of all grocery sales. Its 1,400 Australian stores include Safeway, Big W, Dick Smith Electronics, Tandy, Dan Murphy Liquor, MGW Hotels (50% owned) and Plus Petrol. It also owns 33 Dick Smith Electronics stores in New Zealand. It has sold its wholesale division.

Latest Business Results (June 2003, Full Year)

The June 2003 results span 52 weeks, whereas the June 2002 results are for 53. On a comparable 52-week basis, sales were up 12% and after-tax profit up 16.5%. Supermarket sales (including petrol) rose 11.9%, with food and liquor sales up 9.4%. There were 18 net new supermarket stores opened during the year, bringing the total to 694. Petrol sales surged 56%, with the company opening 31 petrol canopies, to give it a total of 287. It now claims around 11% of national petrol sales. Big W sales rose 11.3%, with eight new stores, and consumer electronics stores recorded 20% sales growth.

Outlook

Woolworths has a diverse range of strategies that it believes will help it to maintain growth. Among its many growth targets are the opening of 15 to 25 new supermarkets each year. It also plans to increase its Big W chain from the present 104 stores to about 150. Another target is annual liquor sales of $2.5 billion, up from $1.7 billion in 2002–03, and there is speculation that it may make some major acquisitions to help achieve this goal quickly. It plans to move into medicines, with its first licensed pharmacist operating a pharmacy within a supermarket planned for 2004. It will also significantly increase its health and beauty offering in around 100 stores during 2003–04. It plans a new joint venture petrol business with Caltex Australia, which will add a further 160 outlets to its chain. It calculates that its 'Refresh' efficiency project has delivered cost savings of $1.7 billion over four years. The project has now entered its second stage, with the company believing it can cut costs by a further 1% within five years.

WOW Year to 29 June*	2002	2003
Revenues ($mn)	24,473.0	26,321.4
Supermarkets (%)	85	86
Big W (%)	9	9
Consumer electronics (%)	3	3
EBIT ($mn)	832.7	945.7
EBIT margin (%)	3.4	3.6
Gross margin (%)	23.1	23.3
Operating profit before tax ($mn)	782.2	906.0
Profit after tax ($mn)	563.0	650.6
Earnings per share (¢)	54.1	62.0
Cashflow per share (¢)	87.8	100.0
Dividend (¢)	33	39
Percentage franked	100	100
Net tangible assets per share ($)	1.21	1.20
Interest cover (times)	16.5	23.8
Return on equity (%)	33.7	35.8
Debt-to-equity ratio (%)	13.0	19.7
Current ratio	0.8	0.8

** 30 June 2002.*

PART II

THE TABLES

Tables Index

Table A

Market Capitalisation

A company's market capitalisation is determined by multiplying the share price by the number of shares. To be included in this book, a company must be in the All Ordinaries Index, which comprises the 500 largest companies by market capitalisation.

	$mn
BHP Billiton	66,465.0
Telstra	60,482.0
National Australia Bank	49,259.8
Commonwealth Bank	37,156.2
Westpac Banking	28,765.8
ANZ	27,612.9
Rio Tinto	16,458.3
Woolworths	12,178.7
St George Bank	10,758.8
Wesfarmers	10,554.3
Foster's Group	9,306.4
Woodside Petroleum	8,946.7
Coles Myer	8,935.6
Westfield Holdings	8,455.2
Amcor	7,437.7
Macquarie Bank	6,707.9
Suncorp-Metway	6,502.5
AXA Asia Pacific	6,230.9
QBE Insurance Group	6,230.9
Australian Gas Light	4,821.1
Tabcorp Holdings	4,167.3
Santos	3,529.1
Boral	3,179.5
Origin Energy	2,769.6
Harvey Norman	2,734.8
Leighton Holdings	2,652.2
Flight Centre	2,122.1
Toll Holdings	2,102.1
PaperlinX	2,089.8
CSR	1,983.8
Coal & Allied Industries	1,857.2
Cochlear	1,806.9
Perpetual Trustees Australia	1,413.8
Washington H. Soul Pattinson	1,408.0
Australian Stock Exchange	1,364.0
National Foods	1,119.3
Brickworks	1,097.3
Bendigo Bank	1,092.8
Spotless Group	1,039.5
Iluka Resources	1,003.4
Australand Holdings	960.6
Sims Group	957.1
Incitec Pivot	903.4
Reece Australia	835.6
GWA International	808.4
Adelaide Bank	752.5

	$mn
Rural Press	740.0
Downer EDI	679.2
Bank of Queensland	676.6
Pacifica Group	661.7
Australian Pharmaceutical Industries	612.3
Crane Group	581.9
Hills Industries	542.2
OPSM Group	515.2
Coates Hire	496.2
STW Communications Group	496.0
Pacific Hydro	476.0
McGuigan Simeon Wines	457.3
Ridley	442.8
Miller's Retail	430.3
GUD Holdings	347.4
AV Jennings Homes	342.2
United Group	336.5
FKP	287.6
Timbercorp	284.2
Alesco	253.5
OAMPS	234.4
Freedom Group	227.5
Campbell Brothers	212.9
Fleetwood	206.6
McPherson's	201.1
ARB	200.5
Select Harvests	192.6
Rebel Sport	185.5
SDI	163.3
Central Equity	151.7
Gazal	144.1
Wide Bay Capricorn Building Society	135.3
Peter Lehmann Wines	128.0
Casinos Austria	110.7
K&S	108.0
Sydney Aquarium	105.3
Blackmores	104.1
Institute of Drug Technology	97.1
Danks Holdings	91.0
Monadelphous Group	80.5
Angus & Coote	73.3
HGL	68.5
Rock Building Society	52.8
Wadepack	51.2
CMI	47.3

Table B

Revenues

This list ranks the companies in the book according to their most recent full-year revenues figures (operating income for the banks). The figures include revenues from sales and services, but other revenues – such as interest receipts and investment income – are not generally included.

	$mn
Coles Myer	27,016.6
Woolworths	26,321.4
BHP Billiton	23,400.3
Telstra	20,495.0
Rio Tinto	19,945.0
National Australia Bank	11,870.0
Amcor	10,709.9
Commonwealth Bank	9,399.0
Wesfarmers	7,425.8
CSR	7,282.9
Westpac Banking	7,263.0
ANZ	6,988.0
QBE Insurance Group	5,642.0
Leighton Holdings	4,848.5
Foster's Group	4,731.5
Suncorp-Metway	4,022.0
Australian Gas Light	3,872.4
Boral	3,831.0
PaperlinX	3,628.1
Origin Energy	3,326.5
AXA Asia Pacific	2,992.0
Downer EDI	2,573.5
Toll Holdings	2,569.8
Australian Pharmaceutical Industries	2,471.5
Spotless Group	2,359.6
Woodside Petroleum	2,240.6
St George Bank	2,185.0
Crane Group	1,911.7
Tabcorp Holdings	1,900.7
Macquarie Bank	1,890.0
Sims Group	1,579.7
Santos	1,478.4
Ridley	1,410.9
Harvey Norman	1,379.1
National Foods	1,225.0
Coal & Allied Industries	1,181.4
Australand Holdings	1,138.5
Westfield Holdings	1,101.9
Pacifica Group	1,077.3
Miller's Retail	1,049.7
Incitec Pivot	950.2
Iluka Resources	894.5
United Group	855.2
Reece Australia	740.2
Hills Industries	660.6
GWA International	659.6

	$mn
Flight Centre	605.9
AV Jennings Homes	529.5
OPSM Group	482.6
Rural Press	463.8
Danks Holdings	433.3
Freedom Group	397.8
Alesco	392.1
Coates Hire	378.4
GUD Holdings	372.4
Washington H. Soul Pattinson	371.0
Campbell Brothers	359.3
Bendigo Bank	346.6
K&S	293.3
McGuigan Simeon Wines	290.5
Cochlear	288.6
FKP	278.6
Rebel Sport	276.9
Perpetual Trustees Australia	265.0
McPherson's	248.7
Monadelphous Group	243.7
Central Equity	220.5
Angus & Coote	217.9
Adelaide Bank	201.1
Australian Stock Exchange	195.1
Gazal	194.7
OAMPS	191.5
CMI	191.2
Fleetwood	188.5
Brickworks	179.6
Bank of Queensland	173.9
STW Communications Group	122.5
Timbercorp	97.2
Blackmores	94.7
ARB	88.0
Wadepack	84.9
HGL	83.9
Select Harvests	81.0
Pacific Hydro	68.9
Peter Lehmann Wines	46.1
Casinos Austria	41.2
SDI	36.7
Wide Bay Capricorn Building Society	33.8
Institute of Drug Technology	25.5
Sydney Aquarium	23.6
Rock Building Society	20.2

Table C

EBIT Margin

A company's earnings before interest and taxation (EBIT) is sometimes regarded as a better measure of its profitability than the straight pre-tax or post-tax profit figure. EBIT is derived by adding net interest payments (that is, interest payments minus interest receipts) to the pre-tax profit. Different companies choose different methods of financing their operations; by adding back interest payments to their profits we can help minimise these differences and make comparisons between companies more valid.

The EBIT margin is the EBIT figure as a percentage of annual sales. Clearly a high figure is to be desired, though of course this can be achieved artificially by inflating borrowings (and hence interest payments). And it is noteworthy that efficient companies like some of the giant retailers can operate most satisfactorily on low margins.

The EBIT margin figure has little relevance for banks – whose high interest payments to their customers mean they have virtually no EBIT – and they have been excluded, as have the insurance companies.

	%		%		%
Woodside Petroleum	49.5	Harvey Norman	18.6	Hills Industries	8.2
Timbercorp	45.0	Australian Gas Light	17.6	National Foods	7.6
Brickworks	43.8	HGL	17.4	OPSM Group	7.3
Pacific Hydro	43.5	ARB	16.7	CMI	7.2
Australian Stock Exchange	40.6	Flight Centre	15.9	Sims Group	7.2
Sydney Aquarium	38.5	AV Jennings Homes	15.3	Campbell Brothers	7.0
Westfield Holdings	36.4	Wadepack	15.3	Freedom Group	7.0
Santos	36.2	Iluka Resources	14.4	Amcor	6.8
Perpetual Trustees Australia	35.2	FKP	14.3	PaperlinX	6.4
Casinos Austria	35.0	GWA International	13.8	K&S	6.1
Washington H. Soul Pattinson	31.8	CSR	13.4	Toll Holdings	6.1
BHP Billiton	31.0	Boral	12.5	Alesco	5.9
STW Communications Group	30.9	OAMPS	12.3	Miller's Retail	5.3
Coal & Allied Industries	28.0	GUD Holdings	11.9	Ridley	5.1
Telstra	27.9	Australand Holdings	11.6	Crane Group	5.0
Cochlear	27.8	Wesfarmers	11.6	Angus & Coote	4.8
Rio Tinto	23.7	Coates Hire	11.4	Downer EDI	4.8
Institute of Drug Technology	23.5	Blackmores	10.7	Leighton Holdings	4.6
Rural Press	23.5	Incitec Pivot	10.3	Spotless Group	4.6
Tabcorp Holdings	22.9	Fleetwood	9.9	United Group	4.3
SDI	22.0	Reece Australia	9.0	Monadelphous Group	4.1
Select Harvests	21.5	Origin Energy	8.9	Woolworths	3.6
Foster's Group	20.5	Pacifica Group	8.6	Coles Myer	2.5
Peter Lehmann Wines	19.6	Rebel Sport	8.5	Danks Holdings	2.0
Central Equity	19.3	McPherson's	8.3	Aust. Pharmaceutical Industries	1.8
McGuigan Simeon Wines	19.3	Gazal	8.2		

Table D

After-Tax Profit

This table ranks all the companies according to their most recent full-year after-tax profit.

	$mn		$mn
National Australia Bank	3,779.0	Spotless Group	51.6
Telstra	3,429.0	Adelaide Bank	51.2
Rio Tinto	2,818.0	Reece Australia	46.7
BHP Billiton	2,788.6	Crane Group	46.4
ANZ	2,322.0	Pacifica Group	44.3
Westpac Banking	2,192.0	Ridley	37.2
Commonwealth Bank	2,012.0	Australian Pharmaceutical Industries	34.0
Woodside Petroleum	729.4	Coates Hire	33.2
Woolworths	650.6	Central Equity	32.8
Foster's Group	568.1	McGuigan Simeon Wines	32.2
St George Bank	563.0	Miller's Retail	30.5
CSR	561.0	Bank of Queensland	28.7
Wesfarmers	538.2	Pacific Hydro	28.4
Amcor	431.4	GUD Holdings	27.4
Coles Myer	429.5	Hills Industries	27.2
Suncorp-Metway	384.0	FKP	26.7
Macquarie Bank	333.0	STW Communications Group	25.3
AXA Asia Pacific	330.0	OPSM Group	24.3
Santos	322.1	Timbercorp	22.8
Australian Gas Light	320.8	United Group	21.9
Westfield Holdings	288.4	OAMPS	18.1
Boral	283.2	Freedom Group	18.0
QBE Insurance Group	277.0	Rebel Sport	16.3
Tabcorp Holdings	263.1	Alesco	12.7
Origin Energy	162.0	Campbell Brothers	11.9
Coal & Allied Industries	159.7	McPherson's	11.8
Harvey Norman	151.0	Fleetwood	11.2
Leighton Holdings	140.0	K&S	11.1
PaperlinX	132.1	Select Harvests	11.0
Iluka Resources	109.0	ARB	10.3
Toll Holdings	106.1	Gazal	9.7
Australand Holdings	90.4	Wide Bay Capricorn Building Society	9.2
Sims Group	75.0	HGL	8.0
Brickworks	72.7	Casinos Austria	7.9
Washington H. Soul Pattinson	72.7	Wadepack	7.6
Flight Centre	70.0	CMI	7.2
Rural Press	68.4	Monadelphous Group	7.1
Perpetual Trustees Australia	68.2	Blackmores	6.2
Downer EDI	66.6	Sydney Aquarium	6.0
Incitec Pivot	65.1	Angus & Coote	5.7
Australian Stock Exchange	61.3	SDI	5.5
National Foods	60.1	Peter Lehmann Wines	5.4
Bendigo Bank	59.0	Danks Holdings	5.2
Cochlear	58.2	Institute of Drug Technology	4.2
AV Jennings Homes	56.8	Rock Building Society	3.9
GWA International	55.0		

Table E

Return on Equity

Shareholder's equity is the company's assets minus its liabilities. It is, in theory, the amount owned by the shareholders of the company. Return on equity is the after-tax profit expressed as a percentage of that equity. Thus, it is the amount of profit that the company managers made for you – the shareholder – from your assets. For many investors it is one of the most important gauges of how well a company is doing. It is one of the requirements for inclusion in this book that companies have a return on equity of at least 9% in their latest financial year.

	%
Cochlear	59.7
Woolworths	35.8
Sydney Aquarium	34.0
Australian Stock Exchange	29.9
Blackmores	29.9
Woodside Petroleum	29.9
ARB	29.5
AV Jennings Homes	28.8
Rebel Sport	27.9
SDI	27.5
Perpetual Trustees Australia	25.1
Wadepack	24.9
Rio Tinto	23.5
Flight Centre	23.2
Telstra	23.2
Monadelphous Group	22.8
GUD Holdings	22.1
CSR	22.0
Westpac Banking	21.8
ANZ	21.1
Coal & Allied Industries	21.1
McPherson's	21.0
Reece Australia	21.0
Freedom Group	20.8
Toll Holdings	20.6
Sims Group	20.4
Tabcorp Holdings	20.3
K&S	20.2
Select Harvests	20.1
OPSM Group	19.9
OAMPS	19.5
Central Equity	19.1
STW Communications Group	19.0
Westfield Holdings	18.7
HGL	17.7
Hills Industries	17.5
Fleetwood	17.4
Harvey Norman	17.0
Institute of Drug Technology	17.0
Leighton Holdings	17.0
St George Bank	16.6
Incitec Pivot	16.4
FKP	16.2
National Australia Bank	16.2
Rock Building Society	16.2
Macquarie Bank	15.8

	%
BHP Billiton	15.3
Miller's Retail	15.1
United Group	15.1
Wesfarmers	15.0
Pacific Hydro	14.6
Pacifica Group	14.6
Iluka Resources	14.4
National Foods	14.4
Adelaide Bank	14.2
Boral	13.9
Timbercorp	13.8
GWA International	13.7
Foster's Group	13.2
McGuigan Simeon Wines	13.0
Australian Gas Light	12.8
Brickworks	12.6
Australand Holdings	12.4
CMI	12.4
Bank of Queensland	12.3
Coles Myer	12.1
Ridley	12.0
Crane Group	11.8
Gazal	11.8
Peter Lehmann Wines	11.7
Wide Bay Capricorn Building Society	11.7
Santos	11.5
Bendigo Bank	11.3
Coates Hire	11.3
Rural Press	11.3
Australian Pharmaceutical Industries	11.1
Casinos Austria	11.1
Washington H. Soul Pattinson	11.1
Angus & Coote	11.0
Suncorp-Metway	11.0
AXA Asia Pacific	10.8
Danks Holdings	10.5
Spotless Group	10.5
Commonwealth Bank	10.3
Alesco	10.0
QBE Insurance Group	9.9
Amcor	9.8
Origin Energy	9.7
Campbell Brothers	9.4
PaperlinX	9.2
Downer EDI	9.1

Table F

Debt-to-Equity Ratio

A company's borrowings as a percentage of its shareholder's equity is one of the most common measures of corporate debt. Many investors will be wary of a company with a ratio that is too high. However, a company with a steady business and a regular income flow – such as an electric power company or a large supermarket chain – is generally considered relatively safe with a high level of debt, whereas a small company in a new business field might be thought at risk with even moderate debt levels. Much depends on surrounding circumstances, including the prevailing interest rates. Of course, it is often from borrowing that a company grows, and some investors are not happy buying shares in a company with little or no debt.

There are various ways to calculate the ratio, but for this book the net debt position is used. That is, a company's cash has been deducted from its borrowings. For inclusion in this book no company was allowed a debt-to-equity ratio of more than 75%. Some of the companies had no net debt – their cash position was greater than the amount of their borrowings – and so have a zero figure in this table. The ratio has no relevance for banks, so they have been excluded.

	%		%		%
Aust. Pharmaceutical Industries	0.0	Danks Holdings	18.8	Angus & Coote	45.9
Australian Stock Exchange	0.0	Rural Press	19.5	BHP Billiton	46.6
AXA Asia Pacific	0.0	CSR	19.7	Central Equity	46.6
Cochlear	0.0	Woolworths	19.7	Sydney Aquarium	47.0
Flight Centre	0.0	Washington H. Soul Pattinson	21.7	Tabcorp Holdings	49.0
HGL	0.0	QBE Insurance Group	22.9	GWA International	50.2
Incitec Pivot	0.0	Wesfarmers	23.5	Alesco	53.4
Institute of Drug Technology	0.0	Fleetwood	24.3	Timbercorp	54.2
Leighton Holdings	0.0	United Group	26.1	Australand Holdings	55.0
Monadelphous Group	0.0	Gazal	27.8	Wadepack	55.0
OAMPS	0.0	Hills Industries	27.9	Miller's Retail	55.1
Perpetual Trustees Australia	0.0	Freedom Group	28.3	Crane Group	57.5
Rebel Sport	0.0	Pacifica Group	33.1	Westfield Holdings	57.5
Reece Australia	0.0	Santos	33.9	Foster's Group	58.9
Sims Group	0.0	OPSM Group	35.7	Spotless Group	61.0
STW Communications Group	0.0	Coates Hire	35.8	Woodside Petroleum	61.9
Brickworks	5.0	Boral	35.9	Coal & Allied Industries	62.3
Casinos Austria	5.1	Blackmores	36.2	Peter Lehmann Wines	62.3
Coles Myer	6.6	Harvey Norman	37.7	Australian Gas Light	63.1
National Foods	7.1	Downer EDI	39.0	CMI	63.3
PaperlinX	8.8	K&S	39.9	McGuigan Simeon Wines	65.4
ARB	10.5	Amcor	40.4	Rio Tinto	66.1
FKP	12.1	Origin Energy	40.9	Campbell Brothers	67.8
Pacific Hydro	14.5	Ridley	41.2	McPherson's	68.6
Select Harvests	14.5	Toll Holdings	41.7	Telstra	73.0
SDI	14.7	AV Jennings Homes	43.3		
GUD Holdings	16.5	Iluka Resources	43.5		

Table G

Current Ratio

The current ratio is simply the company's current assets divided by its current liabilities. Current assets are cash or assets that can, in theory, be converted quickly into cash. Current liabilities are normally those payable within a year. The current ratio measures the ability of a company to repay in a hurry its short-term debt, should the need arise. Banks are not included.

	Ratio		Ratio
HGL	4.0	Boral	1.4
Institute of Drug Technology	3.4	Coles Myer	1.4
Peter Lehmann Wines	2.9	Downer EDI	1.4
Australand Holdings	2.8	QBE Insurance Group	1.4
PaperlinX	2.8	Wadepack	1.4
SDI	2.8	Washington H. Soul Pattinson	1.4
Australian Stock Exchange	2.6	Wesfarmers	1.4
AV Jennings Homes	2.6	Alesco	1.3
GWA International	2.5	Foster's Group	1.3
McGuigan Simeon Wines	2.4	Miller's Retail	1.3
McPherson's	2.4	Pacifica Group	1.3
FKP	2.2	Rural Press	1.3
Gazal	2.2	United Group	1.3
Iluka Resources	2.2	Blackmores	1.2
Incitec Pivot	2.1	CSR	1.2
Campbell Brothers	2.0	Origin Energy	1.2
Perpetual Trustees Australia	2.0	Australian Gas Light	1.1
Reece Australia	2.0	Casinos Austria	1.1
CMI	1.9	OAMPS	1.1
Danks Holdings	1.9	Santos	1.1
Fleetwood	1.9	Spotless Group	1.1
Rebel Sport	1.9	Woodside Petroleum	1.1
Sims Group	1.9	Amcor	1.0
Cochlear	1.8	Brickworks	1.0
Harvey Norman	1.8	Coates Hire	1.0
Hills Industries	1.8	K&S	1.0
Central Equity	1.7	Pacific Hydro	1.0
GUD Holdings	1.7	Rio Tinto	1.0
Ridley	1.7	Telstra	1.0
STW Communications Group	1.7	Timbercorp	1.0
Angus & Coote	1.6	Toll Holdings	1.0
ARB	1.6	Westfield Holdings	1.0
BHP Billiton	1.6	National Foods	0.8
Freedom Group	1.6	Woolworths	0.8
Select Harvests	1.6	OPSM Group	0.6
Crane Group	1.5	Coal & Allied Industries	0.5
Flight Centre	1.5	Sydney Aquarium	0.4
Monadelphous Group	1.5	Tabcorp Holdings	0.2
Australian Pharmaceutical Industries	1.4		

Table H

Price-Earnings Ratio

The price-earnings ratio (PER) – the current share price divided by the earnings-per-share figure – is one of the best-known of all sharemarket ratios. Essentially it expresses the amount of money investors are ready to pay for each cent or dollar of a company's profits, and it allows you to compare the share prices of different companies with widely different profits. A high PER suggests the market has a high regard for the company and its growth prospects; a low one may mean that investors are disdainful of the stock. The figures in this table are based on share prices as of 20 August 2003.

	Times		Times
CSR	3.4	Fleetwood	16.2
Central Equity	4.5	Rio Tinto	16.2
AV Jennings Homes	6.0	Foster's Group	16.4
CMI	6.4	Blackmores	16.5
Wadepack	6.8	Suncorp-Metway	16.5
HGL	8.4	Amcor	16.7
Iluka Resources	8.9	Pacific Hydro	16.7
K&S	9.8	Sydney Aquarium	16.7
Downer EDI	10.2	Australian Pharmaceutical Industries	16.9
Australand Holdings	10.4	Alesco	17.2
Rural Press	10.5	Origin Energy	17.2
FKP	10.7	Select Harvests	17.4
Santos	10.9	Danks Holdings	17.5
Monadelphous Group	11.0	Telstra	17.8
Boral	11.3	Campbell Brothers	17.9
Rebel Sport	11.3	Reece Australia	17.9
Coal & Allied Industries	11.4	Harvey Norman	18.4
ANZ	11.5	National Foods	18.4
Timbercorp	11.8	Commonwealth Bank	18.6
Ridley	11.9	St George Bank	18.6
Crane Group	12.2	Spotless Group	18.7
OAMPS	12.2	Leighton Holdings	18.9
Freedom Group	12.3	Bendigo Bank	19.1
Sims Group	12.4	Toll Holdings	19.1
Woodside Petroleum	12.4	Woolworths	19.1
GUD Holdings	12.7	ARB	19.2
Angus & Coote	12.9	Hills Industries	19.3
McPherson's	13.0	Macquarie Bank	19.4
Westpac Banking	13.2	STW Communications Group	19.4
National Australia Bank	13.3	Bank of Queensland	19.7
AXA Asia Pacific	13.5	Wesfarmers	19.7
Casinos Austria	13.7	Washington H. Soul Pattinson	19.8
Miller's Retail	13.7	Coles Myer	20.5
Rock Building Society	13.7	Perpetual Trustees Australia	20.8
McGuigan Simeon Wines	13.9	OPSM Group	21.0
PaperlinX	13.9	QBE Insurance Group	21.4
United Group	14.0	Australian Stock Exchange	22.2
Adelaide Bank	14.6	BHP Billiton	23.5
GWA International	14.7	Institute of Drug Technology	23.6
Coates Hire	14.8	Peter Lehmann Wines	23.6
Wide Bay Capricorn Building Society	14.9	Westfield Holdings	29.4
Brickworks	15.0	Flight Centre	29.8
Australian Gas Light	15.1	SDI	30.0
Tabcorp Holdings	15.5	Cochlear	30.9
Gazal	15.6	Incitec Pivot	31.4
Pacifica Group	15.7		

Table I

Dividend Yield

Many investors buy shares for income, rather than for capital growth. They look for companies that offer a high dividend yield (the dividend expressed as a percentage of the share price). Table I ranks the companies in this book according to their historic dividend yields. Note that the franking credits available from some companies can make the dividend yield substantially higher if you are in an appropriate tax bracket. The figures in this table are based on share prices as of 20 August, 2003.

	%
CSR	8.3
HGL	8.3
Central Equity	7.6
Australand Holdings	6.6
AV Jennings Homes	6.3
Monadelphous Group	6.0
Angus & Coote	5.9
CMI	5.9
Tabcorp Holdings	5.9
Sydney Aquarium	5.8
Campbell Brothers	5.5
OAMPS	5.5
Crane Group	5.4
PaperlinX	5.4
Rock Building Society	5.4
Gazal	5.3
GWA International	5.3
Hills Industries	5.3
Miller's Retail	5.3
Sims Group	5.3
Blackmores	5.2
Commonwealth Bank	5.2
Iluka Resources	5.1
National Foods	5.1
Telstra	5.1
Australian Gas Light	5.0
Australian Pharmaceutical Industries	4.9
Casinos Austria	4.9
Santos	4.9
Spotless Group	4.9
ANZ	4.8
FKP	4.8
Alesco	4.7
Freedom Group	4.7
Suncorp-Metway	4.7
Wide Bay Capricorn Building Society	4.7
GUD Holdings	4.5
Leighton Holdings	4.5
National Australia Bank	4.5
Wesfarmers	4.5
K&S	4.4
Westpac Banking	4.4
Adelaide Bank	4.3
McGuigan Simeon Wines	4.3
Boral	4.2
Foster's Group	4.2
Pacifica Group	4.2
United Group	4.2
Downer EDI	4.1
Coates Hire	4.0
McPherson's	4.0
Danks Holdings	3.9
AXA Asia Pacific	3.8
Coal & Allied Industries	3.8
Rural Press	3.8
St George Bank	3.8
STW Communications Group	3.8
Bendigo Bank	3.7
Coles Myer	3.6
Amcor	3.5
QBE Insurance Group	3.5
Ridley	3.4
Select Harvests	3.4
Woolworths	3.3
Bank of Queensland	3.2
Rio Tinto	3.2
Wadepack	3.1
Australian Stock Exchange	3.0
Fleetwood	3.0
Macquarie Bank	2.9
Perpetual Trustees Australia	2.9
Woodside Petroleum	2.9
Institute of Drug Technology	2.6
Peter Lehmann Wines	2.6
ARB	2.5
Reece Australia	2.5
Brickworks	2.4
Incitec Pivot	2.4
Rebel Sport	2.4
Cochlear	2.3
Origin Energy	2.3
Washington H. Soul Pattinson	2.3
BHP Billiton	2.1
Toll Holdings	2.1
Flight Centre	1.9
Harvey Norman	1.9
Timbercorp	1.9
Westfield Holdings	1.7
OPSM Group	1.4
Pacific Hydro	1.4
SDI	1.1

TABLE J

YEAR-ON-YEAR REVENUES GROWTH

Companies generally strive for growth, though profit growth is usually of far more significance than a boost in revenues. In fact, it is possible for a company to increase its revenues by all kinds of means – including cutting profit margins or acquiring other companies – and YOY revenues growth is of little relevance if other ratios are not also improving.

	%
McGuigan Simeon Wines	189.1
Monadelphous Group	57.6
CMI	54.2
STW Communications Group	50.3
Amcor	43.3
FKP	42.6
OAMPS	42.2
Origin Energy	39.2
Australian Gas Light	33.2
Coates Hire	29.8
Australian Pharmaceutical Industries	29.6
Flight Centre	29.0
Toll Holdings	26.1
Harvey Norman	22.9
Institute of Drug Technology	22.3
PaperlinX	22.2
Brickworks	21.9
QBE Insurance Group	21.8
Wadepack	21.2
Fleetwood	19.0
Bendigo Bank	18.8
Westfield Holdings	18.5
United Group	18.4
Macquarie Bank	18.1
Rebel Sport	16.6
Reece Australia	16.3
Blackmores	16.2
Crane Group	16.2
OPSM Group	16.2
Adelaide Bank	16.1
Suncorp-Metway	14.9
Freedom Group	13.9
Hills Industries	13.8
AV Jennings Homes	13.6
St George Bank	13.5
Cochlear	13.2
Sims Group	12.1
National Foods	11.7
ARB	11.6
Danks Holdings	11.2
Rock Building Society	10.7
Wide Bay Capricorn Building Society	10.6
Boral	9.8
K&S	9.7
Woolworths	9.6
Downer EDI	9.5

	%
ANZ	9.1
Miller's Retail	8.9
Perpetual Trustees Australia	8.6
Pacific Hydro	8.5
Spotless Group	8.3
GWA International	8.2
Gazal	8.1
Westpac Banking	7.8
SDI	7.2
Campbell Brothers	6.9
Bank of Queensland	6.5
Rural Press	6.4
Central Equity	5.4
Coles Myer	5.2
CSR	4.3
Commonwealth Bank	3.7
Foster's Group	3.5
Select Harvests	3.4
National Australia Bank	3.3
Wesfarmers	3.2
Peter Lehmann Wines	3.0
GUD Holdings	1.8
Telstra	1.5
Santos	1.3
Angus & Coote	1.0
Ridley	0.2
Australian Stock Exchange	–0.3
Iluka Resources	–0.7
Rio Tinto	–1.2
McPherson's	–1.7
Tabcorp Holdings	–1.7
Alesco	–2.1
Leighton Holdings	–2.6
Incitec Pivot	–3.3
Sydney Aquarium	–3.4
HGL	–4.8
Timbercorp	–4.9
Pacifica Group	–5.0
Woodside Petroleum	–6.6
Australand Holdings	–7.7
BHP Billiton	–16.8
Coal & Allied Industries	–18.1
AXA Asia Pacific	–28.8
Casinos Austria	–55.6
Washington H. Soul Pattinson	–59.7

Table K

Year-on-Year EPS Growth

The earnings-per-share (EPS) figure is a crucial one. It tells you – the shareholder – what your part is of the company's profits, for each of your shares. So investors invariably look for EPS growth in a stock. The YOY EPS growth figure is often one of the first ratios that investors look to when evaluating a stock.

	%		%
Wadepack	387.9	National Foods	15.1
Rebel Sport	120.2	Westpac Banking	14.5
AV Jennings Homes	93.4	Bendigo Bank	14.0
Iluka Resources	65.5	Freedom Group	10.4
Spotless Group	57.3	Australian Gas Light	10.2
FKP	55.8	Reece Australia	10.1
Coates Hire	55.7	Amcor	8.6
Sims Group	52.2	Downer EDI	7.1
CMI	49.6	Flight Centre	7.1
Monadelphous Group	46.8	Hills Industries	7.1
Boral	45.9	Ridley	6.5
Brickworks	40.0	Bank of Queensland	5.8
Fleetwood	39.1	Tabcorp Holdings	5.8
Pacifica Group	37.6	Pacific Hydro	5.3
GUD Holdings	36.9	Gazal	5.2
SDI	35.8	AXA Asia Pacific	5.0
Crane Group	33.8	Australand Holdings	3.7
Cochlear	31.8	Wide Bay Capricorn Building Society	3.6
Central Equity	31.4	Australian Stock Exchange	3.1
HGL	30.5	Campbell Brothers	2.3
STW Communications Group	29.3	CSR	2.3
Toll Holdings	28.6	Angus & Coote	2.0
McGuigan Simeon Wines	28.5	Institute of Drug Technology	–0.1
Washington H. Soul Pattinson	28.2	Foster's Group	–0.2
OAMPS	26.2	Danks Holdings	–0.8
Rural Press	25.5	PaperlinX	–3.3
K&S	25.2	Sydney Aquarium	–3.5
ARB	24.3	QBE Insurance Group	–3.8
Macquarie Bank	24.3	OPSM Group	–4.4
ANZ	23.8	Telstra	–6.3
Adelaide Bank	23.7	National Australia Bank	–6.6
Select Harvests	23.4	BHP Billiton	–7.1
Wesfarmers	23.2	Incitec Pivot	–7.6
United Group	23.1	Miller's Retail	–8.7
Origin Energy	23.0	Australian Pharmaceutical Industries	–10.0
Westfield Holdings	21.5	Woodside Petroleum	–10.8
Blackmores	21.0	Rio Tinto	–12.3
Suncorp-Metway	20.2	Timbercorp	–13.6
St George Bank	19.9	Leighton Holdings	–18.1
Coles Myer	19.4	Rock Building Society	–18.3
McPherson's	18.3	Peter Lehmann Wines	–23.5
GWA International	17.9	Santos	–23.9
Alesco	17.5	Commonwealth Bank	–24.4
Woolworths	16.9	Coal & Allied Industries	–24.8
Perpetual Trustees Australia	16.3	Casinos Austria	–41.0
Harvey Norman	16.0		

TABLE L

YEAR-ON-YEAR RETURN ON EQUITY GROWTH

Company managers have a variety of strategies they can use to boost profits. It is much harder to lift the return on equity (ROE). Find a company with a high ROE figure, and one that is growing year by year, and the chances are that you have found a real growth stock.

	%
Wadepack	336.1
Rebel Sport	65.0
AV Jennings Homes	64.4
Coates Hire	61.2
CSR	59.3
McGuigan Simeon Wines	54.1
Iluka Resources	53.8
Spotless Group	47.4
Pacifica Group	46.2
FKP	43.4
Boral	36.9
Sims Group	35.9
GUD Holdings	33.8
Brickworks	28.1
Monadelphous Group	27.8
HGL	26.2
St George Bank	22.9
Crane Group	20.4
K&S	18.7
Washington H. Soul Pattinson	18.7
Central Equity	17.6
ANZ	14.8
Alesco	14.2
GWA International	13.8
BHP Billiton	12.1
CMI	11.6
SDI	11.4
Origin Energy	9.9
Blackmores	9.7
United Group	9.4
Ridley	8.4
Westpac Banking	8.4
Woolworths	8.2
National Foods	7.5
Select Harvests	7.5
Suncorp-Metway	7.1
Macquarie Bank	6.2
Fleetwood	6.1
Bendigo Bank	6.0
ARB	5.7
Rural Press	5.2
Perpetual Trustees Australia	4.8
McPherson's	4.7
Coles Myer	4.3
Amcor	4.1
Australian Gas Light	4.1
Downer EDI	4.0
AXA Asia Pacific	3.8
Australand Holdings	3.1
OAMPS	2.7
Adelaide Bank	–1.0
Tabcorp Holdings	–1.5
Gazal	–1.8
Rock Building Society	–3.0
Angus & Coote	–3.3
Campbell Brothers	–4.9
Hills Industries	–5.0
QBE Insurance Group	–5.2
Danks Holdings	–6.0
Reece Australia	–6.0
Harvey Norman	–6.5
Foster's Group	–7.0
Rio Tinto	–7.1
OPSM Group	–7.6
Pacific Hydro	–9.0
Wesfarmers	–9.3
National Australia Bank	–9.6
Australian Stock Exchange	–10.0
PaperlinX	–10.2
Cochlear	–10.3
Institute of Drug Technology	–11.9
Westfield Holdings	–11.9
Freedom Group	–12.7
Bank of Queensland	–13.2
Sydney Aquarium	–13.3
Telstra	–13.3
Woodside Petroleum	–14.6
Incitec Pivot	–14.8
Australian Pharmaceutical Industries	–15.8
Toll Holdings	–16.9
STW Communications Group	–17.5
Wide Bay Capricorn Building Society	–21.0
Leighton Holdings	–23.1
Commonwealth Bank	–27.4
Flight Centre	–31.3
Peter Lehmann Wines	–33.3
Santos	–34.9
Miller's Retail	–35.8
Timbercorp	–36.2
Coal & Allied Industries	–36.7
Casinos Austria	–45.2

Table M

Year-on-Year Dividend Growth

Most investors hope for a rising dividend, and this table tells how much each company raised (or lowered) its dividend in its latest financial year.

	%		%
Rebel Sport	650.0	Foster's Group	10.3
Pacifica Group	135.3	Telstra	9.1
Origin Energy	100.0	National Australia Bank	8.9
Monadelphous Group	78.6	Alesco	8.3
STW Communications Group	71.2	Central Equity	8.3
Pacific Hydro	66.7	Fleetwood	7.7
GUD Holdings	57.6	Amcor	7.1
Rural Press	53.2	GWA International	6.9
Cochlear	51.0	Coal & Allied Industries	6.7
SDI	50.0	Tabcorp Holdings	6.3
Sims Group	50.0	Blackmores	6.1
Toll Holdings	45.0	Australian Gas Light	5.8
Wadepack	42.9	AV Jennings Homes	5.3
United Group	40.0	Hills Industries	5.0
K&S	39.1	Leighton Holdings	4.8
Select Harvests	37.0	Spotless Group	4.5
McGuigan Simeon Wines	33.3	Suncorp-Metway	3.7
Incitec Pivot	32.1	Bank of Queensland	3.6
Brickworks	29.0	Rock Building Society	2.8
Ridley	27.8	Commonwealth Bank	2.7
McPherson's	25.0	Coles Myer	2.0
Reece Australia	23.5	PaperlinX	1.9
ARB	23.1	Gazal	1.8
St George Bank	23.1	Australand Holdings	0.0
Washington H. Soul Pattinson	21.7	Australian Pharmaceutical Industries	0.0
Westfield Holdings	21.5	Campbell Brothers	0.0
Boral	21.1	Casinos Austria	0.0
Downer EDI	20.8	CMI	0.0
Woolworths	20.5	Danks Holdings	0.0
Crane Group	20.0	Freedom Group	0.0
FKP	20.0	Iluka Resources	0.0
Institute of Drug Technology	20.0	Macquarie Bank	0.0
National Foods	18.2	Perpetual Trustees Australia	0.0
HGL	17.1	Santos	0.0
QBE Insurance Group	16.7	Wide Bay Capricorn Building Society	0.0
ANZ	16.4	AXA Asia Pacific	–0.5
Flight Centre	16.0	Australian Stock Exchange	–2.5
Adelaide Bank	15.6	Sydney Aquarium	–3.6
Bendigo Bank	15.5	BHP Billiton	–5.5
Woodside Petroleum	14.7	Rio Tinto	–8.1
Wesfarmers	14.4	OAMPS	–15.0
Westpac Banking	12.9	Peter Lehmann Wines	–18.2
Angus & Coote	12.5	CSR	–29.2
Miller's Retail	11.8	Timbercorp	–37.5
Coates Hire	11.1	OPSM Group	–62.1
Harvey Norman	11.1		

Table N

Year-on-Year EBIT Margin Growth

The EBIT (earnings before interest and taxation) margin is one of the measures of a company's efficiency. So a rising margin is much to be desired, as it suggests that a company is achieving success in cutting its costs. This table does not include banks or insurance companies.

	%
Washington H. Soul Pattinson	236.9
Wadepack	171.0
Rebel Sport	92.8
Casinos Austria	75.0
AV Jennings Homes	63.2
Iluka Resources	46.3
HGL	44.6
Cochlear	37.5
Sims Group	32.9
Angus & Coote	30.9
SDI	27.5
Boral	26.8
GUD Holdings	24.9
OAMPS	24.6
Central Equity	22.1
Wesfarmers	21.1
Timbercorp	20.6
McPherson's	20.0
Fleetwood	19.7
United Group	18.4
Pacifica Group	15.7
FKP	15.1
Alesco	14.9
Select Harvests	14.3
Coles Myer	14.2
Rural Press	13.0
Toll Holdings	12.9
Australand Holdings	10.4
ARB	10.1
McGuigan Simeon Wines	9.8
Hills Industries	9.4
Spotless Group	9.3
Crane Group	8.2
K&S	7.1
Woolworths	5.6
GWA International	5.4
Perpetual Trustees Australia	4.8
Freedom Group	3.6
Coal & Allied Industries	3.4
National Foods	3.1
Sydney Aquarium	2.7
Tabcorp Holdings	2.3
Blackmores	1.5
Brickworks	1.4
Leighton Holdings	1.4
Australian Stock Exchange	1.3
CSR	1.1
Gazal	–0.1
Harvey Norman	–0.3
Campbell Brothers	–0.4
Downer EDI	–0.8
BHP Billiton	–1.0
STW Communications Group	–2.8
OPSM Group	–4.0
Westfield Holdings	–4.1
Reece Australia	–4.6
Australian Gas Light	–5.1
Foster's Group	–5.2
CMI	–5.3
Woodside Petroleum	–5.6
Monadelphous Group	–6.3
Ridley	–7.6
Danks Holdings	–8.1
Origin Energy	–8.1
Coates Hire	–8.2
Miller's Retail	–8.6
Telstra	–9.3
Amcor	–10.3
PaperlinX	–11.3
Pacific Hydro	–14.1
Rio Tinto	–16.2
Institute of Drug Technology	–17.1
Peter Lehmann Wines	–17.2
Flight Centre	–17.8
Incitec Pivot	–21.2
Santos	–22.4
Australian Pharmaceutical Industries	–23.6

TABLE O

PRICE TO NTA-PER-SHARE RATIO

The NTA-per-share figure expresses the worth of a company's net tangible assets – that is, its assets minus its liabilities and intangible assets – for each share of the company. Intangible assets, such as goodwill or the value of newspaper mastheads, are excluded because it is deemed difficult to place a value on them (though this proposition is debatable), and also because they might not have much worth if separated from the company. The price-to-NTA-per-share ratio relates this figure to the share price.

A ratio of one means that the company is valued exactly according to the value of its assets. A ratio below one suggests that the shares are a bargain, though usually there is a good reason for this. Profits are more important than assets.

In some respects this is an 'old economy' ratio. For many high-tech companies in the 'new economy' the most important assets are human ones whose worth does not appear on the balance sheet.

Two companies, Spotless Group and Tabcorp Holdings, with a negative NTA-per-share figure – as a result of having intangible assets valued at more than their remaining net assets – have been omitted from this table.

	Ratio		Ratio		Ratio
Central Equity	0.8	Washington H. Soul Pattinson	2.3	Rio Tinto	4.0
CMI	0.8	Bendigo Bank	2.4	Institute of Drug Technology	4.1
AXA Asia Pacific	1.2	Pacifica Group	2.4	Toll Holdings	4.1
Iluka Resources	1.2	QBE Insurance Group	2.4	St George Bank	4.2
Santos	1.2	Suncorp-Metway	2.4	Foster's Group	4.4
Angus & Coote	1.4	Bank of Queensland	2.5	National Foods	4.4
Australand Holdings	1.4	Commonwealth Bank	2.5	Blackmores	4.5
HGL	1.4	Pacific Hydro	2.5	GUD Holdings	4.5
Timbercorp	1.4	Incitec Pivot	2.6	Woodside Petroleum	4.5
PaperlinX	1.5	Peter Lehmann Wines	2.6	Wesfarmers	4.7
AV Jennings Homes	1.6	Aust. Pharmaceutical Industries	2.7	Miller's Retail	4.8
Downer EDI	1.6	Casinos Austria	2.7	United Group	4.9
FKP	1.6	Coles Myer	2.7	Select Harvests	5.0
Boral	1.7	Gazal	2.8	Telstra	5.0
Coates Hire	1.7	Rebel Sport	2.8	Sydney Aquarium	5.2
Ridley	1.7	Sims Group	2.8	Westfield Holdings	5.2
Wadepack	1.7	Amcor	2.9	McPherson's	5.5
Wide Bay Capricorn Blding Soc.	1.7	Harvey Norman	2.9	Alesco	5.6
Adelaide Bank	1.8	Origin Energy	2.9	ARB	5.6
Brickworks	1.8	STW Communications Group	2.9	Perpetual Trustees Australia	6.1
Crane Group	1.8	Westpac Banking	2.9	Australian Stock Exchange	6.5
Danks Holdings	1.8	Macquarie Bank	3.0	OAMPS	7.3
CSR	1.9	Leighton Holdings	3.2	Woolworths	9.8
K&S	2.0	Hills Industries	3.4	SDI	10.2
McGuigan Simeon Wines	2.1	Reece Australia	3.5	Flight Centre	10.8
ANZ	2.2	Campbell Brothers	3.6	OPSM Group	12.6
National Australia Bank	2.2	BHP Billiton	3.7	GWA International	14.5
Coal & Allied Industries	2.3	Fleetwood	3.9	Cochlear	15.1
Monadelphous Group	2.3	Freedom Group	3,9	Rural Press	125.9
Rock Building Society	2.3	Australian Gas Light	4.0		

Table P

Five-Year Share Price Returns

This table ranks the return to investors from a five-year investment in each of the companies in the book. It is the accumulated return, which means it incorporates not only capital gain but also reinvested dividends, bonus stock and rights issues. Five-year return figures were not available for Australian Stock Exchange, Incitec Pivot, Origin Energy and PaperlinX.

	% pa
SDI	102.0
Toll Holdings	69.5
OAMPS	60.9
Flight Centre	50.4
Institute of Drug Technology	47.2
Select Harvests	46.5
Miller's Retail	45.3
AV Jennings Homes	45.2
McPherson's	40.9
ARB	40.2
Fleetwood	39.9
Pacific Hydro	38.0
Cochlear	37.9
STW Communications Group	34.9
Reece Australia	34.9
FKP	33.7
Brickworks	32.3
K&S	31.8
Timbercorp	30.6
GUD Holdings	30.5
Rebel Sport	28.2
Wadepack	27.5
CMI	27.5
Coal & Allied Industries	26.7
McGuigan Simeon Wines	25.5
Angus & Coote	25.1
Washington H. Soul Pattinson	24.3
Macquarie Bank	23.7
CSR	23.7
Wesfarmers	23.6
Wide Bay Capricorn Building Society	23.2
Perpetual Trustees Australia	23.1
Hills Industries	22.8
Gazal	22.0
Bendigo Bank	21.4
ANZ	20.4
Australand Holdings	20.2
St George Bank	19.8
Amcor	19.1
Monadelphous Group	19.0
Woolworths	18.8
Casinos Austria	18.7
Boral	18.7
Sims Group	18.2

	% pa
Leighton Holdings	18.2
Peter Lehmann Wines	18.1
Danks Holdings	17.9
BHP Billiton	17.5
Westfield Holdings	17.2
Freedom Group	17.2
Westpac Banking	16.8
Crane Group	15.2
Central Equity	15.2
Rock Building Society	14.7
QBE Insurance Group	14.6
National Foods	14.6
Downer EDI	14.6
Bank of Queensland	14.6
Rio Tinto	14.5
Spotless Group	14.2
Alesco	14.1
National Australia Bank	13.6
Adelaide Bank	13.6
United Group	13.2
Blackmores	13.2
Commonwealth Bank	13.1
Rural Press	12.9
Campbell Brothers	12.3
Woodside Petroleum	11.8
Suncorp-Metway	11.6
Iluka Resources	11.1
Ridley	10.5
GWA International	10.3
Santos	10.2
Australian Pharmaceutical Industries	9.9
Sydney Aquarium	9.5
Tabcorp Holdings	9.1
Pacifica Group	8.7
Harvey Norman	8.6
HGL	8.4
OPSM Group	8.1
Foster's Group	7.5
Coates Hire	6.3
Coles Myer	4.7
Australian Gas Light	3.3
Telstra	–0.3
AXA Asia Pacific	–1.2

Table Q

Non-Interest Income to Total Income

The final three tables rank the banks only. Most of the banks are working to diversify away from their traditional lending business into other operations, such as insurance and funds management. This table ranks them according to their success, showing how much of their income derives from non-interest sources.

	%		%
Macquarie Bank	86.9	National Australia Bank	39.2
Suncorp-Metway	85.3	St George Bank	39.0
Rock Building Society	63.6	Bank of Queensland	37.2
Commonwealth Bank	46.5	Bendigo Bank	35.9
ANZ	42.5	Wide Bay Capricorn Building Society	26.8
Westpac Banking	41.0	Adelaide Bank	16.7

Table R

Cost-to-Income Ratio

All the banks are working to reduce their high costs. The cost-to-income ratio – expressing costs as a percentage of operating income – is one of the measures commonly used by analysts to ascertain their success.

	%		%
ANZ	41.6	Wide Bay Capricorn Building Society	60.7
National Australia Bank	50.1	Bendigo Bank	69.8
Westpac Banking	55.0	Bank of Queensland	71.3
St George Bank	57.1	Rock Building Society	72.7
Commonwealth Bank	59.1	Macquarie Bank	75.7
Adelaide Bank	59.7	Suncorp-Metway	83.6

TABLE S

RETURN ON ASSETS

Banks have large assets, and the return on assets ratio – profits as a percentage of total assets – is another popular measure of their efficiency.

	%		%
ANZ	1.3	Rock Building Society	1.0
Wide Bay Capricorn Building Society	1.3	Suncorp-Metway	1.0
Westpac Banking	1.2	Commonwealth Bank	0.8
Macquarie Bank	1.1	Adelaide Bank	0.7
St George Bank	1.1	Bendigo Bank	0.7
National Australia Bank	1.0	Bank of Queensland	0.6

APPENDIX

SEPARATING THE WHEAT FROM THE CHAFF

BY ALAN HULL, AUTHOR OF *ACTIVE INVESTING*
www.alanhull.com

In order to lessen the impact of short-term factors which affect opinion on our portfolio – rumours, market cycles, speculation, etc. – we need to ensure that a company's fundamentals are the main driving force behind the market dynamic. The specific market dynamic we want to isolate is depicted by the following diagram.

Figure 1

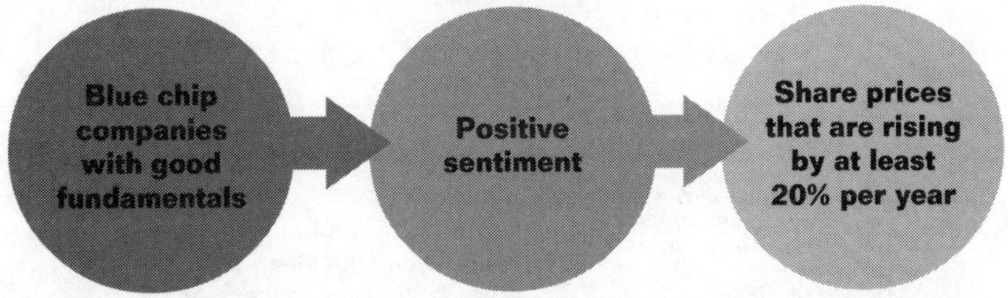

The fact that our blue chip companies have good fundamentals doesn't necessarily mean that those fundamentals are the sole cause of rising share prices. We must perform qualitative analysis to eliminate as many of the unpredictable short-term factors which affect opinion as we possibly can. Consider the chart of Cochlear overleaf (Figure 2).

We want to pinpoint shares like Cochlear that will keep us smiling for years and doing very little work to manage our portfolio. Therefore we must seek out shares which are similar in nature to Cochlear, insofar as they are devoid of volatility. The key phrase here is 'shares which are rising steadily over time' where 'steadily' is the key word.

Our arch enemy is volatility. Fundamentals are a factor that affect share prices over the long term and don't cause price activity to behave violently. Figure 3 is also a chart of a blue chip share with good fundamentals, but its share price is being influenced by other factors. This is evident in the short-term, erratic price activity.

Technically, Coles Myer might fit all of our search criteria, but its price chart bears scant resemblance to Cochlear's. At this juncture we can either indulge in endless debate with exponents of other market disciplines about the probable future direction of the share price, or we can simply accept that it is not conforming to our particular market dynamic. I choose the latter option because I'm here to run a business and make money rather than enter into fruitless and time-wasting debate. There are usually plenty of shares which do conform to our specific market dynamic.

Figure 2

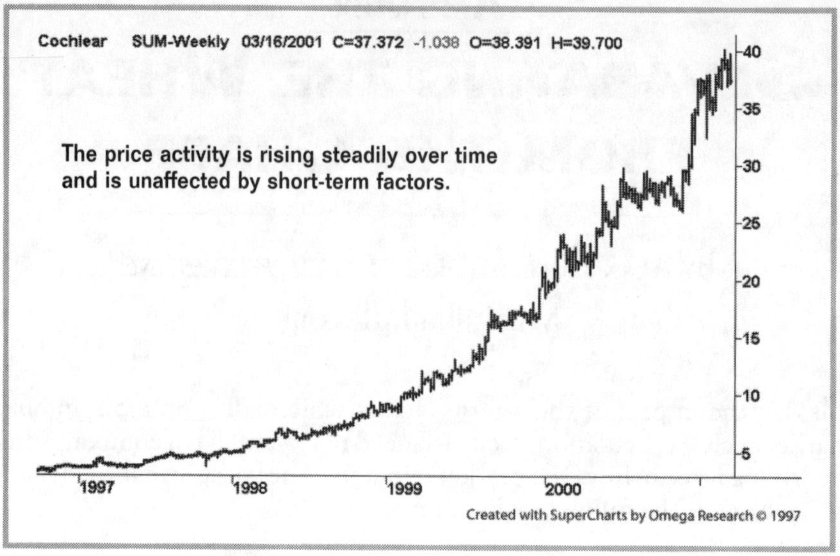

Figure 3

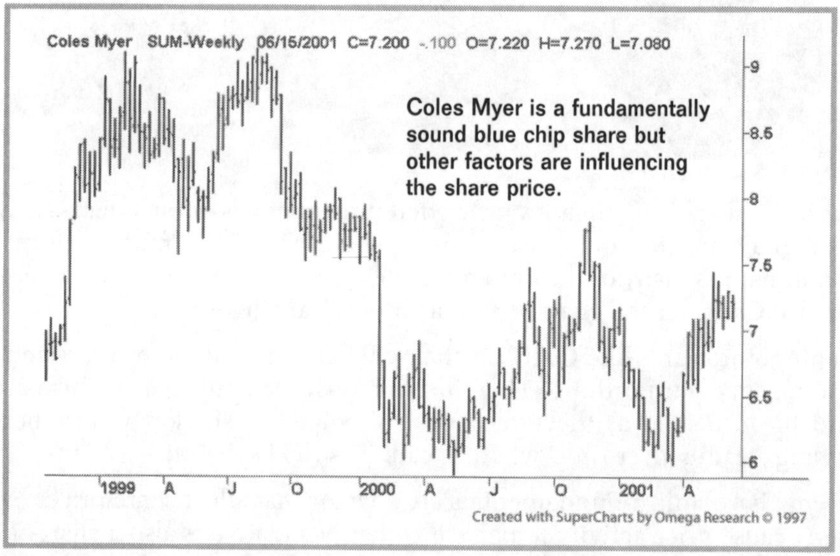

Multiple Moving Averages

Our assessments of Cochlear and Coles Myer are based wholly on our interpretation of their respective price charts. We can make the job of selecting shares to buy a lot easier by using a charting method which will visually isolate the effect of short-term and long-term factors on shares. The chart opposite (Figure 4) has two moving averages – a short-term average of five weeks and a long-term average of 30 weeks.

Figure 4

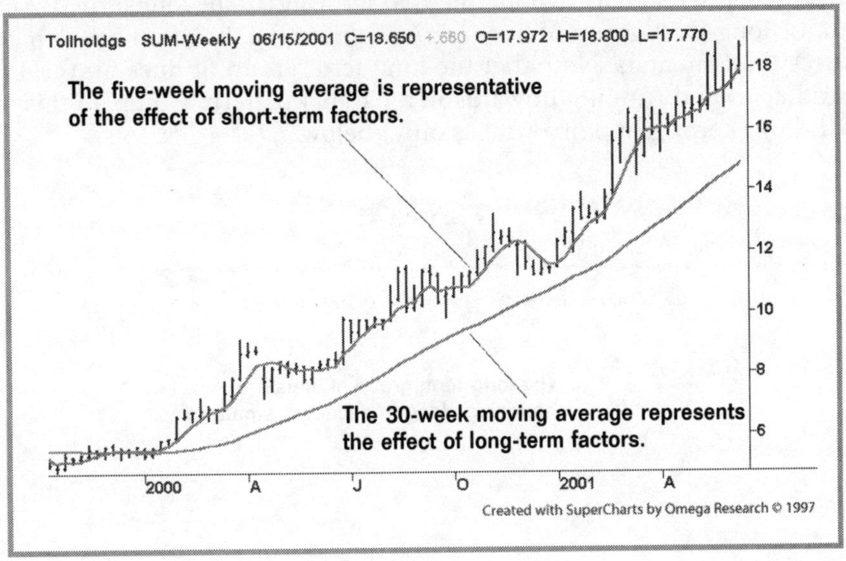

On a short-term basis, we can see that Toll Holdings' share price is repeatedly rising and falling. But in the long term, it is rising steadily.

To enhance this picture even further, we can add more moving averages with different values, and switch off the price bars. The following chart shows Toll Holdings with a group of six short-term moving averages and a group of six long-term moving averages.

Figure 5

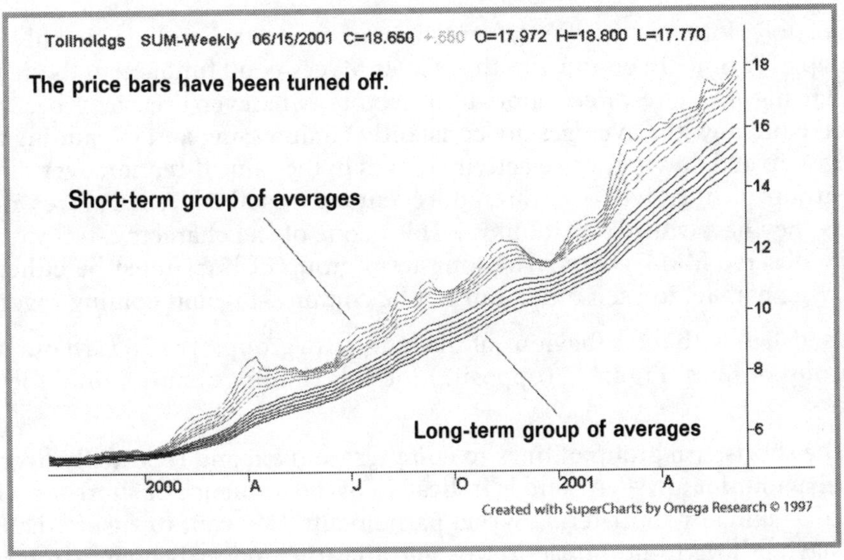

Chartists refer to this type of chart as a 'Multiple Moving Average' or MMA chart. The technique of having two groups of averages to represent the effect of short-term and long-term market factors was originally developed by Daryl Guppy. By employing this method we can clearly see the behaviour of price activity in both the short term and in the long term. We are primarily interested in the long-term group of lines because this is the time frame which is influenced by a company's fundamentals. Note that the long-term group of lines on the Toll Holdings chart is spread apart and running upwards in a parallel pattern. Compare this to the MMA chart of CML (long-term group of averages only) below.

Figure 6

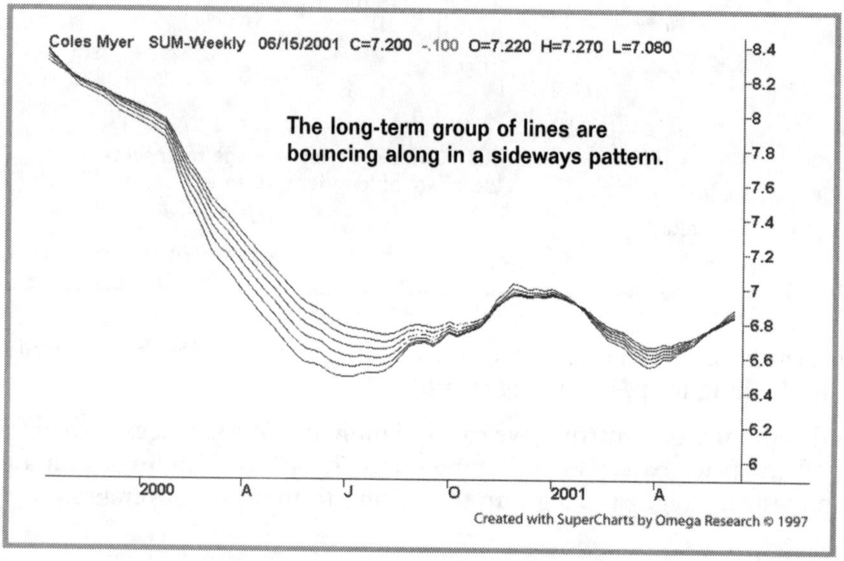

In the case of Toll Holdings, the fundamentalists are in control and are steadily moving the share price up over time. In contrast to this, Coles Myer's good fundamentals are not the key factor influencing its share price. Short-term factors, whatever they may be, are having a large impact. Note how the averages are constantly compressing and expanding as the price activity moves up and down. If price activity moves in the same direction over time, then the long-term group of lines will separate and eventually establish themselves in a parallel formation as they have with Toll Holdings. This is one of the characteristics we are looking for when we observe MMA charts. The long-term group of lines must be either spreading apart or moving parallel to each other, but not be compressing and coming together.

Once we're satisfied with the behaviour of the long-term group, we can turn our attention to the short group of lines. Figure 7 (opposite), of Toll Holdings, shows only the short-term group of lines.

We expect the short-term group of lines to compress and expand repeatedly over time. This is normal behaviour for any share and is indicative of the influence of short-term factors and frequent profit-taking by short-term market participants. We want to ensure that short-term factors are having little to no impact on us and that they never become strong enough to overpower the longer-term factors, namely good fundamentals. To this end, we want to see the short-term group of averages bouncing along in a consistent and uniform pattern.

If short-term factors are capable of taking control of the share price then we will be able to observe this on an MMA chart in crossovers between the short-term and long-term groups of lines. This type of extreme volatility in the short-term group of averages indicates that the balance of control between the short-term and long-term factors is fairly even. Figure 8, below, shows an example of this. This is not a situation we want to buy into... literally.

Figure 7

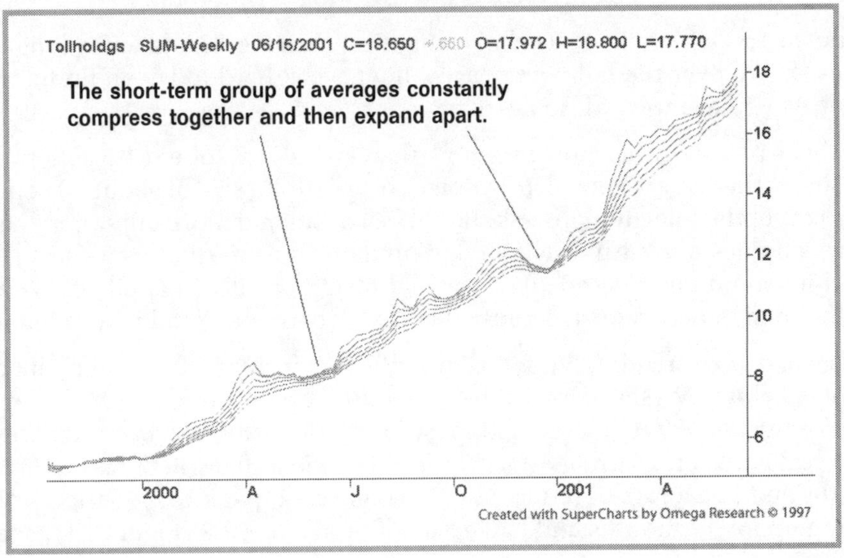

Figure 8

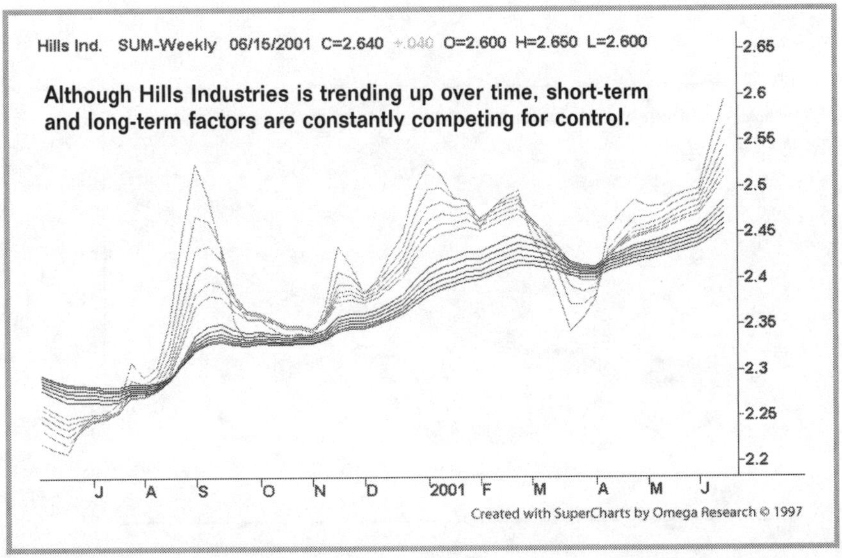

To summarise the qualities that we are looking for:

- The long-term group of averages must be spreading apart or running parallel with each other.
- The long-term group must be trending upwards.
- The straighter the long-term group of lines, the better.
- The short-term group should be behaving in a consistent, repetitive manner.
- The short-term group must not cross into the long-term group.

If we seek out shares which have the above qualities, then we should enjoy long-term trends like the ones shown over the following pages. If we work hard today on finding these kinds of shares, we won't have to work tomorrow.

This is the final phase of the hunt for good shares, and we should be able to narrow the number of shares that we are considering down to a portfolio size of about 10 using the MMA charts. This part of the selection process should be considered more important than choosing shares with high rates of return. Having good fundamentals in the driver's seat is of primary concern and it should take precedence over optimising profits. I happily own shares which don't have sky-high rates of return, because they do have smooth, gradually rising share prices.

Toll Holdings had been trending up for 17 months and in June 2001 had a rate of return of 55% (Figure 9, below). Wesfarmers had been trending up for nine months and in June 2001 had a rate of return of 48% (Figure 10, opposite). Woolworths had been trending up for 13 months and had a rate of return of 40% (Figure 11, opposite). Miller's had been trending up for 10 months and had a rate of return of 61% (Figure 12, page 132). Suncorp Metway had been trending up for 12 months and had a rate of return of 40% (Figure 13, page 132).

Assessing MMA charts is a subjective process and the guidelines given here, mixed with plenty of practice, will help make your opinion profitable. However, MMA charts do not provide us with any exit signals – they are only used for selecting shares to buy. There are better and less ambiguous techniques for knowing when to sell.

Figure 9

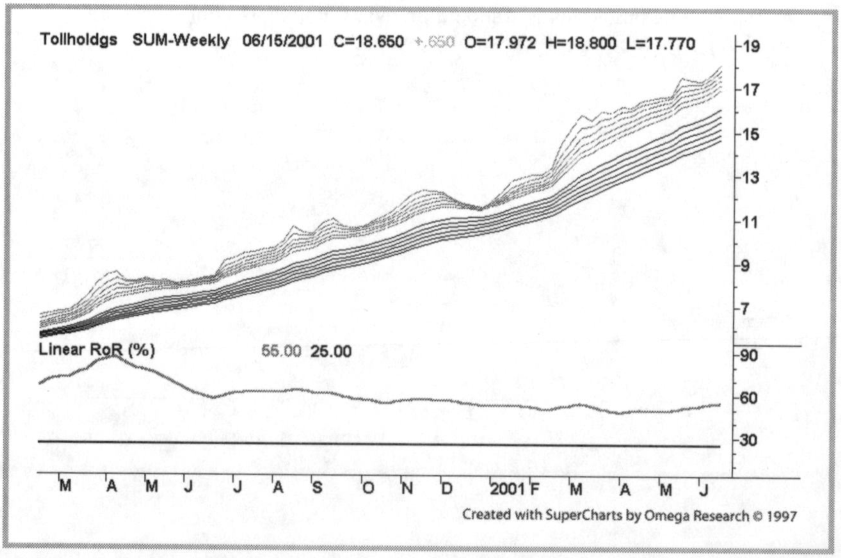

Figure 10

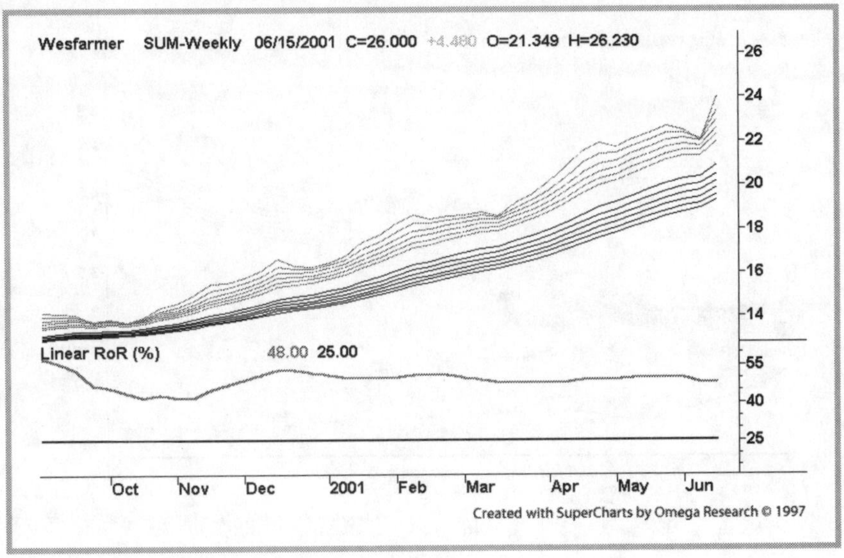

Figure 11

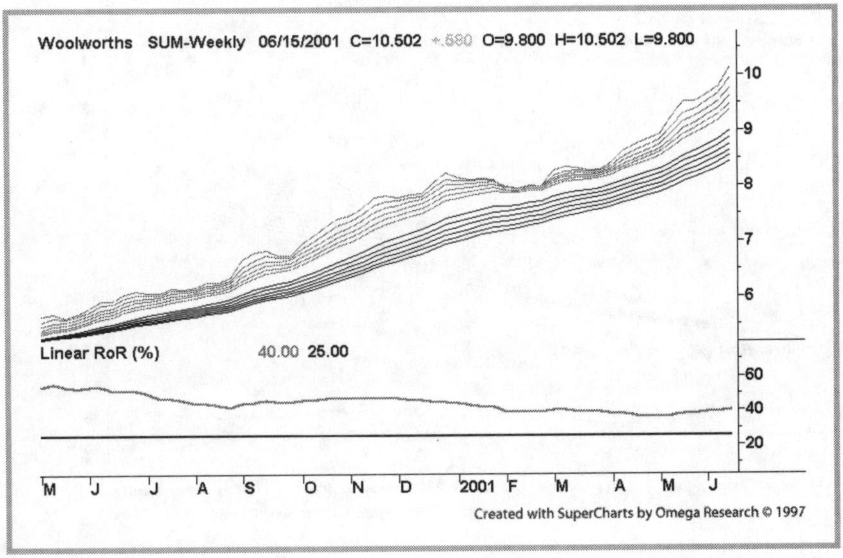

Figure 12

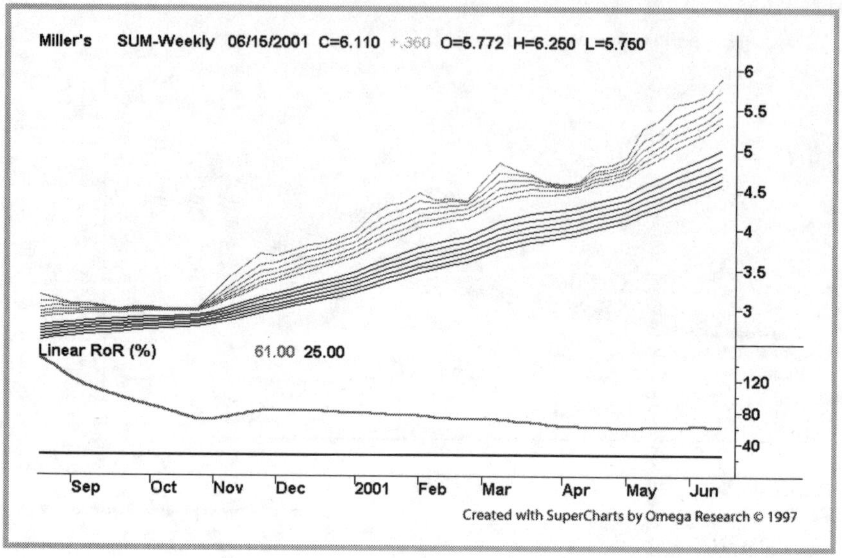

Figure 13

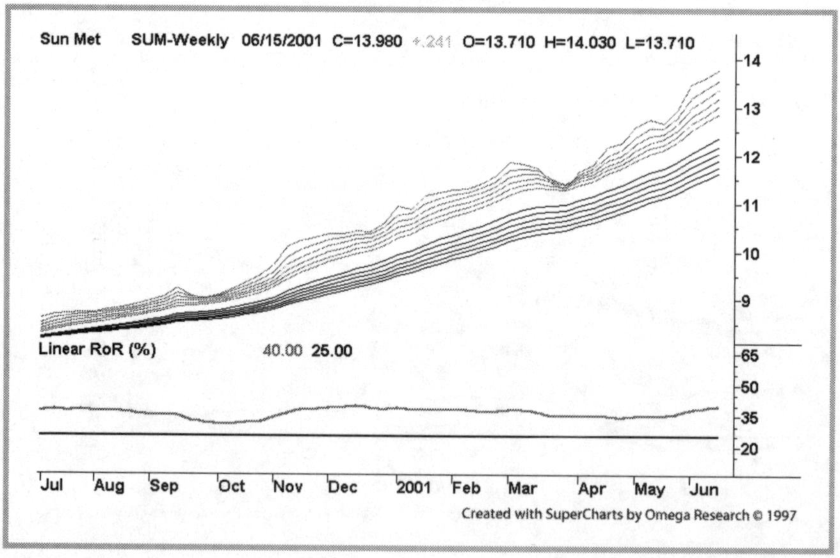

Also by Martin Roth...

Sector Investing

When looking to construct a share portfolio, Martin believes an excellent starting point is the Standard & Poor's ASX sectors. By studying the GICS sectors, investors can identify market trends and compare Australian stocks to international securities. Careful selection can then lead to a well-diversified portfolio with excellent growth prospects.

How the Stock Market Really Works (4th edition)

This book is a one-stop reference guide that explains the workings of the Australian stock market in clear and simple terms. Forging a path through the information overload that often confronts the inexperienced investor, Martin seeks to help readers attain real and valuable insight into the Australian stock market.

Available from all good bookshops.